M000034165

HOUSEWORKS

An Owner's Manual for Your Home

CREATIVE
PUBLISHING
international

MINNETONKA, MINNESOTA

Creative Publishing international, Inc.

Group Executive Editor: *Paul Currie*
Associate Creative Director: *Tim Himsel*
Managing Editor: *Kristen Olson*
Editorial Director: *Bryan Trandem*

Lead Writer: *Steve Boman*
Additional Writers & Editors: *Jerri Farris,*
Karl Larson, Joel Schmarje
Lead Art Director: *Gina Seeling*
Additional Art Directors: *Eileen Bovard,*
Dave Schelitzche
Project Manager: *Michelle Skudlarek*
Copy Editor: *Janice Cauley*
Set Builders: *Mike Schauer, Greg Wallace*

Vice President of Photography &
Production: *Jim Bindas*
Studio Services Manager: *Marcia Chambers*
Photo Services Coordinator: *Carol Osterhus*
Photographers: *Rex Irmin, Andrea Rugg,*
Rebecca Schmitt, Steve Smith
Production Manager: *Kim Gerber*
Purchasing Manager: *Dave Austad*
Production Staff: *Gretchen Gundersen,*
Laura Hokkanen

Popular Mechanics™

a publication of Hearst Magazines

Editor-in-Chief: *Joe Oldham*
Home Improvement Editor: *Steven Willson*
Associate Home Improvement Editors:
Thomas Klenck, Roy Berendsohn,
Editorial Assistant: *Lynne Abbate*
Art Editor: *John Bostonian, Jr.*
Electronic Production Associate:
Mike Vukobratovich
Contributors: *Neal Barrett, Norman Becker,*
Fran Donegan, Merle Henkenius, Edward Lipinski,
George Retseck, Eugene Thompson
Hearst Brand Development: *David Graff,*
Fran Reilly, Risa Turken, Kim Bealle,
Jenifer Kramer, Jane Ubell

CREATIVE PUBLISHING international

President: Iain Macfarlane

Cover photo courtesy of Marvin Windows & Doors

Library of Congress Cataloging-in-Publication Data

Houseworks : an owner's manual for your home / Popular mechanics.
    p. cm.
  ISBN 0-86573-772-X (softcover)
  1. Dwellings--Maintenance and repair--Amateurs' manuals.
I. Creative Publishing international. II. Popular mechanics.
TH4817.3.H6754 1998

643' .7--dc21   98-36739

Contents

INTRODUCTION

No one needs to tell you how important an investment your house is. Financially, you'll probably never make a bigger purchase. And emotionally, you have an attachment that runs deep; your house, after all, is the place you and your family call home.

Houseworks: A Guide to Understanding Your Home was written to help you understand how your house of today works. At one time, not so long ago, it was common for husband and wife to build their own house from the ground up. Through this process, homeowners gained an intimate, working knowledge of virtually every aspect of their homes. Their only assistance came from friends, neighbors, and members of the extended family—many of whom had built their own homes and were now passing along their knowledge.

Times have changed, however. Today, even a modest new house may boast a complicated array of space-age plumbing pipes, electronically controlled lights and appliances, zone-controlled heating ducts, decorative low-voltage lighting, motion-sensor security devices, and state-of-the-art window "systems." Such variety surely would have amazed our grandparents. Houses were simpler in their day, and most homeowners had a better sense of how all the pieces fit together.

But something else has changed, too. Careers and lifestyles have become ever more specialized and hectic, and fewer homeowners have the opportunity to serve a hands-on apprenticeship in home construction and maintenance. First-time homeowners today might find themselves living hundreds or even thousands of miles away from the network of family members and longtime neighbors who might teach them what they need to know.

Meeting this vital need for information is what *Houseworks* is all about. Houses today are complex structures; few people really know how all the systems in a house work, and fewer still can explain it clearly.

We'll examine all the elements of this intriguing, complex, and important structure. *Houseworks* takes you inside the walls of your dwelling, around the electrical system, through the plumbing, down into the foundation, and up to your roof. It also examines the nuances of your furnace and air-conditioning system, your doors and windows, the exterior and interior surfaces, and the insulation and weatherstripping.

Houseworks is not a typical how-to book. Although you'll read about some important repair and maintenance techniques, this guide focuses on explaining how each system in your home works. You'll follow electricity as it completes a circuit through your home; you'll do the same with water as it travels through your plumbing system. We'll also tell you where problems are most likely to occur and show you what to look for.

Each chapter contains tips and sidebars featuring important safety and technological information. Do you want to learn more about deadly radon gas? Or why lead paint can be so dangerous to children? Or how a house can be insulated and weatherstripped too well? In this book, you'll learn the "hows" and "whys" of all these issues and more.

Along the way, we'll highlight some of the most interesting technological advances. Curious as to how much R-values have increased in new window systems? Or why steel framing is migrating from skyscrapers to houses?

This book is intended for both the first-time homeowner and the experienced do-it-yourselfer. Our expertise comes from two sources: *Popular Mechanics*, the esteemed magazine and book publisher that has been showing the world how things work for nearly a century; and Cowles Creative Publishing, the producer of more than 20 best-selling home improvement books.

It's just possible there are homeowners out there who don't need this book. Perhaps they have a close friend or sibling who is a skilled home builder; someone who is knowledgeable in every aspect of today's technology, who communicates with crystal clarity, who charges nothing, and can be depended on to help them at a moment's notice, morning or night.

You're not this fortunate? Rest assured; you have the next best thing right in your hands: *Housworks: A Guide to Understanding Your Home.*

How to Use This Book

Houseworks: A Guide to Understanding Your Home is structured to tell the complete story of your house, from the concrete footings hidden under the basement floor to the shingles covering the peak of the roof. You'll learn about the materials used to build your house, how to evaluate their condition, and how to spot problems.

The book examines the elements of your house in the same order in which they were constructed and installed:

We suggest that you begin by taking a few days to leisurely read the book through from beginning to end. Move about your house as you read, taking notes on what you see and learn along the way. Keeping a notebook or journal is a good way to keep track of important information. By the time you finish the book, you should have a complete understanding of all your home's systems and materials, and a new-found confidence in your ability to maintain your home.

The last chapter of this book, Troubleshooting, is a reference that identifies the causes of common problems and suggests possible solutions.

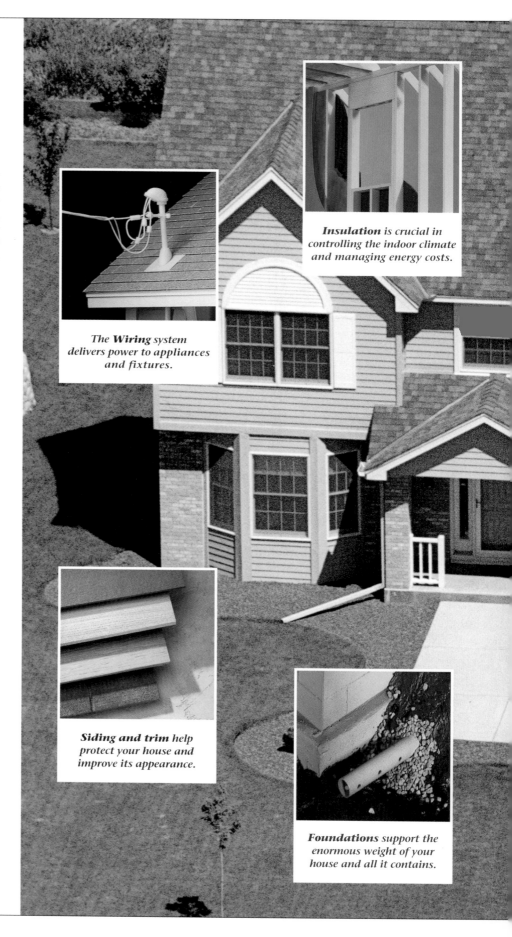

*The **Wiring** system delivers power to appliances and fixtures.*

***Insulation** is crucial in controlling the indoor climate and managing energy costs.*

***Siding and trim** help protect your house and improve its appearance.*

***Foundations** support the enormous weight of your house and all it contains.*

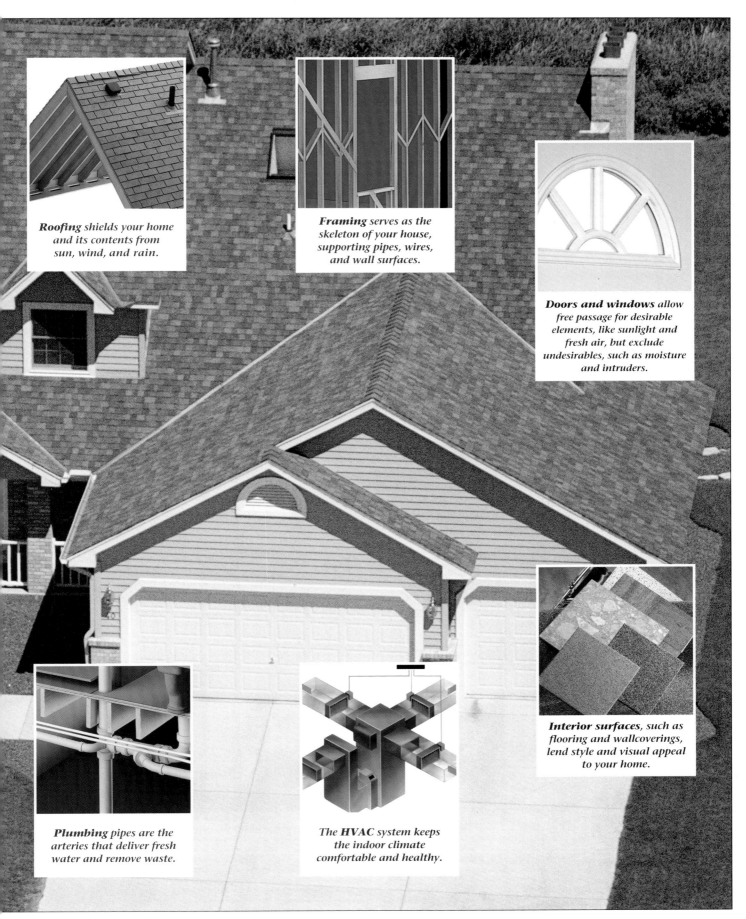

Roofing shields your home and its contents from sun, wind, and rain.

Framing serves as the skeleton of your house, supporting pipes, wires, and wall surfaces.

Doors and windows allow free passage for desirable elements, like sunlight and fresh air, but exclude undesirables, such as moisture and intruders.

Interior surfaces, such as flooring and wallcoverings, lend style and visual appeal to your home.

Plumbing pipes are the arteries that deliver fresh water and remove waste.

The **HVAC** system keeps the indoor climate comfortable and healthy.

Posts

Sill plate

Footings

A basement includes broad footings under each load-bearing element. If the footings under the exterior walls and interior posts are insufficient, the foundation will settle unevenly, leading to a variety of problems.

Soil grading

Foundation wall

Footing

Drain tile

FOUNDATIONS

The first physical step in the creation of your house had nothing to do with lumber and nails. While the carpenters were still mulling over blueprints, huge earth-moving machines (or a crew of diggers, if yours is an old house) conducted a mysterious excavation of the earth, and skilled masons built a series of subterranean walls that would soon be expected to defy gravity.

A good house foundation is a precise, carefully built structure designed for enormous brute strength. As the link between your house and the earth itself, a good foundation is expected to hold hundreds of thousands of pounds aloft, a feat that is possible only if its massive walls are perfectly flat and vertically straight (plumb) to within the barest of tolerances. For the most part, the materials and tools used to build this amazing structure have changed little in thousands of years. Ancient Romans constructed their buildings using mortar, natural stone, levels and trowels that would be easily recognized by builders of today.

And like the ancient coliseums and aqueducts, the foundation of the modern home is expected to exhibit heroic longevity. Your house's roof, its siding, its wall surfaces, its mechanical system may all undergo several renovations over the life of a house, but the foundation is expected to survive a century or more without settling or shifting more than a fraction of an inch. In some instances, houses destroyed by fire have even been rebuilt on the same foundations that supported the original structure.

If a foundation's function is heroic, its failure can be tragic. A foundation that fails to withstand the elemental forces of wind, flood, or earth tremors can lead to the literal collapse of an entire home. Fortunately, such catastrophes are rare. But a house with a poorly constructed or damaged foundation can exhibit a host of smaller problems, such as leaky basements, cracked walls and ceilings, twisted door frames, broken windows, and warped floors.

The design of your house's foundation may vary, depending on your region and on the quality of the soil supporting your house. In the Snow Belt, for example, foundations survive best when they extend deep into the ground below the frost line. In a region with soft soil or a high water table, a foundation must be built to "float" the weight of the house over the widest possible area. In areas where earthquakes are a threat, a foundation should be designed to help a house absorb the sways of a quake. And a house built on a flood plain or on swampy terrain requires a foundation that will withstand high water levels and keep the house dry.

This chapter will discuss the most common foundation designs, beginning with the most common—the basement wall foundation.

Granted, you can't easily change a faulty foundation the way you can replace a broken window. But a careful inspection can help you identify serious problems that may threaten the integrity of the building. And you'll be reassured to learn that many small problems can be easily remedied—provided they are spotted in time.

RADON

Radon is a colorless, odorless gas that has been shown to increase the risk of cancer. It results from the presence of uranium-238 in the soil. As this atomic element begins to decay, it breaks down into radon-222, which eventually transforms into a gaseous form.

As a gas, radon rising up through the soil normally dissipates harmlessly once it reaches the air. However, if the gas seeps into a subsurface structure and has no escape, it can accumulate to levels that pose a genuine threat to human health.

Radon was identified back in the 1800s by Marie Curie while she was investigating high frequencies of lung disease in Bavarian uranium miners. Curie's research identified a correlation between the frequency of the disease and the exposure to radon.

Concern over radon's presence in American homes started in the mid-1980s when a Pennsylvania construction engineer set off radiation detectors at a nuclear power plant before the facility had even begun to function. An investigation into the source of the radiation pinpointed the engineer's home. Subsequent radon level readings determined that the house had more than 650 times the acceptable level of radon.

Radon appears to be more prevalent in certain regions of the country. Cracks, openings around water and sewer pipes, and the type of soil on which the house rests can influence radon levels in your basement. These factors can make radon levels vary greatly between even neighboring houses. If you spend much time in your basement, it is recommended you do an accurate testing for radon.

The EPA regards 4 picocuries of radon gas per liter of air (pCi/L) as incentive to act, and has set 20 pCi/L as the absolute maximum amount of exposure.

Various options exist to decrease radon levels. Sealing the basement is the least effective but easiest. Other options include venting your drain tile, installing a pipe under the foundation to suck the gas away before it even reaches the basement, or using an air-to-air heat exchanger.

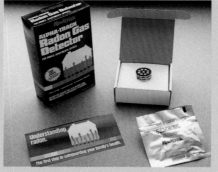

There are a variety of radon detectors available on the market today. The best read gas levels over a four- to six-month period, which gives you the most accurate reading.

Wall Foundations

More than half of all homes rest on wall foundations that enclose a crawl space or walk-down basement. Wall foundations are popular for a number of reasons—both structural and practical. A basement foundation is virtually impervious to frost heave, and the space can provide valuable extra room for utility use, storage, or expanded living quarters.

Walls

In a typical basement foundation, the exterior walls must withstand a variety of forces. Not only must they carry an enormous overhead weight, but they must withstand the lateral pressure created by the displacement of many tons of soil from inside the foundation.

Imagine standing chest deep in a slow stream with a heavy person on your shoulders. Essentially, that's the type of forces your foundation walls stand up to year after year, season after season.

Your basement walls, like the bones and muscles in your legs, are stronger vertically than they are laterally. Built correctly, your walls will have no problem with the vertical load of the house and its contents. However, much as your legs are pushed by the imaginary stream, so, too, do your basement walls feel the pressure of the surrounding soil and subsurface moisture. In a standard basement, the slab floor you are standing on pro-vides sufficient horizontal reinforcement to keep the walls from sliding inward.

Larger basements, in which a wall may span a long distance, may incorporate a buttress wall standing perpendicular to the exterior walls.

Depending on where your house is built, there may be internal reinforcements that strengthen your basement walls. For example, if your house is built on a steep slope, the wall on the upper part of the slope may be held by metal pegs extending down into bedrock. In areas with high water tables, or areas prone to earthquakes, metal rods, called rebar, are run vertically and horizontally throughout the walls.

Inspect your basement walls yearly, looking for signs of bowing or cracks. Aside from an earthquake, the most serious threat to a basement foundation is water. If the soil surrounding your foundation becomes saturated during heavy rains or spring melt-off, the weight of the earth can be doubled or even tripled, and can overcome the foundation walls.

During catastrophic floods in the Midwest, thousands of homes were destroyed when saturated soil caused foundation walls to cave in. A few homeowners had the foresight to flood their basements before the foundations were compromised. With the pressure of the surrounding soil balanced by the pressure of water in the basement, these are the homes that still stand today.

While inspecting your walls, use a long level to make sure the walls are flat and plumb. Small cracks, especially along mortar lines, don't necessarily indicate serious problems, but large cracks or broken blocks indicate a more ominous situation, and should be watched carefully.

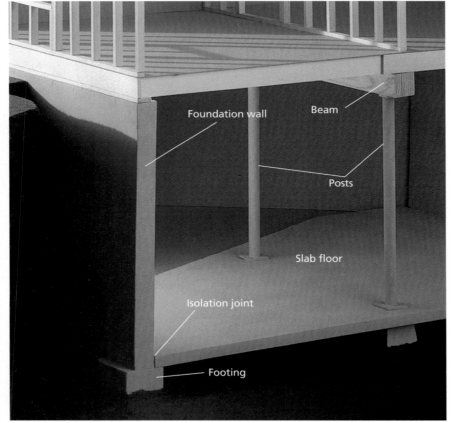

In a typical wall foundation, the footings under load-bearing walls and posts are wider than the components they support. This distribution of weight prevents settling.

Footings

Though you won't be able to see this feature, each load-bearing wall and post in your basement foundation rests on a wider concrete or stone base, called a *footing*. By distributing the load over a wider area, the footing reduces the likelihood that the foundation will settle. Footings perform the same function for a foundation that snowshoes do for a winter hiker.

A small amount of settling is normal, especially in an older house, but excessive or uneven settling of the footings can cause serious problems. If you notice cracked plaster, noticeably sloped floors, or door and window frames that are out of square, there is a good chance your foundation footings are settling unevenly. Using a level to check floor joists in the basement can also tell you if your foundation footings are settling. Watch for these symptoms carefully, and call in a building engineer promptly when you spot them.

Beams & Posts

Unless your house is very small, the foundation walls alone cannot carry the entire weight of your house. Along the center of your basement, you'll find one or more large beams, supported on the ends by the foundation walls, and with vertical posts spaced at regular intervals along the span. In a finished basement, the beam may be disguised in a wall or hidden above a suspended ceiling.

If yours is an older home, the beam may be hewn from a single piece of timber. In newer homes, the beam is often made from 2 × 10s or 2 × 12s ganged together, or from laminated layers of plywood. In some instances, metal I-beams are used. The posts supporting the beam will be either wood or metal.

The location and size of each beam, and the distances between support posts are regulated by the local Building Code. Most problems with beams occur because they are supported by too few posts, or because the post footings under the slab floor are settling. Periodically inspect the beam and posts to make sure they are level and plumb, and look for cracking and signs of rot.

Sill Plate

The house above your head is joined to the foundation by a 2 × 4 or 2 × 6 sill plate anchored to the top of the foundation walls. To prevent rot, the sill should be made of treated lumber and the top of the foundation wall should be covered with a fiberglass sealer. In regions where termites are a problem, metal or plastic termite guards cover the foundation to keep insects from migrating up into wood framing members.

Window & Door Openings

Next, examine all the window and door openings in your foundation walls. On concrete block walls, these openings are created as the wall is built, and are topped with a *lintel* made of precast concrete or blocks reinforced with poured concrete. On a poured concrete foundation, wood stops are inserted at window and door locations to prevent the concrete from filling the desired opening.

Periodically inspect the condition of the lintels over window and door openings for cracks. The lintels carry substantial weight, so problems need to be dealt with immediately.

If your basement has been finished or remodeled to include living spaces, make sure there is a second route of escape other than the main stairway. According to most local codes, basement areas used as living quarters must have either a second doorway or stairway, or an egress window that provides an escape opening at least 20 inches wide and 24 inches tall.

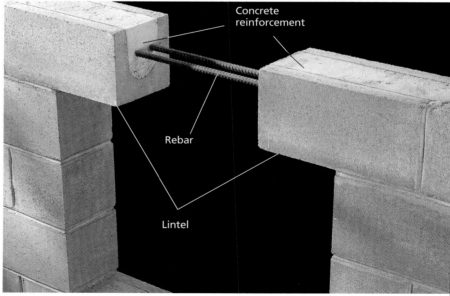

Labels: Concrete reinforcement, Rebar, Lintel

Lintels, in the form of concrete block reinforced with rebar and concrete, carry the weight across basement window and door openings. Lintels may also be made of precast concrete or metal angle irons.

Drainage & Waterproofing

In addition to withstanding the pressure of earth pressing in on the walls, your foundation needs to keep moisture out. In addition to visible flooding, water stains and perpetual mildew indicate your foundation is less than perfect at defending against water.

Many of the best methods for waterproofing a basement must be incorporated when the foundation is built, but there are ways to remedy water problems in an existing basement.

Grading the earth around your house so it slopes away from the foundation is vital to keeping your basement dry. In fact, in an older house, grading and roof gutters may be the primary means of keeping the basement dry.

When it rains, rainwater rolls off your roof, collects in the gutters, and pours out the downspouts only a few feet from your house. If this run-off water remains close to the house, it will create a small swamp and eventually seep into your basement.

However, adequate grading away from the house will ensure that rainwater flows away from the foundation and into your yard or city sewers.

You can measure the grade by using a carpenter's level taped to a straight 8-foot-long board. On grass, the grade should slope down 3/4 inches per foot—or 6 inches over 8 feet. If the slope is insufficient, add soil to increase the grade, or use a ground pipe to direct water farther away from the foundation. If the surface around your house is a nonporous surface, such as concrete, the grade can be much more gradual—about 1/2 inch per foot.

Window wells and doors can be easy entries for water. Proper grades around these openings will keep water from gathering, and during winter can prevent ice haz-

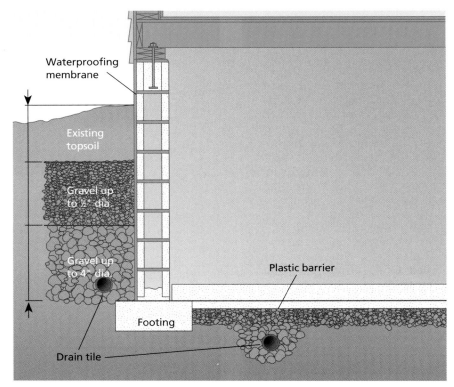

In new construction, a wall foundation includes several waterproofing and drainage features: drain tile installed around the outside base of the foundation; a porous backfill, such as gravel; a waterproofing membrane applied against the outside surface of the walls; soil grading to direct water away from the foundation. A plastic barrier under the slab keeps moisture from rising up through the floor. More expensive homes may also include an interior waterproof coating on the foundation walls and interior drain tile.

ards from forming near doorways.

Properly maintained basement window wells are typically filled with rocks or gravel to encourage draining, and in newer houses, window wells may also have base drains that carry water away from the house.

Keep window wells clear of dirt and debris, which can slow drainage. Water that accumulates in your window well will eventually seep through your window frame and run down the inside of your wall.

Another option is to purchase a plastic well cover that looks like a bubble and covers the window and the well. The covers are available at most home improvement stores and are quite inexpensive.

Drain tiles are perforated pipes laid just above the footings at the base of the foundation. The area around the tile is filled with gravel or other porous material. Water filtering down through the soil is channeled into the drain tile, which flows into an egress pipe leading either to a storm drain or to open air (if the house is on a hillside).

If yours is a newer house, your foundation should already be protected by drain tile around the outside of the footings. However, drain tile can also be retrofitted inside an older basement. It's a simple but time-consuming process of breaking the concrete in the slab floor so you can dig a trench just around the inside of your walls.

A sump pump is an automatic electric pump that ejects water from a drainage pit, called a *sump*. In some homes, especially older ones, the sump pit is located in a central location to collect rising ground water before it can flood the basement. In homes where interior drain tile directs water to the sump, the pit is often located in a corner of the basement. In many regions, sump pumps are mandatory in new construction. Dry areas do not require them.

The sump pump senses the quantity of water in the sump and automatically turns on when needed. Once operating, the pump forces the water up through a hose out of the house and away from the foundation. When the water level in the sump is sufficiently lowered, the pump automatically shuts itself off.

There are two types of sump pumps: pedestal and submersible. Pedestal pumps use float mechanisms, similar to those in toilets, to measure the amount of water, while submersibles are regulated by either a float mechanism or by water pressure. You can adjust the mechanisms in both pumps to attain desired water levels.

Check to see if your sump pump is in good working order every season and clean it annually. During your annual cleaning, it's a good idea to clean out the sump pit as well.

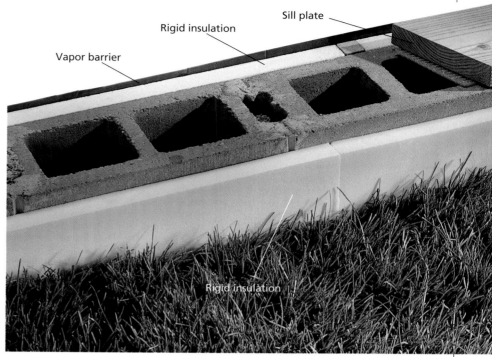

Vapor barrier

Rigid insulation

Sill plate

Rigid insulation

Insulating the inside surfaces of foundation walls is a good idea, even if the outside surfaces are already insulated.

Though a sump is designed to remove subsurface water and send it away from the house, some homeowners also use the sump to handle "gray" drain water from a clothes washer or basement shower. Under no circumstances should a sump pump handle septic wastes from a toilet.

Waterproof coverings seal foundations and slab floors against moisture penetration. On newer homes, the exterior surfaces of the foundation are coated with tar, mortar, clay, or are covered with sheets of butyl rubber or PVC. A layer of polyethylene laid over a bed of gravel prevents water from rising up through the slab floor.

If the exterior waterproof coverings break down over time—or if you want to waterproof the foundation in an older home—waterproof coverings can be applied over the inside wall and floor surfaces. These products may help reduce moisture problems, though they are not nearly as effective as those applied externally when the foundation was built.

Insulation

The ground around your foundation is a natural insulator that will keep your basement cooler in the summer months and warmer in the winter months. However, by installing insulation you can significantly lower heating costs.

In a newer home, the foundation may be covered with rigid-board insulation applied to the outside of the walls. Digging down a foot or so around the outside of your foundation will confirm this.

Older homes rarely have exterior foundation insulation. Here, the best option is to insulate the inside surfaces of the foundation walls—either with batt insulation installed in new 2 × 4 stud walls, or with rigid insulation panels glued directly to the wall between furring strips. Either type of insulation can be covered by drywall and will help your heating bill.

For information about how much insulation is needed read the chapter on insulation and weatherproofing.

Materials

Well over 75% of all basement wall foundations are built of either poured concrete or concrete blocks. In old or very new homes, however, you may find other materials used. Each material has advantages and disadvantages and different maintenance needs.

Poured concrete foundations have an expected life span of about 200 years. Poured concrete is the strongest foundation material, but it is also fairly expensive and complicated to build. If your basement walls are one solid mass, and you can see the texture of the wood or metal forms that shaped the wet concrete, then you have a poured concrete foundation. Some older homes, however, may appear to have solid concrete walls when, in fact, they are rubblestone walls that have been finished with a concrete or mortar top coat.

While inspecting a poured concrete foundation, you may get the idea that the walls and floor are one monolithic unit, but that isn't the case. A concrete foundation uses an isolation joint between the bottom of the walls and the slab to allow for expansion and shifting. Without this isolation joint, the walls or floors would soon crack or buckle under the lateral stress.

While this isolation joint serves a vital purpose, it also creates an easy passageway for water. If you're trying to locate the source of water seepage, it's one of the first places to look.

When inspecting the walls, you may see hairline cracks. These often occur while the concrete sets and are not a major concern. You can clean and seal the surface to fill these small cracks.

If you suspect a crack is active, mark the ends with tape to see if the crack is progressing. Active cracks should be filled with hydraulic or quick-setting cement.

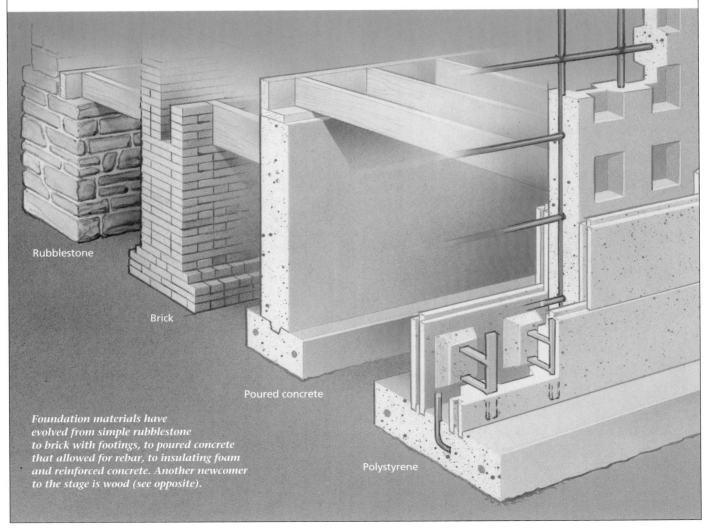

Rubblestone

Brick

Poured concrete

Polystyrene

Foundation materials have evolved from simple rubblestone to brick with footings, to poured concrete that allowed for rebar, to insulating foam and reinforced concrete. Another newcomer to the stage is wood (see opposite).

Concrete blocks, otherwise known as cinder blocks, are hollow and are held together by mortar. Concrete block foundations are considerably cheaper and easier to build than poured concrete, but their life expectancy is only about 100 years—half that of poured concrete.

Faults in the mortar are due to the pressures exerted and the ability of the material to withstand them. It's natural for these faults to occur over time, and they generally don't indicate a serious problem. These small cracks should, however be repaired with mortar to prevent them from becoming more serious.

But if you find cracks in the concrete blocks themselves, it means that the blocks have been seriously weakened and should be replaced. Moreover, cracked blocks indicate major settling or shifting of the foundation—a problem that should be inspected by a building engineer.

Rubblestone and brick basements are found only in very old residences. With these types of foundations, attention should be paid to any cracks or breaks in the mortar or stones.

Examine your foundation semi-annually to see if any cracking has occurred. Like mortar faults in concrete block walls, cracks in rubblestone and brick are natural and can be repaired by packing the joints with new mortar—a process called *tuckpointing*.

Cracks in bricks or stones themselves suggest a structural breakdown of the material itself. These problems are more serious and should be attended to immediately. With care, both bricks and stones can be replaced.

Wood wall foundations, sometimes known as *permanent wood foundations*, were first used in the mid-1970s and are enjoying a gradual increase in popularity. Today about 5% of new U.S. homes and

Polystyrene Foundations

The insulation value and convenience of polystyrene, the same foam used in coffee cups, is stirring up interest in the building trade.

Though there are many variations of polystyrene block, the most common system features rigid polystyrene molded into blocks, planks and panels. On the building site, the polystyrene pieces are assembled to form hollow forms; then concrete is poured into them. Once the concrete cures, the forms remain in place and are ready to accept drywall and exterior finish.

A wall constructed with polystyrene forms has an insulating value of R-20 to R-25. By contrast, a typical concrete foundation has an R-value of about 1.3, and a wood foundation, when insulated, is rated at R-15 to R-18.

One variation of polystyrene foundations uses blocks in which concrete is sprayed on a polystyrene core. The insulating value of a foundation built with these blocks ranges between R-10 and R-15.

20% of new Canadian residences have wood foundations.

Wood foundations can be constructed during very cold periods when concrete is difficult to pour. Wood foundations are also cheaper and easier to construct than poured concrete or block foundations, making them popular with people building their own homes.

Since wood foundations are treated with preservative chemicals and have an exterior waterproof coating, the wood industry maintains that they will be very durable. Still, wood foundations are so new that chronic problems may not yet be obvious. If you have a wood foundation,

always be on the lookout for signs of stress or rot. If possible, keep an eye out for consumer updates regarding wood foundations and the use of chemical preservatives in them.

Wood wall foundations consist of plywood and framing members that have been pressure treated with arsenates and other chemicals to prevent rot.

Slab Foundations

Concrete slab foundations are very common in warm climates where deep frost footings aren't necessary. They are also used on loose or sandy soil to distribute the weight of a house over a broad area and keep it from sinking. Depending on the size of the building, the slab may be thickened around the edges or along beam and post locations to provide support.

In areas with winter frost, the thickened portion of a slab foundation should extend several feet down to a point below the frost line. A slab that does not have these frost footings may shift or heave considerably from season to season.

Slab foundations generally require little care, since the vertical pressures are reduced and the lateral forces found in a basement foundation are absent.

If the workers built your slab foundation correctly, they began by laying a thick layer of gravel to provide drainage and distribute the load. Then they put down a layer of rigid insulation covered with a plastic vapor barrier. Finally, they laid a 4-inch to 8-inch layer of concrete reinforced with wire mesh or steel rebar. Built in this way, a slab foundation will be relatively warm and waterproof.

Many slab foundations, however, were not constructed so diligently. For this reason, some slab foundations have noticeable problems with heat loss and moisture infiltration.

If it isn't insulated, a slab foundation can be unpleasantly cold in the winter and uncomfortably warm in the summer, since it transfers heat directly to and from the earth. If this is the case with your foundation, installing a layer of rigid insulation under the surface flooring can substantially improve your year-round comfort level.

Water problems with an existing slab foundation can be difficult to remedy. You can lift the flooring and apply a liquid sealer or plastic barrier against the concrete slab, but the effectiveness of these measures may be limited.

A better solution to water problems is to make sure the landscape and soil around the house are designed to direct water away from the edges of the slab foundation. Since the home is raised only a few inches off the ground, any buildup of water around the foundation is likely to seep into your home.

This proximity to the earth also makes your home susceptible to pests and wood rot. Make sure to inspect the framing members and siding around the foundation.

Pier Foundations

With a pier foundation, your home rests on beams that are supported by a number of columns, called *piers*. Pier foundations are common in houses built in flood plains and other high-water areas, since they can raise a structure well off the ground and don't require extensive excavation. Due to their design, older pier foundations provide little defense against tremors and wind uplift.

Your pier foundation may be

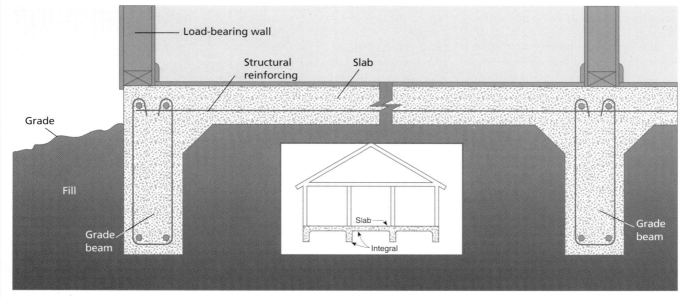

A slab foundation consists of a layer of reinforced concrete laid over a bed of gravel. The areas directly under load-bearing walls or posts are supported by a thickened area of concrete, called a grade beam. Slab foundations are most common in warm climates where there is no need for deep frost footings.

made of natural stone, brick, concrete, and possibly even wood.

With a pier foundation, the space under the house is often hidden by an apron that blocks wind and prevents debris from collecting and animals from finding a home underneath the house. Usually, the apron will have an opening that you can remove to gain access to the space and examine the piers. Examine the piers regularly for signs of damage or decay.

With a pier foundation, the floor joists are supported by beams between the piers. The piers should be of equal height and the stone or wood should be solid. Excessive cracking or crumbling may indicate that the materials are not strong enough to support the weight of the house. Consult a building contractor or structural engineer if you see these symptoms.

Remove any debris from the area under the house. Leaves and other trash will retain moisture and provide insect and animal pests with shelter. In a colder region, make sure the spaces between floor joists are insulated, and make sure the insulation remains dry.

A newer version of the pier foundation, called the *grade beam foundation,* is often used on hillside homes in the West. In this design, the piers are poured concrete columns that are connected to an underground beam. This variation provides a stronger, more unified foundation.

Pier foundations may prop up a deck and porch, as shown in this photo, to provide open area beneath the structure.

A pole foundation can be used to raise a house high above flash floods, or for houses on steep grades.

Pole Foundations

Like a pier foundation, a pole foundation raises a house off the ground, but with this design the vertical support columns are more fully integrated into the framing structure of the house. Rather than simply holding the house aloft, the poles—made of poured concrete, steel or wood—are directly connected to each story of the house. Pole foundations are often used when there is a need to raise a house to a substantial height above the ground.

If you have a pole foundation, walk around the base of the columns periodically to look for signs of deterioration. Call a contractor or engineer if you have any concerns.

Because of their design, pole foundations are very earthquake resistant, work well on steep slopes, and are well suited in areas where flash flooding is a possibility.

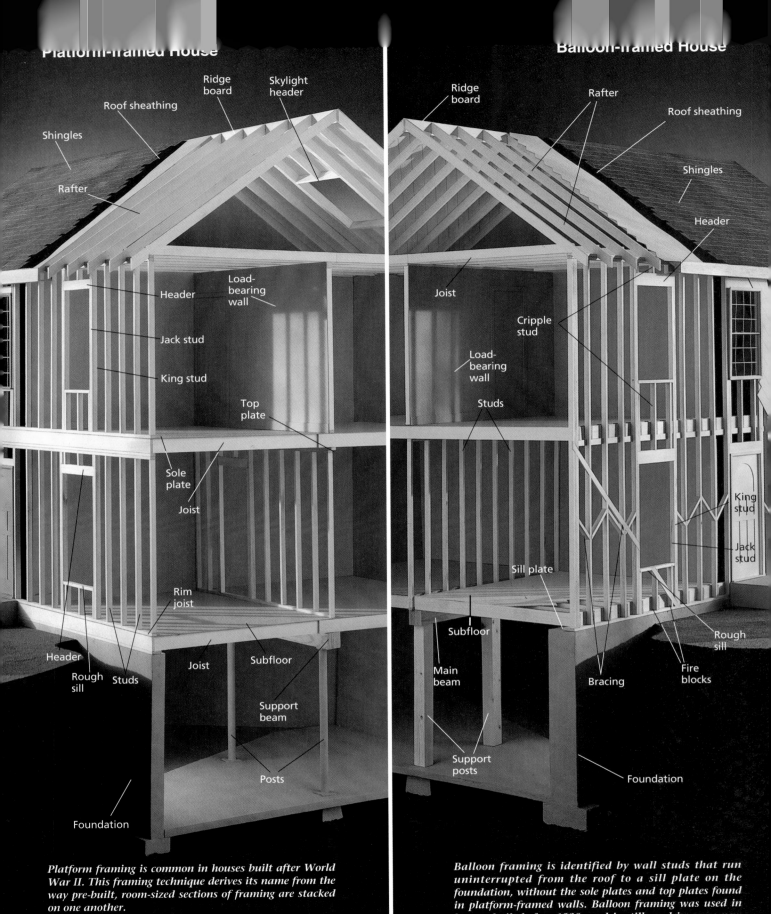

Platform-framed House

Shingles

Roof sheathing

Rafter

Ridge board

Skylight header

Header

Jack stud

King stud

Load-bearing wall

Top plate

Sole plate

Joist

Header

Rough sill

Studs

Joist

Subfloor

Rim joist

Support beam

Posts

Foundation

Platform framing is common in houses built after World War II. This framing technique derives its name from the way pre-built, room-sized sections of framing are stacked on one another.

Balloon-framed House

Ridge board

Rafter

Roof sheathing

Shingles

Header

Joist

Cripple stud

Load-bearing wall

Studs

King stud

Jack stud

Sill plate

Subfloor

Main beam

Bracing

Fire blocks

Rough sill

Support posts

Foundation

Balloon framing is identified by wall studs that run uninterrupted from the roof to a sill plate on the foundation, without the sole plates and top plates found in platform-framed walls. Balloon framing was used in houses built before 1930, and is still used in some new

FRAMING

Filmmakers and novelists have long known of the romance inherent in raising the framework of a building. You know the scene: Laborers gather as the first rays of morning cut the sky. They spend the day hammering and sawing. By afternoon, they have raised the walls and, as the day ends, the last rafter is hammered in place.

With little more than a pile of lumber, a bucket of nails and a team of good carpenters, a house can be raised—*your house*. Framing is a dramatic task, and it is vitally important that it is done right.

If your home has a well-built, sturdy frame, you will reap the benefits for decades. Solid framing will remain straight and true. It will support the weight of a house without straining. And, ideally, it will withstand all the fury that Mother Nature throws at it.

Slapdash framing may fail on all these fronts.

Granted, the framework in your home is already complete. What can you realistically do about its quality? Not a lot, at least not without expending a good deal of time and money. If your carpenters erected a shoddy frame, you'll have to deal with the consequences.

You can, however, make certain that your current framing does not deteriorate through rot or infestation. You can learn what kind of modifications your house frame will permit. And you can avoid damaging your framing by abusing it.

We'll cover these topics and others in this chapter. We'll investigate how a grand piano or hot tub can overstress a frame, and we'll explain why gaps along your ceiling may come and go with the seasons. We'll even look at steel-framed houses. Along the way, you'll learn a fair bit about something that started as a pile of lumber and a bucket of nails.

Platform or Balloon Framing?

All framing is not created equally. Most houses in the U.S. have one of two types of framing.

Platform frames are comprised of individual room-sized sections of framework. These sections, once fully built, are erected in rows along long walls and are stacked atop one another on multi-story houses.

Balloon frames rely on walls made of studs that run from foundation to rafter. The walls are strengthened by diagonal bracing. A balloon frame wall section will run the length of the house. Balloon framing is not without its benefits. These walls, while delicate in appearance, are actually very strong. Vertical movement is almost non-existent, making a balloon frame wall an excellent base for stucco and brick veneers, both of which can crack if the walls shrink.

Balloon framing is a disappearing art, however. Though balloon framing was prevalent in houses built before World War II, since the 1950s most homes have been built with platform frames. Builders today prefer platform frames because they can cut construction time and cost. Platform frame walls can be fabricated off-site and erected with less effort and expense than balloon frame walls. But some styles of modern homes, particularly those with high, vaulted ceilings, are still built with balloon frames.

How can you tell what style you have? You may be one of the lucky people who possess the blueprints of their home. But for everyone else, finding out may require the removal of a section of wallboard. If the studs are resting on sole plates, you have a platform-framed house (*photo, below*).

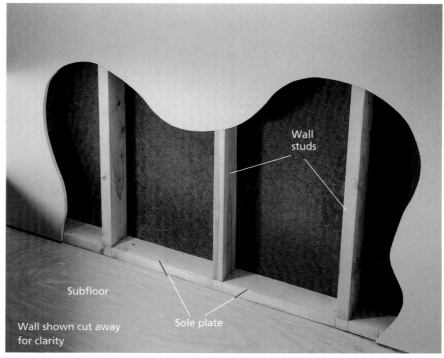

Studs on sole plates indicate a platform frame.

Joists & Beams

If you have a crawl space or unfinished basement, take an up-close view of your joists and beams. Your flooring is supported by dozens of joists you see standing on edge. The massive beam running down the middle of the house supports your joists. And the post, or posts, support your beam. Upper floors are constructed in the same manner, except the beams are often replaced by load-bearing walls. Although building materials have changed over the years, the basic design of joists and beams has been used for centuries.

What has changed over the centuries is the load we put on the floors. Hot tubs, waterbeds and lots of new appliances can put unexpected strain on flooring.

Floors under main living areas are generally engineered to support 40 pounds per square foot (psf) of live load—the weight of everything on the floor.

Upper-floor bedrooms in some homes have joists that are designed to carry 30 psf. Some attic joists can withstand only 20 or even 10 psf.

When positioning a very heavy object like a waterbed or piano, consider the ability of your floor joists to support the object. Contractors often swap stories of homeowners who placed grand pianos in the middle of their floors and discovered years later that their floors had settled. One way to alleviate stress on joists is to place very heavy items perpendicular to the joists so their weight is shouldered by as many joists as possible. Avoid placing very heavy items over the middle of an unsupported span. Doing so can cause the joists to bow over time.

Extremely heavy objects, such as a hot tub, may require additional framing to support their weight.

While conducting a visual tour of your joists and beams, check for:
• Evidence of rot or termite damage in your joists and beams. (Look closely at the ends.)
• Warped or cracked joists.
• Bowed or deeply cracked wood beams.
• Rust or rot on posts.
• Joists that have been cut or removed.

Examine joists to be sure previous plumbers, electricians or HVAC installers did not inflict any harm. Notches should never exceed a sixth of a joist's depth and should not be placed within the middle third of its span. Holes drilled in joists should not exceed a third of a joist's depth and should be no closer than 2" from its edge. Joists that have been notched or cut too deeply need to be braced.

If you walk across your floor

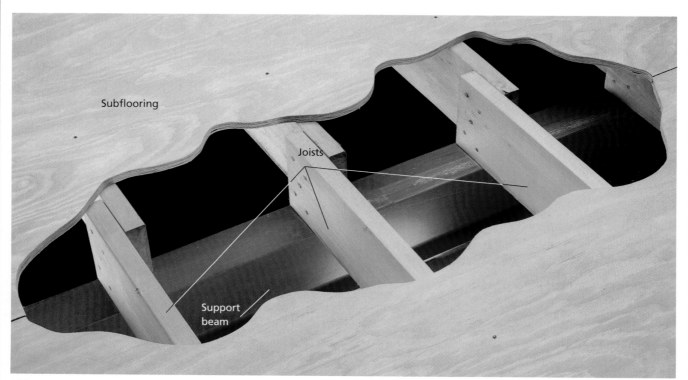

This cutaway allows you to see joists resting on a steel beam. Your subflooring rests upon the joists. Every item of framing must be level, dry and free of rot and insect infestation.

and find that your plates clatter or your floor seems to bounce, you probably have a joist problem called *deflection*.

Essentially, what is happening when floors bounce is that the joists are spanning too great a distance for the weight they are carrying. Thus, when you walk across the middle of a joist, it sags under your feet and simultaneously rises at its ends. When you step off the joist, it rebounds to its initial state. Although your floor is not about to collapse, a room with sturdy floors is much more appealing than one that feels like a trampoline.

Correcting deflection involves adding extra support to your joists. Solutions include adding an extra beam or adding an additional post.

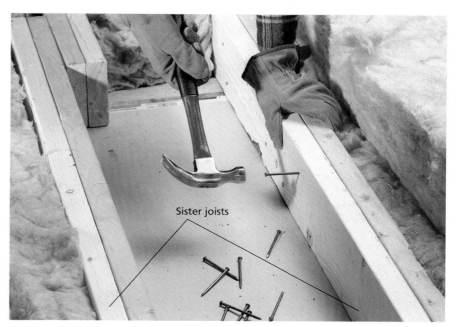

*Hot tubs or whirlpools require additional support under them. Extra joists called **sister joists** are bolted or screwed to existing joists to help bear the heavy load.*

HURRICANE BRACING

When strong winds blow, the walls and roof of a house can act like a large kite. Or when an earthquake strikes, a house frame that shifts just a few inches can cause the entire structure to collapse.

If you live in a hurricane area or a region where earthquakes are prevalent, you should double-check to make certain you have adequate framing connectors. These connectors work like tie-downs to keep your framework from shifting or lifting free of the foundation.

After Hurricane Hugo destroyed thousands of homes in Florida, some homeowners learned the hard way that sloppy contractors had omitted connectors in their houses or had failed to attach them sufficiently. The devastation wrought by Hugo pointed to the importance of proper bracing.

Joist hanger

Rafter tie

Mending plate/strap

Post beam cap

Special connectors are required in many areas at risk from hurricanes or earthquakes. If you live in such an area, check to see that you have these. Examples include (from left): wrap-around joist hanger, rafter tie, mending plate, post beam cap.

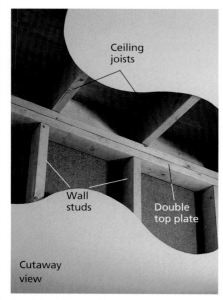

Ceiling joists

Wall studs

Double top plate

Cutaway view

Load-bearing walls are an integral part of your home's framework. Altering these walls requires additional bracing.

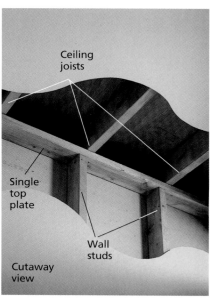

Ceiling joists

Single top plate

Wall studs

Cutaway view

Partition walls can be removed without compromising the strength of your home.

When carpenters installed your window and door frames, they framed your openings to transfer the weight of the missing vertical studs.

Wall Framing

If you're like a lot of homeowners, you mull over remodeling options for your house. *Could these two rooms be combined? Can we expand the kitchen into the dining room? I wonder if we could enlarge the door there?*

It will clearly help when you engage in these mental sketches if you know which walls in your house are load-bearing and which are not.

Load-bearing walls transfer the weight of the house to the foundation. Exterior walls are load-bearing, as are interior walls aligned above support beams. In many houses, load-bearing walls will have a double top plate to support the ceiling joists (this is not a hard-and-fast rule, however).

Any modifications to load-bearing walls should be attempted only after consultation with a structural engineer or good carpenter. When studs are removed from these walls, you must install headers to support the weight of the joists above.

Non–load-bearing walls are installed in a house to divide floor space into rooms. They can be removed or opened without affecting the stability of the house.

You can identify a non–load-bearing wall, also called a *partition wall*, by the fact that it usually does not have a double top plate and openings are not supported by load-bearing headers or jack studs.

Partition walls running perpendicular to the floor and ceiling joists are not aligned above support beams. Any interior wall that is parallel to floor and ceiling joists is a partition wall.

If you plan to remove or alter a load-bearing wall, keep in mind that the span must be solidly braced. Most wood headers can span a maximum of 8 to 12 feet, depending upon the material.

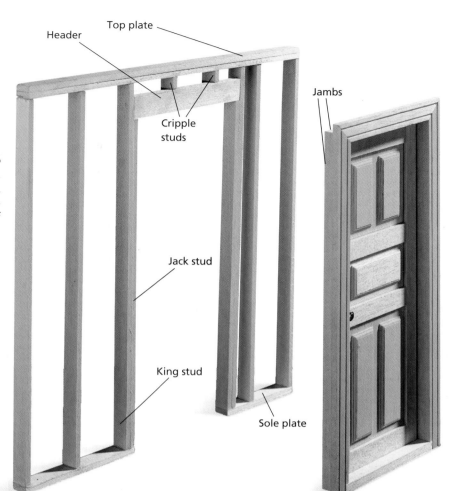

Door & Window Framing

Framing studs are typically 16 inches apart, measured on-center. Any opening wider than that on a load-bearing wall requires reinforcement to ensure the stability of the wall. A header spans the opening to transfer the weight from the absent framing members to additional framing members called *jack studs.* Naturally, the larger the opening, the more weight is carried by the supports.

If a window or door opening is not properly framed, it can cause the entire wall to sag. This is not something you want to experience first-hand. Should this happen, major repairs will be needed.

Door and window openings require a header installed atop the opening and jack studs to support the header.

Labels: Header · Top plate · Jambs · Cripple studs · Jack stud · King stud · Sole plate

MASONRY-FRAMED WALLS

In some homes, the load-bearing walls are actually constructed from stone or brick rather than wood. These walls are very durable. For proof, visit the ancient churches of Europe. In old stone houses, the walls may indeed be completely solid, but in most masonry construction there is an air space between two layers of brick. These two layers are braced with wall ties.

In modern masonry-framed houses, insulation is set into the space for greater efficiency. In some cases, cement blocks are used on the inner layer as a way to save money.

Masonry-framed walls resemble the foundation walls found in most homes, and require the same kind of maintenance and repair as concrete foundations (see pages 8 to 17).

Masonry framing has its drawbacks. Uninsulated masonry walls are very cold and the technique can be costly. Another drawback is that masonry buildings fare poorly in earthquakes.

Most brick houses in the U.S. are actually wood-framed houses with a brick veneer. Remove the bricks and you'll find wood studs supporting the house.

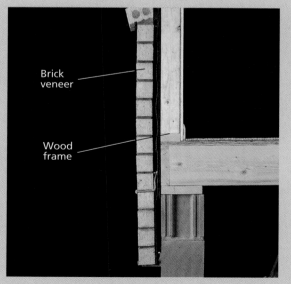

Brick veneer

Wood frame

Most brick houses in the U.S. are simply wood-framed houses with a brick veneer. As such, they are susceptible to some of the same problems as other wood-frame houses, such as termites and rot.

Termites leave characteristic tunnels in wood. The damage caused by termites can be devastating, but it can often go undetected.

Termite & Rot Damage

If lumber is kept dry and free of insect damage, it will last for centuries. But wood can be destroyed in short order by rot or termites.

The framework resting on your foundation faces the greatest risk because it is in such close proximity to the ground. If your wood is damp or you suspect an infestation of termites, the problems must be eradicated quickly.

Termites destroy lumber by eating it from the inside out. Framework ravaged by termites may look fine, but it can be nearly hollow.

Subterranean termites avoid light and open air. This species, the most common in the U.S., tunnels up from the ground directly into the wood. Or, they can create tunnels up foundation walls that serve as a pathway to the wood.

Damp-wood termites live along the Pacific Coast. They damage only moisture-soaked wood.

Dry-wood termites are present only in some southern parts of the U.S., but they don't need the safety of damp ground. These devastating insects will bore directly into above-ground wood and cover their tracks by plugging their holes.

Call a reputable exterminator if you find termites. Most anti-termite chemicals are very dangerous and difficult to apply. For example, a chemical commonly used to control termites, Chlordane, was found to cause cancer in humans. It is now banned for almost all uses and can only be injected into the ground beneath homes.

Rot can be just as insidious as termites, but is easier to guard against. Make certain your framework is protected from wetness. Plug leaks and halt condensation with better ventilation. Rotten sections of framing must be cut away and replaced or adequately braced.

Rotting joists need to be repaired or replaced. The source of the moisture that led to the rotting also needs to be eliminated.

How to Locate Framing Studs

Most house walls are built of vertical 2×4s, or 2×6s in some newer houses. Eventually, you will need to locate the exact position of these framing members. You might be simply hanging a heavy painting or you could be tackling a more difficult task, such as installing a new window. You would obviously like to pinpoint the studs without tearing a wall apart.

Fortunately, every wall carries some telltale clues that make this job easier.

• The simplest option is to tap your knuckles across the wall and listen for a change in sound. While this will generally reveal the rough location of a stud, it will not clearly identify both edges. To find the center of the stud, you can probe the wall with a small nail. When you locate one edge, measure over 1½" to find the other edge. Lightly mark the wall. Small nail holes in drywall can be repaired with spackle or wallboard compound and touch-up paint. This method works on plaster walls too, but you run the risk of cracking the brittle plaster. A better option is to drill repeated ⅟₁₆" to ⅛" diameter holes across the surface. When the bit meets resistance at a depth of about 1", you have found a stud. (Two important cautions when drilling: Avoid working where there may be concealed electrical wires or water and gas pipes, and use only a double-insulated drill.)

• If you'd rather not put small holes in your walls, careful visual examination may do the trick. By shining a light at a low angle across drywall, you can often see bumps or depressions where nails are driven into studs. You'll get the best results in a dark room.

• Visual inspection of the baseboard can also reveal depressions over the heads of finishing nails.

• Another good option is to remove outlet cover plates. Generally, the boxes underneath are nailed to studs. With the cover off, you can see which side the stud falls on and then measure over in increments of sixteen inches to find where other studs fall. Remember to confirm the width of the studs. You cannot depend on all studs being exactly 16" apart on center.

• If you do a lot of remodeling and repair work, your best bet is to invest about $20 in an electronic stud finder. These units normally run on a simple 9-volt battery and accurately establish both outside edges of the studs. All you need to do is sweep the device across the wall. Generally, electronic stud finders work well on drywall or wood-paneled walls. They also work on plaster walls as long as wood lath lies beneath the plaster. Metal lath will confuse the sensors.

• Another option is to use a simple magnetic stud finder. These inexpensive devices have pointers that react when they pass over nails used to install drywall panels. They will not work on plaster walls or on paneling that has been installed with adhesive.

Although it creates a series of holes that will need to be filled, an accurate low-tech way of finding a wall stud is to probe the wall until you run into resistance.

If you don't mind spending about $20 (and you don't have metal lath under your plaster), an electronic stud finder will locate framing members quickly and easily.

The underside of a stairway. The risers and treads of this stairway rest upon three stringers.

To quiet squeaky stairs, you can drive a hardwood wedge, coated with carpenter's glue, between the treads and the risers from under the stairway. This will tighten the joints.

Stair Framing

Stairs use a method of framing that transfers much of the load of the staircase to the floor diagonally. The risers and treads of a staircase rest on stringers that span the run of the stairs.

Creaks on individual treads are the result of an uneven plane across the tops of the stringers. This problem can be caused by changes in moisture levels, by poor construction, or wear and tear.

Squeaky stairway treads can be quieted without too much trouble. Try one of the following:

• Drive flooring nails at opposing angles into the treads to anchor them to the stringers. With hardwood treads, drill pilot holes. Recess nail heads, and fill holes with wood putty.

• Reinforce the treads by gluing small wood blocks to the underside of the risers and treads. Then, secure the blocks to the risers and treads with wood screws.

• Shim the treads with hardwood wedges coated with glue (*photo*).

Sometimes, a stair tread can break or crack. If that happens, fix the problem at once. Inspect other treads. If one tread is weak, others are probably weak, too.

If treads break, the problem may be traced to the stringers. Many stairways have only two stringers running down the edges of the stairway. A third stringer added to the center of the stairway greatly improves the strength of the whole structure. This task is obviously much easier if the underside of the stairway is exposed.

Other items to check:

• Every stairway must have a secure railing. Make certain your railings are attached to studs, not simply hung on flimsy drywall.

• Make certain any carpeting or rubber tread floor coverings are tightly attached.

Steel Framing

You don't have to be a carpenter to know that most houses are built with wood. Even the most infrequent visitor to the local lumberyard can identify a 2 × 4. The sight of new construction and the basic material that goes into it is as common as a hammer and nail.

However, if you've been watching closely, you may have noticed that a portion of the new construction and renovation isn't being framed with wood. The construction looks similar, but each member is metal—steel, to be exact.

The fact is, fluctuating lumber prices and sagging wood quality have sent many contractors looking for alternative building materials. While most have simply incorporated more engineered-wood products, such as manufactured beams and trusses, a growing number are moving to steel.

For contractors trained in standard wood framing, the logical choice is light-gauge, cold-formed steel in components sized to match the dimensional lumber they're familiar with. These components allow the builder to frame in a more or less traditional fashion with only modest retooling.

Though few houses use steel framing at every corner and wall, about 5% of new homes use steel in some fashion or other. The steel industry is projecting, perhaps optimistically, that up to 25% of new homes will use steel within a few years. While this seems unlikely, the very idea makes the beleaguered timber industry nervous.

Cold-formed steel framing material mirrors dimensional lumber in shape, size and function. At the manufacturing stage, the steel is stamped into a "C" shape for use as studs, joists, and rafters. It is then coated with zinc to prevent rusting.

Traditional sizes and familiar framing methods ease the learning curve for builders and allow them to mix steel and wood. In many cases, steel components allow a piece-for-piece substitution, with conventional spacing on 16" and 24" centers. Although new fasteners and specialty tools are on the drawing boards, most builders use screw guns and self-tapping screws to fasten framing members. In most cases, builders line door and window openings with wood, which allows them to nail casings and trim conventionally.

Few carpenters will admit to liking steel. Radical changes in materials and installation methods require a new sensibility and higher prices, at least initially. But builders are leaning toward steel because lumber prices have fluctuated greatly in the past few years and finding straight studs has been increasingly difficult. Unstable lumber can add to building costs and create drywall stress cracks.

Once in place, steel frames will not bend or warp due to moisture, and they are not prone to insect damage. Steel is considered to fare better than wood in mild earthquakes and in wind storms. And because steel will not combust, it is possible to find lower insurance premiums for steel-framed houses.

Still, steel framing has its drawbacks. Steel, simply put, is a poor insulator. A steel stud conducts 20 times more heat than a wood 2 × 4.

Another problem is that many local Building Codes lack standards for steel-frame construction. Thus, most steel-frame homes built today require an engineer's stamp before they can be approved. That stamp can add thousands of dollars to the cost of a steel house.

Finally, buying steel requires more planning and precision on the part of builders. It's no simple task for a builder today to pick up an extra 50 steel studs during the lunch hour.

Component assemblies

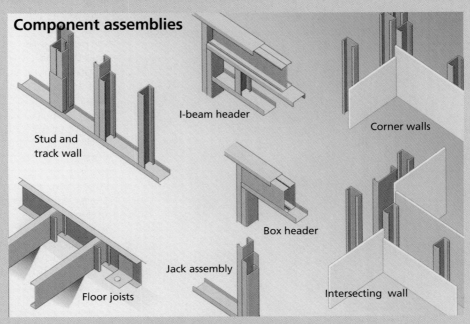

I-beam header

Stud and track wall

Corner walls

Box header

Jack assembly

Floor joists

Intersecting wall

Steel framing has been used to erect commercial buildings for years, but its use in home building has been limited until recently. The diagrams above show how steel framing members are joined.

Roof Framework

The framework of a pitched roof relies on the engineering principle of triangulation. The sloping rafters support the weight of the roof and transfer that weight to the walls. The bottom of the triangle, your attic floor joists, keeps the rafters from pushing out the walls.

Take a tour of your attic and examine your roofing framework. Older houses almost always have roofs that were built on-site from individual sticks of lumber. Rafters in these houses are normally fashioned of 2 × 6 lumber. Newer houses generally rely on prefabricated trusses, which are cheaper and faster to assemble. Trusses are held together by stamped metal connectors and are often built with 2 × 4 lumber.

What does it mean to you? A remodeling job can be more difficult with prefab trusses because none of the pieces can be removed without reducing the strength of the entire truss. On the other hand, a good carpenter can more easily alter traditional rafters without weakening the roof. When adding a skylight, for example, rafters can be cut and braced to allow the installation of a larger unit. With trusses, skylights must be small enough to fit between the framework. Otherwise, extensive alterations are required. In addition, trusses reduce the amount of easily accessible storage space in your attic.

The biggest threat to your roof framework (aside from the occasional tornado or hurricane) is rot. The fungus that causes rot thrives in moist areas. If you have any moisture on the underside of your roof, whether it's from a leak or condensation, you need to get rid of it. Staunch any leaks or improve ventilation.

Inspect your roof for rotting wood annually. Look closely on the upper side of your roof framing and where the framing meets the wall plate. Probe the wood with a penknife to test its soundness. The knife blade should not penetrate more than a quarter inch.

In some instances, roof framework is not up to the task of supporting heavier roofing shingles or deep snow. Under too great a load, the roof will slowly sag or, in extreme cases, collapse. Some homeowners find out too late that their rafters are woefully overburdened 2 × 4s. If this is the case in your house, by all means brace the framing to strengthen the rafters. Homeowners in the Snow Belt need to pay closer attention to this. Otherwise, they might wake up to discover an attic full of snow after a big blizzard.

A technique common on many houses built before 1950 was to construct rafters using 2 × 6 lumber.

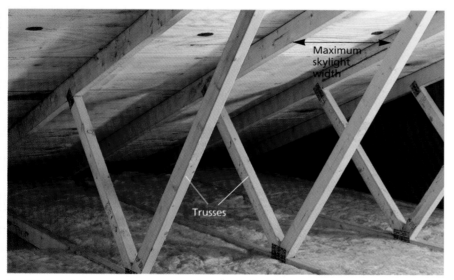

Prefabricated trusses are common on houses built after 1950. The trusses, made of 2" dimensional lumber, are connected with metal plates.

Truss Uplift

In the winter, you've got a crack along the edge of your ceiling. In the summer, it's gone.

This phenomenon is not something you're imagining. It's in your trusses.

The problem, called *truss uplift,* is caused by differences in the rate of expansion between the bottom and upper chords of the roof truss. The bottom chords are covered with insulation, while the upper chords are exposed to the air in the attic. In the winter, the top chords gain moisture from condensation on the roof sheathing. This causes them to swell in length. Meanwhile, the bottom chords can shrink slightly as they are exposed to high temperatures and a low relative humidity. This causes the upper chords to pull the bottom members up, lifting the ceiling below.

In the summer, the lower and upper chords equalize in length. As a result, the ceiling drops back into position.

Truss uplift is more common during the first winter in a newly built house. If it happens, sit tight. The wood will stabilize as time goes by and the crack along the edge of your ceiling will likely disappear. If your older house is plagued by truss uplift, then you may have a more persistent problem.

A simple cosmetic solution is to fasten moldings to the ceiling. The moldings will move with the ceiling and keep the crack covered. A better solution is to make certain your attic is properly ventilated. Keeping condensation from settling in your roof will go a long way to diminishing truss uplift.

Trusses can be braced to help prevent uplift. In addition to helping reduce uplift, the bracing will strengthen the roof and provide a measure of security against high winds.

A typical skylight installation requires framed openings in the roof and the ceiling, plus a framed shaft. In homes with rafters, one or two rafters can be cut, provided the openings are reinforced with double headers and "sister" framing members. In homes with trusses, skylights are most conveniently installed between framing members.

JOIST STRENGTH

If you have an unfinished, walk-up attic, you may have considered turning this space into living quarters or using it for storage. This is a great way to add space to your house, provided the attic flooring can support the weight.

It all depends upon the size of the lumber used for the joists, the distance between them, and the length of their span.

To qualify for conversion into a living space, your attic should have floor joists rated for a live load of 30 pounds per square foot (psf). As shown in the chart, this will be possible if the floor joists are 2 × 6s that span no more than 9 ft. 9 inches, 2 × 8s that span no more than 12 ft. 10 inches, 2 × 10s that span no more than 16 ft. 5 inches, or 2 × 12s that span no more than 19 ft. 11 inches.

If your attic floor has a live load of 20 psf, it is suitable for light storage, but if it has a live load of 10 psf, it should not be used for storage at all.

There are options if your floor has an insufficient live load for the purpose you envision. For example, doubling up the framing with "sister" joists installed next to each existing joist can strengthen a floor with 2 × 4 joists so it can be used for storage. And sistering a 2 × 6 floor can make it strong enough to be used as a living space.

Span Table					
Joist Size (16" on center)	2 × 4	2 × 6	2 × 8	2 × 10	2 × 12
40 psf	NA	8'-10"	11'-8"	14'-9"	17'-9"
30 psf	NA	9'-9"	12'-10"	16'-5"	19'-11"
20 psf	8'-1"	12'-9"	16'-10"	21'-6"	NA
10 psf	10'-3"	16'-1"	21'-2"	27'-1"	NA

40 psf of live load will support main living rooms; 30 psf will support bedrooms and attic floors; 20 psf is suitable for limited attic storage; 10 psf is suitable only for supporting drywall ceilings and no storage.

Gable roof

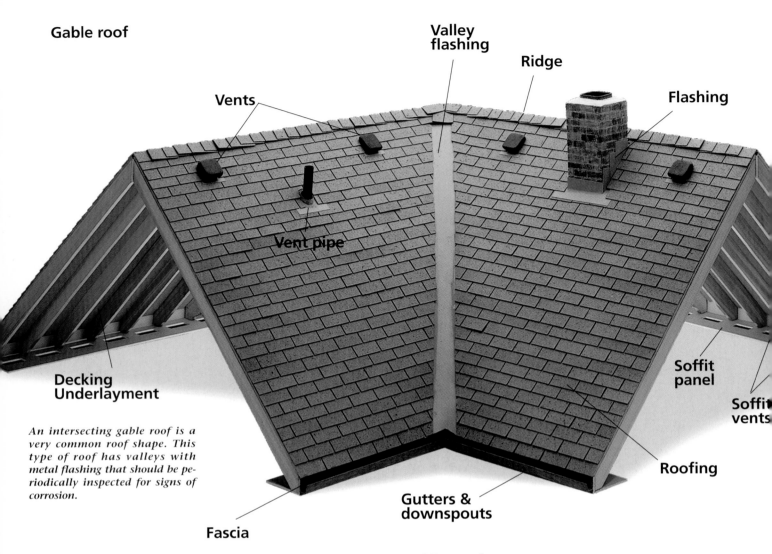

Vents

Valley flashing

Ridge

Flashing

Vent pipe

Decking
Underlayment

Soffit panel

Soffit vents

Roofing

An intersecting gable roof is a very common roof shape. This type of roof has valleys with metal flashing that should be periodically inspected for signs of corrosion.

Gutters & downspouts

Fascia

Shed roof

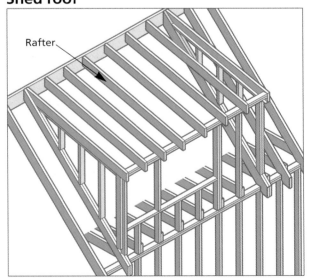

Rafter

A shed roof is often used on porches and dormers. If the pitch of the roof is very shallow, it should be covered with roll roofing rather than traditional shingles.

Hip roof

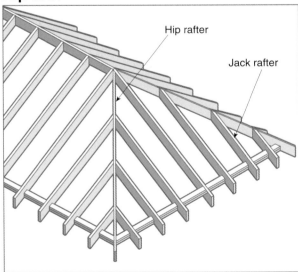

Hip rafter

Jack rafter

A hip roof provides a protective overhang on all four sides of a house. It is built by angling the gable ends of the roof back toward the center of the roof. This type of roof has no valley flashing, and is thus a very durable, trouble-free roof.

ROOFING & VENTILATION

Even if it makes you feel a bit silly, take a few minutes now to stand outside your house and take a good long look at your roof. This hardworking system protects your entire home and its contents from the destructive power of the elements. Before the original carpenters began any of the interior work, they finished the roof in order to safeguard the dwelling. Now, however, it's up to you to make sure the roof is up to the task of protecting your family and all your worldly possessions.

To begin with, simply identify the various components of your roof system. Note the type of surface roofing material used, and evaluate its general condition. Are there any shingles that are missing, buckled or clearly worn?

Problems with shingles and other roofing materials account for many roof troubles, but there are several other elements that also need periodic inspection, maintenance, repair or replacement.

Identify all the different types of metal flashing used to seal the joints between the roofing material and chimneys, vent pipes, roof vents, and dormers. Is there any evidence of corrosion or breaks? If your home has a gutter system, examine the soundness of gutters, downspouts and extension pipes. Is there any visible damage?

If you can only shrug your shoulders to these questions, read on. We'll take a look at how your roof works, how it is designed and how you can keep on top of any troubles.

Perhaps you've heard the adage, "a bad roof only leaks when it rains." The saying is funny, but only partly true. A poorly maintained roof will leak when it rains, but it will also leak when snow melts or when ice builds up on the eaves. And the legacy of even a small leak may be rotted rafters and damaged ceilings. On a related note, improper roof drainage can produce wet basements and ruined siding.

Let's take a closer look at your roof, which is composed of three different parts: the framework (pages 28 to 29), the decking and the roof covering. Later, we'll also examine the different kinds of materials used for roof coverings.

LADDER SAFETY

Too many homeowners take too many foolish chances when they use ladders to work on their roofs. Every year, a surprising number of people are injured or killed in ladder accidents. You can cut your risks substantially if you follow these rules:

• Use a good-quality ladder that is the right size for the job. Never extend a ladder to reach higher than it is designed and never exceed the rated weight capacity listed on the ladder.
• Only use ladders that work properly. If any part is damaged, don't use the ladder. Before using an extension ladder, make sure it slides up and down easily and test the integrity of the pulleys and latches.
• Make certain your ladder is properly positioned against a wall or roof. A ladder that is only a few degrees off-center could cause the ladder to slide sideways or buckle.
• Always have level, stable footing under your ladder. If the ground is uneven, install a sturdy riser under one leg. If the ground is soft or slippery, drive a stake next to each ladder foot to keep the ladder from slipping.
• When using a ladder to climb onto a roof, make sure it extends at least three feet above the roof edge.
• Stay clear of power cables! If you must work anywhere near electrical cables, use only a fiberglass or wood ladder.
• Watch out for wires, branches and overhangs when carrying a ladder.
• Attach an adjustable stabilizer to the top of your ladder if you are leaning it against a wall.
• Never carry heavy or large items up a ladder. Instead, use a hoist to raise and lower heavy or bulky materials.
• Wear sturdy footwear. Clean off mud or sand from your shoes before climbing.
• Don't attempt to climb up a roof that is too steep. Remember that it is often easier to climb off a ladder and walk up a roof than to climb down a roof and get back on a ladder.
• Climbing a ladder requires your full attention and quite a bit of physical exertion. Don't attempt to use a ladder if you are tired or are under the influence of alcohol or medications.

Use riser blocks and stakes to stabilize a ladder on uneven or soft ground.

The typical roof consists of three layers: plywood or lumber decking, underlayment, and surface shingles.

Decking

After the basic support framework of rafters or trusses was in place, the first step in the construction of your roof was the installation of a base layer of plywood or plank *decking*, or *sheathing*. The decking provides a flat and sturdy attachment point for shingles or other roofing material. You can inspect the decking from your attic or upstairs crawl space. During your inspection, look carefully for any rotten, infested or warped boards that need to be replaced.

In older homes, the decking is usually ¾-inch lumber planks nailed to the rafters. For new construction, decking usually takes one of two forms.

Plywood is the material of choice for decking with asphalt shingles, roll roofing, slate and sometimes tile. Plywood decking is usually at least ½ inch thick. The sheets lie in a staggered pattern, and a slight gap between panels allows for expansion. Plywood used for roof decking should be stamped with a grade of *Construction I*, *Construction II*, *Standard*, or *Exterior Construction*. If your decking doesn't meet these standards, inspect it frequently for problems.

Spaced slats can be installed under wood shakes and shingles, tile and metal panels. Slats are usually 1 × 4 lumber, and are sometimes nailed to a plywood deck in order to improve insulation, ventilation, or strength.

Underlayment

Roof underlayment attached over the decking serves as a last line of protection to prevent wind-driven rain from penetrating the sheathing and framing members. The underlayment of choice is 30-pound *builder's paper*—a felt product impregnated with asphalt.

In colder climates, recent changes to local codes require a special type of underlayment, called "ice guard" or "ice shield," instead of the standard building paper for the first course or two of underlayment. An adhesive membrane, this material bonds with the decking to create a barrier to water infiltration due to ice dams. If you live in such a climate and are planning to have a new roof installed, make sure to insist that your contractor install ice guard.

Flashing

Wherever there is an interruption in the continuous roofline—such as in valleys, and around roof dormers, vents, chimneys and skylights—metal flashing is installed to ensure that surface water is directed onto the surface of the shingles and doesn't migrate into the wood decking and framework below. Though flashing is generally made of corrosion-resistant metal, it doesn't last forever. Roof leaks are very often caused by flashing problems, so inspect your flashing regularly for rust and corrosion.

Small holes in flashing can be patched with a roofing cement or a fiberglass patching kit, but if you have frequent problems it's probably time to replace the entire flashing. And if you are having new roofing installed, make sure the contractor also replaces all the flashing. Some roofers try to cut corners by reusing the old flashing.

Flashing made of corrosion-resistant metal is used to seal the joints between roofing materials and other roof structures, such as a roof vent or chimney (right). Flashing installation is designed to direct water safely onto the surface of the shingles.

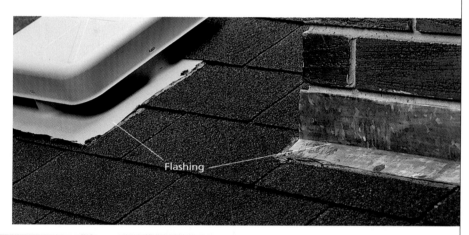

Flashing

Flashing products for roofs include (clockwise from top left): roll flashing, drip edge, preformed valley flashing, skylight flashing, step flashing, and vent pipe flashing.

SLOPE (OR PITCH)

The steepness of a roof can be described by referring to its SLOPE (or pitch)—the ratio of vertical rise to its horizontal run. Therefore, a roof that rises three inches for every foot of run is said to have a 3-in-12 slope. Knowing the steepness of your roof will help you determine what coverings are appropriate for your home. Refer to the chart (below) when evaluating your roof.

Run (12")
Rise (5")

Determining your roof's slope is easy with a square. For every foot of length, see how many inches your roof rises.

Roofing Material	Minimum Slope
Asphalt shingles	3-in-12
Wood shakes	3-in-12
Wood shingles	3-in-12
Cement shingles	2-in-12
Roll roofing	1-in-12
Slate	5-in-12
Metal	2-in-12

Minimum allowable roof slope varies, depending on the type of roofing material used.

Photo courtesy of CertainTeed Corporation

Asphalt shingles cover most homes in the U.S., largely because they are far less expensive than most other roofing materials. You can expect to get 10 to 30 years of life from an asphalt shingle roof. On standard three-tab shingles, the shingles are staggered so each joint is covered by the shingle above.

Valley flashing protects the areas where two roof planes meet. Periodically inspect the valley flashing for signs of rust or pinhole leaks, and keep it free from leaves and other debris, which hold moisture and hasten rust.

Roofing Materials

If you stay long enough in your house, it's almost certain you'll have to re-roof it. For most home-owners, the decision to re-roof comes when the roof starts to leak or shows signs of decay. But a new roof can also give your house an attractive face-lift. Today there are more roofing materials than ever—you don't have to settle for simple black asphalt shingles. You can have your choice of color, texture and, of course, price.

Asphalt shingles

Asphalt shingles are found on about two-thirds of all homes in the U.S. The life expectancy for an asphalt shingle roof ranges from 10 to 30 years, depending on the environment, the quality of the shingles, and the quality of the installation.

Asphalt shingles come in two broad categories: *organic* base and *fiberglass*.

Organic base shingles are made of a cellulose mat saturated with asphalt and covered with mineral granules. Organic shingles are cheaper than fiberglass and more flexible, but they are less fire-resistant than fiberglass shingles.

Fiberglass shingles have a mat of woven glass fiber saturated with asphalt and covered with mineral granules. Fiberglass shingles are very long-lived, but they are some-what brittle in cold weather. Some roofers in the snowbelt refuse to install fiberglass shingles at all, while others will install them only in warm weather. Fiberglass shingles have excellent fire resistance, with a Class A rating, in contrast to the Class C rating carried by organic shingles.

The two most common types of asphalt roof shingles are the *three-tab*, also called strip shingles, and *architectural*, also called laminate shingles. A three-tab shingle is a rectangular mat with two slots cut in its front edge. The slots provide stress relief as the shingle expands and contracts with the weather. An architectural shingle has a heavy base mat and another mat or sections of mat applied on top of it. Aside from making the shingle heavier and more durable, this construction gives the roof shadow lines and improves its visual appeal.

Finally, there are regional and specialized forms of asphalt roofing, such as a highly wind-resistant shingle called a *T-lock*. These slotted T-shaped shingles lock to the shingles below and above. Some manufacturers also offer asphalt shingles without any tab cutouts.

When a new asphalt shingle roof is installed, the roofer has the option of either laying the new roofing over the old roof, or stripping the roof down to the decking before laying new underlayment and shingles. In most regions, local building codes allow for no more than two layers of asphalt shingles on a roof. If your house already has two layers, you'll need to have a "rip" done before the new roofing can be laid.

Wood Roofing

At one time, wood shakes (rough, with an uneven texture) and shingles (smooth and uniformly shaped) went directly from the tree to the roof with no enhancements. Today's wood shingles and shakes are more sophisticated. Cedar roofing is factory-treated with chemicals to boost its fire rating. Southern yellow pine shakes are pressure-treated to help them resist rot and decay, and although these shakes have been on the market for less than a decade, their manufacturers expect the product to have a life span of 30 years.

To get maximum durability out of a cedar roof, roofers recommend you clean it once or twice a year with a pressure washer to remove debris and apply preservatives to help it resist sun and weather.

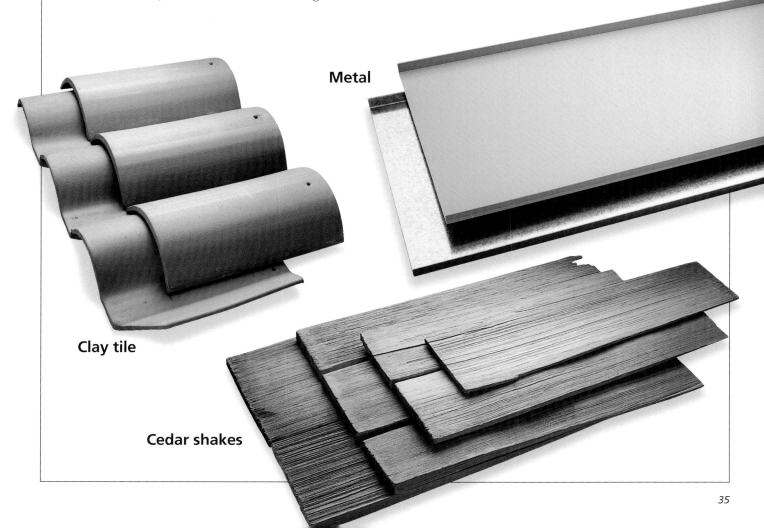

Metal

Clay tile

Cedar shakes

Clay Tile

Clay tile is among the oldest and most durable of roofing materials. Made from kiln-dried clay, these tiles are weather-resistant, fireproof and insect-proof. Most people think these tiles are limited to the barrel-shaped type common in the West, but clay tiles can be flat, and they may have a glossy surface. Clay tiles are generally secured with clips or fasteners, but among the most interesting methods is a tie-wire system in which the tiles literally hang from the wires suspended from the ridge of the house.

Roll Roofing

Roofs with a shallow pitch are often covered with sheets of asphalt-granular material laid in overlapping rows. Roll roofing is often found on porches, shed dormers, and other locations where the roof pitch is very shallow. Roll roofing generally has a shorter life span than asphalt shingles; few roll roofing installations will survive more than 10 or 15 years before they need to be replaced.

Slate

Slate roofing comes in gray, purple, green and red. Properly installed, it has incredible durability. If it is protected from falling tree limbs or other impacts, it can last almost indefinitely. Slate is very expensive to install, and while it doesn't require much maintenance, an old slate roof might need a little tender loving care, such as fixing the odd cracked piece.

Cementitious Roof Tile

Cementitious roof tile offers a traditional look using modern materials. These products are made from portland cement, sometimes reinforced with cellulose fibers. Available in a variety of colors, cement tiles can be molded to look like wood shingles, barrel-shaped tiles or slate.

The strong suit of cementitious roofing tiles is their durability—you can expect 30 to 60 years of life from a cement tile roof. Such a roof is also virtually impervious to moisture, fungus, insects and fire. A cement tile roof is very heavy, however, and requires roof framing and decking sturdy enough to support it.

Metal Roofing

Metal roofing is available in the widest range of materials and configurations. The most common types are steel panels with exposed fasteners, steel panels with hidden fasteners, and aluminum panels designed to look like shakes, shingles or tiles. Other options include copper and terne-coated stainless steel (terne is an alloy of lead and tin).

To combat rust, steel panels are galvanized, either with zinc or a zinc-aluminum compound.

Metal roofs are relatively inexpensive and may last as long as 60 years. They are popular in regions of heavy snow fall, because the snow tends to slide off rather than pile up.

Built-up Roofing

Homes with nearly flat roof pitches are usually roofed with alternating layers of asphalt-saturated building paper and liquid asphalt. Gravel, crushed stone or marble chips are then spread over the surface to help reflect heat. Depending on your climate, a built-up roof needs to be resurfaced every 7 to 15 years.

Slate shingles

Gutters & Downspouts

If you want to start an argument going among home builders, bring up the subject of roof gutters. Some builders insist that gutters are necessary to divert water away from the siding and basement walls. Others insist gutters create more problems than they solve. In regions with snowy winters, for example, they claim that gutters may contribute to the formation of ice dams that can ruin a roof.

Arguments aside, if you have a gutter system you've got to make certain it's working properly. You could have real troubles on your hands otherwise.

Gutters are installed below the edge of the roof and are slightly angled so water flows to the downspouts. They must be free of leaks or blockage. You should clean the system at least twice a year. If the downspouts are plugged, you can clean them with a drain auger. Installing strainers will help keep leaves and twigs from clogging the downspouts in the future.

Should your gutter system clog, water will spill over the edge onto the eaves and possibly work its way down your house's siding. In the winter, the problem can be worse. Build-ups of ice can bend or destroy gutters, and ice-clogged gutters can act as miniature dams (hence "ice dams"). Melted snow, kept liquid by an overly warm roof, can rise behind these dams and force its way under shingles.

These problems can be avoided by making certain your gutters are clear. You should also make certain your roof is well ventilated—meaning cold—and keep snow from piling up.

Also make sure that the water flowing through the downspouts is directed away from the house. Otherwise, rushing water can damage your yard or garden and it can

drain down foundation walls and contribute to a leaky basement.

Make certain your house has splash blocks, diverter hoses or a drainage system designed to channel roof runoff into the ground away from your foundation. Many homeowners are surprised to discover that damp basement walls can be eliminated by proper drainage.

Downspouts must be large enough to carry your roof's runoff. Roofs 1000 square feet or less need only 3-inch-diameter downspouts. Larger roofs must have

4-inch-diameter downspouts.

Gutters and downspouts can be made of aluminum, copper, galvanized steel, vinyl or wood. What kind of material you have will affect its performance.

Aluminum is light and doesn't rust, but it's easy to damage. Copper is very durable but very expensive. Steel is strong and less expensive, but it must be kept painted to prevent rust. Vinyl is easy to maintain, and relatively cheap. Wood can add a natural look, but it must be periodically treated to prevent decay.

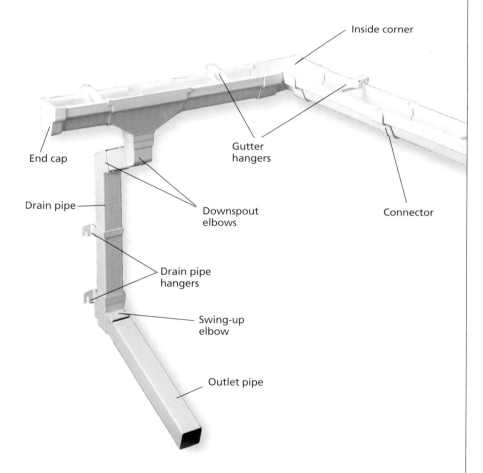

Vinyl gutter and downspout components make it easy and inexpensive to install your own gutter system.

Your roof must always have an air gap between the insulation and the roof decking. Without this ventilation gap, moisture can be trapped against the roof decking and will eventually cause rot. Insulation baffles can be installed to provide this air space.

Roof vent

Insulation baffle

Insulation

Soffit vent

A common roof vent will ventilate 150 square feet of attic space; 300 square feet if you have vapor barriers in your attic.

A gable vent is a good way to increase cross-ventilation without altering the roof surface.

Vents

Here's a paradox: The best roofs always have plenty of holes.

What do we mean? That good roofs always have proper ventilation.

Roof vents are openings in the attic or in the enclosed roof over-hang (soffit), designed to allow moisture and excess heat to escape. For new construction, most Building Codes require at least one square foot of venting for every 300 square feet of ceiling area on a pitched roof. However, if you don't have vapor barriers in your attic, you need to have a ventilation ratio of 1 to 150 square feet.

Without proper ventilation, water vapor that seeps up through your house (from showers and cooking and other daily activities) can condense and collect on insulation and roofing framing. Over time, the moisture will reduce the effectiveness of the insulation and can cause rotting in your framing. Vents make certain this moisture-laden air is dispersed outdoors before it can condense.

Vents also transfer heat. In the summer, a poorly ventilated roof can cause your house temperatures to rise because hot air gets trapped in your attic. Proper venting can drop attic temperatures by 40°F or more. And in the winter, vents ensure that your roof stays cold, which is essential to prevent snow from melting and flowing down to the overhangs, where it cools, re-freezes, and forms ice dams.

There are a host of venting options. Turbine vents harness the wind to draw air out of your attic; soffit vents under the eaves allow for excellent air flow up under the rafters; ridge vents, working in concert with soffit vents, permit hot air to exit at the very peak of a roof; cupola vents add an architectural flourish to a roof; gable vents allow for cross-ventilation.

LEAKS

Using a ladder, or a pair of binoculars if you don't care for heights, check your roof for these signs that your roof needs replacement or repair.

• Torn or loose shingles, especially along the roof's ridges and in its valleys.

• Shingles that are curled, blistered or broken.

• Protruding nail heads.

• Worn shingles. See if the granules have worn off and asphalt is showing through.

• A crooked ridge. This may indicate serious problems with the roof decking.

• Soft spots in the roof. These can usually be spotted because the shingles will tear away easily from rotten decking in a wind storm.

Sometimes you don't have to look for a problem; it finds you. Plenty of homeowners have experienced the queasy feeling that comes with finding a wet spot emerging on a perfect ceiling. If your roof is leaking, you need to repair the problem immediately. Even minor leaks can rot wood and cause ceilings to fall. A small leak that goes unnoticed for years can cause a great deal of damage.

Roof leaks are not always caused by shingle problems. Pay attention to metal flashing, as well.

Flashing leaks are most common near chimneys or vent stacks. The resulting gap allows water to flow unimpeded into your house. Often, a tell-tale damp spot will appear on a ceiling or wall near a chimney or roof vent. This type of repair can be fairly simple, if the flashing itself is in decent shape. You can just smooth a layer of roofing cement over any exposed seams, making certain not to produce any depressions that could pool water. If the flashing has pulled away from the mortar on your chimney, or if the flashing has rusted through, repairs will be more difficult. Consult a roofer or find a good how-to book and learn how to make these repairs.

If the flashing is okay and the roofing appears to be in good shape, check for small sections of damaged shingles (or shakes, tiles, etc.). Pinpointing a leak is easiest if you have an unfinished attic. During a rainstorm, inspect the underside of the decking for moisture. Rarely is a leak directly over the spot where your ceiling is damp. Rather, water may stream several feet down along the decking or rafters before falling to the floor of the attic. Patch the hole with caulk, and mark the spot by driving a small nail through the roof. Pinpointing the leak is more difficult if you don't have access to the underside of the roof decking. In this case, you must venture atop your roof to search for the culprit.

Water stains on rafters and decking are tell-tale signs of roof leaks. Repair or replace the roof immediately, and carefully check for signs of rot and other water damage.

Warped shingles can be repaired and patched, but you should view this as a sign that your roof may soon need replacement.

Cracked and broken shingles indicate that your roof is on the verge of complete failure. A roof in this condition will almost certainly leak, and is not a candidate for repair.

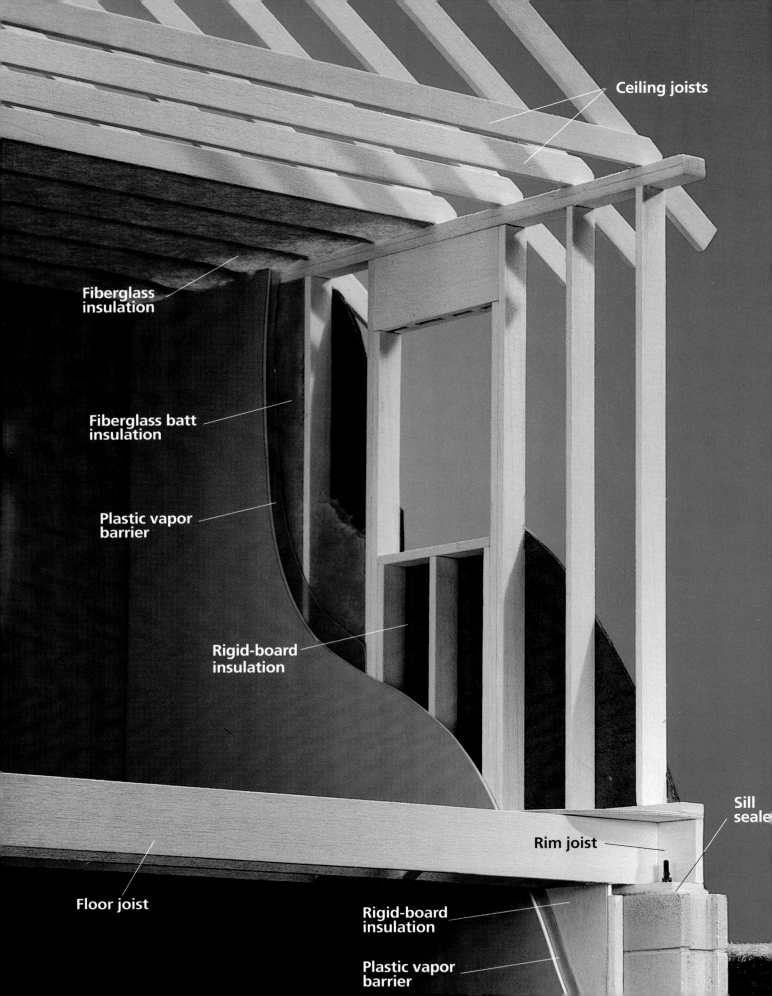

Ceiling joists

Fiberglass
insulation

Fiberglass batt
insulation

Plastic vapor
barrier

Rigid-board
insulation

Floor joist

Rigid-board
insulation

Plastic vapor
barrier

Rim joist

Sill
seale

INSULATION & WEATHERPROOFING

Before you take a look at your home's insulation, pour yourself a cup of hot coffee.

Notice what you use to hold the coffee? It's probably a ceramic mug with a handle or a Styrofoam cup. You obviously want a device that will keep your coffee hot and your hands cool.

The same principles apply to your home. If it's freezing cold outside, you still want the interior of your house comfortably warm. Or if it's blazing hot outdoors, you prefer a cool indoor retreat.

Insulation and weatherproofing are the keys to achieving this goal. Mind you, how well your house is insulated depends in part on its age and location. A home built in a temperate region in the 1940s or 1950s, when energy was very cheap, may have very little or no insulation. A northern home built after 1970, on the other hand, probably has fairly ample insulation. Even the choice of building materials can affect the home's energy efficiency. Wood shingles and siding materials, for example, have a noticeable insulating value, while slate shingles and masonry siding materials have almost none.

Although it's possible for a home to be too airtight (*below*), this is the exception rather than the rule. No matter what the age of your home, a close inspection will almost certainly reveal some areas where additional insulation and weatherstripping will be helpful. And unlike many elements of your home—such as the foundation, framing or roofing—insulation and weatherproofing are aspects that can be easily improved at a reasonable cost.

Making sure your home is properly insulated and weatherproofed offers many benefits: your home will be more comfortable, you'll pay less in utility bills and you'll have the satisfaction of knowing you're doing your part to conserve energy.

AIRTIGHT HOUSE SYNDROME

It's an old story by now. Medical experts have long known that modern commercial office buildings with fixed windows and sealed air circulation systems can create health problems—especially respiratory ailments. Less widespread is the knowledge that many private homes share some of the same air-quality problems.

Over the last 50 years or so, improvements to building materials, such as the introduction of plywood, asphalt-impregnated roofing felt and new types of insulation gradually tightened the typical new home construction. Homes built in the 1950s and 1960s were considerably more energy efficient than earlier homes, but they were not yet so tight that air quality became a serious issue.

Then came the oil crisis and soaring energy costs of the 1970s, when builders and homeowners began to caulk, plug and cover virtually every crack and gap where cold air might enter or heat might escape. At about this time, health officials began to notice an upsurge in cases of asthma, carbon monoxide poisoning and other health problems. The money that homeowners saved on energy was instead being spent on doctors' fees and medications to combat headaches and respiratory ailments caused by constantly breathing stale air.

We now know that a tightly sealed house can trap a host of harmful contaminants, including radon gas, molds and dust mites, nitrogen dioxide from gas stoves and furnaces, and formaldehyde vapors given off by certain building materials. Tightly sealed homes can also cause the buildup of moisture, which leads to mold and wood decay. Most seriously, if a home is so tightly sealed that the furnace gets insufficient air, deadly carbon monoxide gas can back up into the home.

Should you panic? Not necessarily. If your home was built before 1960, it's not likely you can seal it tightly enough to cause serious air-quality problems. And if your home was built after 1985, the builder was more than likely aware of the potential hazard and used materials and construction techniques designed to ensure good air quality. For example, newer homes sometimes include a heat recovery ventilation (HRV) unit to provide regular air exchange. And newer furnaces and fireplaces often draw their combustion air from the outdoors rather than indoors.

If you suspect that your home may have an air-quality problem, look for one or more of the following signs.

•EVIDENCE OF BACKDRAFTING. Look for soot marks around the burner units on gas furnaces and appliances. This indicates that a lack of fresh air is causing combustion gases to back up into your home.

•CONDENSATION. Noticeable moisture condensing on windows, or mildew on wall surfaces indicates that your home is not "breathing" adequately.

•PERSISTENT SMELLS. If food odors or the odor of cleaning solutions persist for many hours, it often means that fresh air is not entering your home.

•UNEXPLAINED HEALTH SYMPTOMS. Headaches, nausea, dizziness, eye inflammation, nose irritations and vomiting can all be caused by poor air quality.

Soot near the hood of a gas water heater exhaust stack may indicate a dangerous backdraft.

INSULATION GUIDE

If we learned anything from the energy crisis of the late seventies and early eighties, it was the importance of making buildings energy efficient. Building Codes began to require insulation in new homes, and local utilities, government agencies and insulation manufacturers spread the word about the benefits of adding insulation in older homes. People saved money on energy bills and may have even earned a federal income tax credit.

But things are different now. Most people inclined to upgrade the energy efficiency of their homes have already done so. The question now has become whether adding more insulation makes economic sense.

The answer varies. Adding insulation certainly makes sense for walls and ceilings that have no insulation at all, and it's probably a good idea if you are increasing existing insulation to levels that meet current Department of Energy guidelines. But extra insulation is not a wise idea if the cost of the upgrade exceeds projected savings.

To determine the energy efficiency of your house, you'll first need to locate and measure the insulation in your house. Check all surfaces that are adjacent to cold, unheated areas: upstairs ceilings, exterior walls, floors above unheated basements and crawl spaces.

Next, try to determine the R-value of the existing insulation. The R-value is a rating that indicates a material's resistance to heat conduction. Some insulation lists this information on a paper or foil facing. Or you can use the chart below to estimate the R-value of your insulation.

Now, compare these R-values with the Department of Energy recommendations, as shown in the chart (left). Although it's a safe bet that installing insulation where none was present will save you money, it's trickier to determine the wisdom of increasing insulation in walls and ceilings that are already insulated.

The best way to make this decision is to calculate the payback period of the new insulation. Use the Insulation Comparison chart below to determine how much it will cost to bring your insulation up to DOE standards. Next, contact your utility company or fuel supplier for an estimate regarding the per-year savings you'll realize based on the insulation upgrade. Once you have the total cost of the new insulation, including installation costs, divide this number by the per-year savings estimate to learn how long it will take to recover the investment. If you expect to live in your house long enough to recoup these costs, then it makes sense to add insulation.

RECOMMENDED INSULATION AMOUNTS

	Northern Zone	Temperate Zone	Southern Zone
Attic:	R38	R30	R26
Walls:	R19	R19	R19
Floors:	R22	R13	R11

INSULATION COMPARISON

Type of Insulation	R-Value Per Inch	Cost Per R-Value Per Square Foot	Comments
Fiberglass Batts, Loose Fill	2.9 to 3.2	$.01 to $.019	Easy to work with, but will irritate skin, eyes and lungs. Nonflammable, except for paper facings.
Loose-Fill Mineral Wool	3.3	$.019	Uses and precautions similar to fiberglass.
Cellulose	3.2	$.014	Inexpensive. Must be treated with fire-retarding chemicals. Installation labor can be expensive.
Extruded Polystyrene Panels	5	$.077	Used on exterior foundation walls and under slabs. Cover with fire-rated wallboard when used inside.
Expanded Polystyrene Panels	4	$.046	Used on foundation walls; not as strong as extruded types. Cover with fire-rated wallboard indoors.
Polyisocyanurate Panels	7	$.077	Commonly used as sheathing. R-value may drop over time. CFCs used in manufacturing.
Air Krete	3.9	$.08	Foam applied by trained installer. Prices may depend on availability of trained personnel.

Attic

The place to start checking your home for insulation is at the top. If your house has insulation in only one location, it's safe to assume it will be in the attic. Attics are easy to insulate, and the materials used to insulate these spaces are inexpensive and readily available.

If your attic is unfinished, begin by inspecting the space between the floor joists for insulation. If you have a finished attic, examine the joist cavities in any unheated crawl spaces behind the finished walls. Mineral fibers—fiberglass and rock wool in batts, blankets and loose-fill material—are the insulations most often used in attics, although joist cavities may be filled with cellulose loose-fill insulation. In a colder climate, most experts suggest at least 12 inches of insulation; if you find less than this in your attic, you should consider adding more. In addition to filling the joist cavities with insulation, you can also lay an additional fiberglass blanket over the tops of the joists.

Whether you are merely inspecting insulation already in place or considering the addition of new insulation, make sure that the insulation does not cover recessed light fixtures. Local Building Codes usually require a minimum 3-inch airspace between recessed light fixtures and insulation, unless the fixture is rated IC (insulated ceiling). Even though mineral fibers won't easily burn, they can cause an unrated fixture to overheat and start a fire in the ceiling. Sheet metal shields that surround the fixture are available to create a safety zone. Don't pile insulation above the fixture.

While inspecting the attic, also look for thermal bypasses—gaps and cracks around chimneys and plumbing pipes where heat may rise freely into the attic from the heated spaces below. These gaps are notorious heat bandits; simply

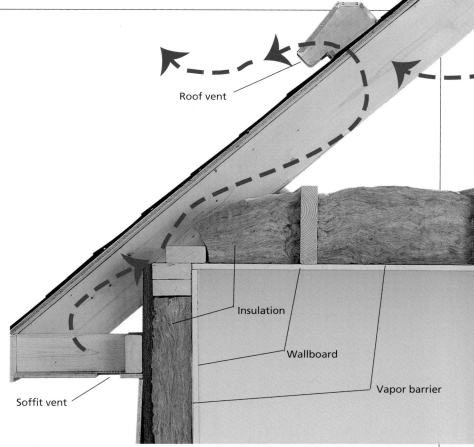

In a well-designed attic, vapor barriers, insulation and vents work together to prevent moisture damage and keep the interior of your home comfortable.

When measuring insulation in an unfinished attic, put your weight only on the joists, never on the space between joists. A piece of scrap plywood can make this work easier.

sealing the gaps with foam or packed fiberglass insulation can lead to significant energy savings.

With a skylight shaft that runs from roofline to the floor of your attic, make sure the shaft is wrapped with fiberglass insulation.

If you have a heated, finished attic, try to determine whether the rafter spaces behind finished ceiling surfaces have been insulated. This diagnosis is easiest if you have access to the unheated crawl spaces behind the knee walls. Try to determine if ceiling insulation was installed so there is an air gap of

one inch or so between the insulation and the roof sheathing. Without this gap, moisture can become trapped inside the rafter spaces and can cause roof sheathing, wallboard or plaster to break down or rot. If you find this situation, make careful annual inspections and correct the problem at the first sign of moisture damage. Rusty spots in the wallboard indicate that nails are corroding. Your wisest move is to remove the ceiling material and rebuild the surface with proper insulation and vapor barriers.

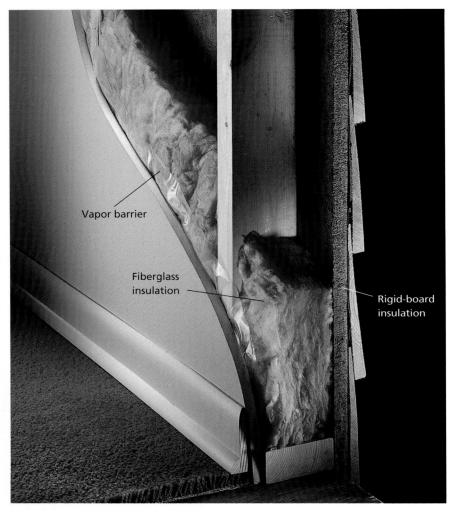

Vapor barrier

Fiberglass insulation

Rigid-board insulation

In new construction, walls usually have an exterior sheathing of rigid-board insulation, with wall cavities insulated with fiberglass batts. A plastic vapor barrier covers the insulation just under the wallboard.

In older construction (left), the exterior sheathing is made of wood planks. Insulation, if present at all, is probably loose-fill cellulose. Cellulose insulation was added to many homes in the 1970s and 1980s.

Walls

Although exterior walls are slightly less susceptible to heat loss than ceilings, insulation is no less important. Determining the precise insulation values of your existing walls can be difficult, though identifying uninsulated walls is usually painfully easy. If you feel icy drafts penetrating around electrical outlets and door casings, or if the walls feel cool to the touch in winter, it's a strong sign that your wall insulation is substandard.

Removing electrical coverplates and heating registers can often reveal what kind of insulation you have inside the wall cavities. Be forewarned: in older homes, this investigation may reveal no insulation whatsoever, or an outdated insulating material, such as shredded paper. If you have a newer home (built after 1980) or an older home that was re-sided in the last 20 years or so, the exterior walls may be sheathed with rigid fiber or foam panels that offer some insulation value. Prying up a board or two can let you identify the sheathing material.

Though improving wall insulation has obvious merit, the methods available for accomplishing this task are limited. To insulate the wall cavities in an existing house without removing the interior wall surfaces, it's necessary to drill holes through either the interior or exterior and blow in loose-fill fiberglass or cellulose. The goal here is to completely fill every bay between studs—a job that can be difficult because of the fire stops and other blocking that may be present. This work is usually done by a contractor who has the proper equipment, although homeowners can also lease this equipment at rental centers.

When it's time to add new siding, many people take this opportunity to install rigid-board insulation before the siding goes on. This not only increases the R-value of the wall, but it also insulates over the studs, something fiberglass batts placed between the studs can't do.

Whenever you are remodeling or adding on to your home, consider the insulation value of the walls. The walls of a new addition, for example, offer the chance to achieve high R-values in a number of ways. For example, framing with 2 × 6s rather than 2 × 4s allows room for an extra R-6 when insulating with fiberglass. You can also combine fiberglass with rigid-board insulation to get even higher R-values. Rigid insulation used on interior walls must be covered with fire-rated drywall.

Spaces around door and window framing members should be filled with fiberglass insulation. If this was not done when the walls were framed, you can remove the casings to pack insulation in these spaces. Doing so can miraculously reduce drafts around doors and windows.

Expandable foam can seal drafty gaps, like those below baseboard moldings.

VAPOR BARRIERS

All exterior walls—wood framed or masonry—should have a vapor barrier between the insulation and the "warm-in-winter" side of the wall.

A vapor barrier is any material that significantly resists the flow of moisture, such as polyethylene film or aluminum foil. Fiberglass insulation is available with a kraft paper or foil facing that's intended as a vapor barrier.

In colder regions, vapor barriers should be installed so they face the inside of the wall. This keeps moisture vapor from passing through the insulation and condensing on the cold surfaces beyond. This moisture reduces the effectiveness of your insulation, and it can eventually cause framing members and sheathing to rot. If paper-faced batts are installed in a floor over an unheated basement or crawl space, the paper faces up.

In warm, humid climates, however, the outside relative humidity levels are as high or even higher than the humidity levels inside houses. In these locales, vapor often drives into a house from the outdoors, rather than the other way around.

There is considerable disagreement about the proper use of vapor barriers in warm climates. Many insulation contractors in these regions install vapor barriers on both sides of the insulation, while other contractors omit the barrier altogether.

But the latest recommendation from insulation manufacturers is to always put a vapor barrier on the warm side if the average January temperature is less than 35°F, such as in Green Bay, Wisconsin. No vapor barrier is necessary if the average January temperature is higher than 35°F, such as in Miami.

To be on the safe side, though, it's best to check with local building officials and reputable contractors in your area.

Vapor barriers are designed to keep moist air from migrating into wall spaces, where it can condense.

Basements & Crawl Spaces

Many people overlook their basements or crawl spaces when it comes to insulation and weatherproofing. They know to look in the attic, but they fail to check down below. As a result, most basements and crawl spaces are woefully underinsulated.

Check your own basement. See how much insulation—if any—you have. Probe, too, for gaps in your walls near pipes or laundry vents.

Does your ground floor meet—or even approach—the R-value guidelines found earlier in the chapter? If not, it's time to get working.

Check the rim joists and head joists in your basement to see if the spaces above the foundation walls are insulated. If these spaces are empty, loosely filling the sections between joists with fiberglass insulation can cut energy losses substantially.

In an unheated basement, the spaces between floor joists should be packed with fiberglass insulation, or a combination of fiberglass and rigid board.

If your basement is finished—or if you are planning a remodeling project to turn your basement into living space—the walls should be insulated. One method for doing this is to build a frame wall and install fiberglass batts between the studs. Since the wall will not be load-bearing, it can be pulled out a few inches from the foundation, providing extra space that can be filled with insulation. Another technique calls for attaching rigid-board insulation to the concrete walls with construction adhesive (*opposite page*).

The walls of crawl spaces should be insulated with either fiberglass or rigid-board insulation. Even after the walls are insulated, wrap the pipes and HVAC ducts in crawl

Weatherproofing basement windows is easy with preformed plastic window guards. Fasten them to your foundation walls with masonry anchors and weigh down the bottom flange with stones. Also caulk around the edges.

Insulate the spaces around rim joists and header joists. Pack the insulation just tightly enough to keep it from falling out; compressing the insulation reduces its effectiveness.

spaces with fiberglass or foam insulation. Cover dirt floors in crawl spaces with a 6-mil polyethylene vapor barrier to prevent ground moisture from entering the house. Keep the barrier in place with bricks or stones.

Depending on when it was constructed, your house may have extruded or expanded polystyrene insulation attached to the exterior of foundation walls. Digging down one to two feet along the foundation will tell you if this is the case. Extruded polystyrene is the better choice here, because it stands up to the pressure of backfill, while expanded styrene will crumble. Adding exterior foundation insulation is not practical with an existing house, but if you have plans for a room addition, make sure the outside of the new foundation is insulated. Another option with a concrete block foundation is to fill the inner cavities of the blocks with foam as the foundation is created.

Walls in heated basements can be insulated with rigid-board insulation installed between furring strips glued to the masonry walls. The insulation and furring strips should be covered with a vapor barrier before wallboard or paneling is attached.

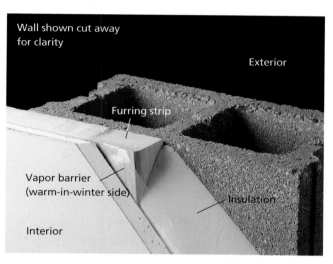

Wall shown cut away for clarity

Exterior

Furring strip

Vapor barrier (warm-in-winter side)

Insulation

Interior

Caulk around dryer vents or service pipes entering your basement, using a good-quality silicone caulk.

In an unheated basement, the spaces between ceiling joists should be insulated with paper-faced insulation, installed so the facing is against the heated floor side of the spaces. If you do this work yourself, make sure to wear long sleeves, gloves, and eye and lung protection to guard against irritation caused by the mineral fibers.

Seal gaps around the foundation sill plate, using plastic or foam backer rope. Sealing these gaps will also provide a barrier against insects and other pests seeking entry to your house.

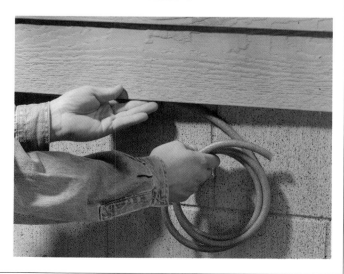

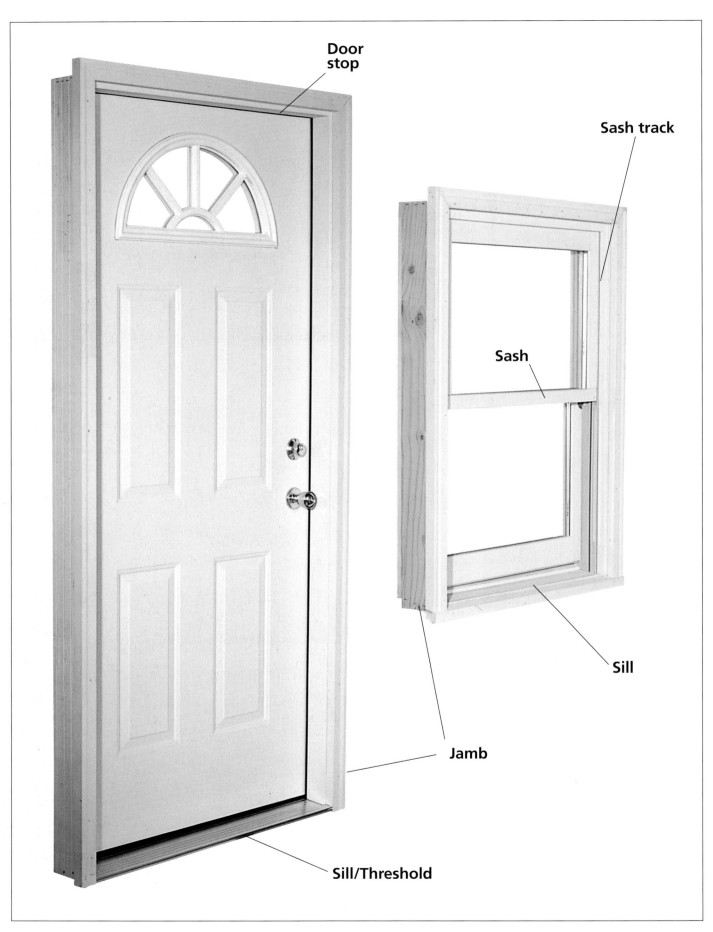

Door
stop

Sash track

Sash

Sill

Jamb

Sill/Threshold

DOORS & WINDOWS

The next time you step through your front entryway or pause to gaze through a living room window, consider, for a moment, the challenging role that doors and windows play in your home.

We want our doors to allow us easy passage in and out of the house, but we expect them to repel unwanted intruders. Windows are expected to allow sunlight to pass through them, but they must repel rain, snow and insects.

On the outside, doors and windows must contend with storms, bitter cold or searing heat, while on the inside they face completely opposite conditions. We expect them to perform day after day without getting weepy with condensation or frosty with ice, and we want them to look nice all the while. And one other thing: windows and doors need to last for decades.

In this chapter, we'll look at how to evaluate your doors and windows and keep them in good working condition—whatever their age. Plus, we'll look at locks, hinges and other essential hardware.

If you're under the impression that doors and windows have remained pretty much unchanged over the years, you're in for a surprise. Advances in technology—some of them truly "space age"—have made doors and windows a great deal more durable and free of trouble.

But don't lament if you have an older house with original doors and windows. Though they won't be as energy-efficient as newer models, they can still provide many years of trouble-free service—provided you keep them in good operating condition.

HIGH-TECH GLASS

The glass in a modern window or door is a good deal more than a simple pane of glass mounted in a wood frame. Today's marketplace boasts a wide variety of products and some pretty impressive price tags to boot. Over the past several years, advances in technology have shown that glass can play a much more important role in conserving energy than ever before.

As recently as the early 1980s, people who replaced their old single-pane windows (R-value less than 1.0) with double-glazed windows were at the forefront in the fight to save energy. Those who opted for triple-glazed windows—the limits of technology at the time — were considered energy fanatics. But even those fanatics were just toying with the weakest link in the energy chain in their homes. Those triple-glazed units had insulation values of about R-3, while the walls that held them had R-values that ranged from 11 to 19. In many well-insulated houses, the windows were simply holes in the walls where vast amounts of energy escaped. The average home lost about 25% of its energy through the windows.

Today, things are different. Most windows are still energy drains, but some models offer much more energy efficiency than the glazing systems of the past. A few models boast insulation values as high as R-8. When you factor in the solar heat gain, some of these new high-tech windows outperform an R-19 wall in terms of net energy loss.

Plain double-glazed windows (R-value about 1.75) now make up the bulk of the market, but most window manufacturers are selling double-glazed windows with some version of high-performance glazing, made possible by the development of low-E (low emissivity) coatings. When applied to a window, these coatings reflect heat back into the home. Some low-E coatings are also used to reflect outside heat radiated by the street and buildings into the house.

Some low-E coatings are bonded to the glass, others are incorporated into the glass, and still others are applied to a film that's suspended between two panes of glass. There are pros and cons for each type of coating. *Soft coat* products, which are bonded to the surface of the glass, offer the best insulating properties. *Hard coat* products, which are part of the glass itself, are more durable. In general, any low-E coating will improve the R-value of a double-glazed window to roughly equal that of a standard triple-glazed window. The low-E double-glazed glass, however, is about 50% lighter than a triple-glazed window.

To increase the thermal effectiveness of low-E windows, manufacturers offer double-glazed windows in which the empty space between the panes is filled with argon or another inert gas. When combined with reflective low-E coatings, gas-filled double-glazed windows can have an insulation value around R-4.

When this low-E and inert gas technology is applied to triple-glazed windows, the R-value can reach as high as 8.0. At least one manufacturer suspends two low-E films between panes and fills all three spaces with krypton gas.

Of course, all this technology comes with a price. Although costs will vary, low-E coatings add 15% to 20% to the cost of a standard double-glazed window and gas-filled windows are even more expensive. The heftier price tags may be worth the investment, however. The Department of Energy estimates that on a new home, windows using low-E technology will save enough energy to pay for themselves in about four years. For the higher-R products, the payback is roughly eight years.

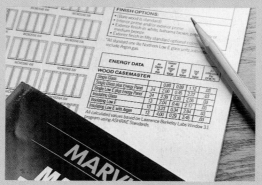

Most window manufacturers now offer at least one high-efficiency glazing option. Product catalogs show the glazing options available.

Bi-fold door

Entry door

Passage door

Exterior doors need to be strong, durable and well insulated. A solid wood door can have an R-value as low as 2, while an insulated foam-core door can have an R-value approaching 15.

Your house needs to have one exterior door that is at least 36" wide and 6 ft. 8" high. For ease of moving large items, wider and higher is better.

Entry Doors

A logical place to start your inspection is with the entry doors. Begin by measuring them. Front doors are normally at least 80 inches high, 36 inches wide, and 1¾ inches thick; rear doors may be narrower. Current local codes require that at least one entry door have a clear opening at least 36 inches wide and at least 80 inches high. Although there's no reason to replace a door that doesn't meet Code minimum, it does make sense to know the exact dimensions of your entry doors. Many an appliance was returned to the store because the sheepish home-owner didn't know the size of the entry door.

Front or rear, your entry doors should be made of solid fiberglass or wood, or solid wood clad with steel or vinyl. An inexpensive hollow-core door invites heat loss, and it's easy for a burglar to kick in. In addition, solid-core doors are less likely to warp.

Also inspect the door hinges. Because of their weight, entry doors should be hung on three hinges. Make sure the hinges are solidly anchored to the frame.

For security, an exterior door should have a good lockset attached: a deadbolt is best. You should also have a way to see who-ever is outside the door. If you don't have a window that provides a clear view of visitors, then add a peephole.

Passage Doors

Interior passage doors are generally thinner and narrower than exterior doors—and they don't have to be as sturdy. Passage doors are commonly 30 to 34 inches wide and 1⅜ inches thick.

It's a mistake to seal all gaps around a passage door in the same fashion you would weatherstrip an entry door. On passage doors, a slight gap should exist at the bottom of the door. In bathrooms with an exhaust vent, for example, a door that fits too snugly will not allow enough air to flow under the door, interfering with ventilation.

Many newer houses have flush doors that are hollow or filled with honeycombed cardboard. Older houses, and better quality newer houses, rely on wood panel doors, which generally provide better soundproofing.

If you have any locks on interior doors, make certain that you can unlock them from the outside. This ensures that you'll be able to provide assistance should someone sustain an injury behind a locked door. And, of course, you won't have to worry about children accidentally (or not so accidentally) locking themselves in.

Replacement Tip

Replacing doors in an older house can be a little complicated. If the doorways are of nonstandard size, you must either special-order custom doors or cut down a stock door to fit the space. In many older houses, upstairs rooms have smaller doors than those found downstairs. When replacing a door, make certain the style of the door "fits" as well as the size.

DOOR OPTIONS

Not long ago, hanging a door was considered a tricky proposition. With today's prehung doors, replacing or upgrading a door is much easier. When you buy a new door, consider how you want it to perform. An insulated steel entry door will provide good security, but it won't look as inviting as a solid wood door. A solid wood door, though, will require more maintenance and won't provide the same level of insulation as a fiberglass door. Most doors must endure heavy use, so don't skimp on quality. Interior passage doors, too, offer more options than you might imagine. Soundproofing, for example, is often overlooked when choosing a new passage door. You'll find that bathrooms and bedrooms can benefit greatly from choosing doors with good soundproofing values.

Core-block doors have glue-laminated wood blocks covered with veneer. These doors are less likely to warp than solid-core doors because the wood grain runs in alternate directions.

Insulated heavy-gauge steel doors can offer good protection against the cold and against intruders trying to kick them in. You'll need a "thermal break" to keep cold metal edges of door away from metal thresholds.

Fiberglass doors are expensive, but they have good insulating properties and are tough. Though the fiberglass may be pretinted, the surface can also be painted or stained.

Storm Doors

Combination storm doors are considered nearly mandatory in some parts of the country. With proper weatherstripping, storm doors cut winter drafts significantly and can roughly double the R-value of an entry door. In the summer, a screen insert will provide ventilation. Be forewarned: during hot summer days, direct sunlight can heat unventilated air space between the two doors to the point where door trim warps and paint melts.

Specialty Doors

A modern home may have a number of different door styles.

Glass entry doors incorporate windows or sidelights, which can help brighten a dark entry hall. As you probably know, however, glass door panels are almost always the weak link in your home's security. If the door lock can be reached through a broken window, it provides a tempting target for intruders. In better models, the glass is tempered and double-glazed for better security and energy efficiency. A great many homeowners eventually replace glass doors with more secure solid-core doors.

Sliding patio doors are enormously popular, offering easy access to a deck or patio, and let in lots of natural light. In millions of homes across the country, patio doors have also let in burglars and other intruders. Even when "locked" most patio doors can be lifted off their tracks quite easily. And once the doors are removed, the opening is large enough to allow thieves to carry off almost anything they choose.

There is some good news, though. If your patio door was installed in the last few years, it may feature an anti-lift plate that prevents the glass panels from being removed. Newer doors may also have multipoint locking systems that "deadbolt" the door into the top and bottom frames. If you have an older patio door, look into retrofit products that can improve the security of your door.

To keep your patio doors operating smoothly, periodically inspect and clean the tracks, to help keep the rollers in proper adjustment.

French doors are double doors that swing open from the center. They provide an elegant appearance and let in lots of sunlight. Weathertight models are used to connect the outdoors with interior space, while indoor models join two rooms. Not surprisingly, exterior French doors tend to be poor insulators, and cheaper models don't provide much security against break-ins.

Sliding glass doors dramatically increase the amount of natural light and ventilation but they have their drawbacks. They are not well insulated, they can be very drafty, and their tracks can gather frost during the winter.

Published courtesy of Marvin Windows & Doors

Combination storm doors are available in many styles to complement the look of your home.

Door Hardware

Many, if not most, door problems originate with the hardware rather than the door itself. Most problems are caused by a simple lack of maintenance. Loose doorknobs, balky locks and squeaky hinges can all be prevented with little effort. Most problems, such as out-of-plumb doors and worn weatherstripping, are easy to fix.

Bi-fold doors, common on closets, need to be periodically lubricated. Remove the door, wipe the tracks with a cloth and spray the track and rollers with a greaseless lubricant. If the gap between doors is uneven when the doors are closed, adjust the top pivot blocks with a screwdriver or a wrench.

Locksets work by extending the latchbolt into a strike plate set in the door frame. If a doorknob or key binds when turned, the problem usually lies in the spindle and latchbolt mechanism. Cleaning and lubricating the moving parts will clear up most problems. If you have a minor alignment problem, first check the hinges. They may be loose. Otherwise, small adjustments can be made by enlarging the strike plate hole with a file.

Old doors often have passage locksets. They'll last nearly forever, if you keep them lubricated. To do so, loosen the doorknob setscrew and remove knobs and attached spindle. Loosen the faceplate screws and pry lockset from the door. Gently remove the lockset cover (don't let the spring escape from its channel) and give the entire mechanism a liberal dose of solvent-lubricant. Wipe away excess. Reinstall.

Deadbolts provide the best security for your door. Unlike a latchbolt, the deadbolt can't be jimmied open with a credit card or pick. Stay away from double-key locks, which can only be opened from the inside with a key. A missing key could prove fatal if your family has to flee in an emergency.

Windows

Windows come in so many different shapes and styles that they are almost impossible to catalog. If you live in an older house, for example, your windows may be classic double-hung windows with wood frames and single-pane glass, operated with pulleys and counterweights hung inside the walls. In a newer house, you might have space-age vinyl-clad casement windows, with double- or triple-glazed sashes and high-tech cranks. Or perhaps your house, like many, has an assortment of different window styles.

No matter what types of windows you have, it makes good sense to periodically take inventory of them and note their condition. Properly maintained, even old windows can last for many years. If you allow them to deteriorate, however, you can plan on spending thousands of dollars in the not-so-distant future.

Here are just a few of the choices available from window and door makers. Single-pane glass (A), normal on older houses, is today only installed in very mild climates. Double-pane glass (B) has a sealed air space between layers of glass to reduce heat loss. Variations include low-E glass, with an invisible coating of metal on one surface, and gas-filled windows containing an inert gas like argon. Tinted double-glazed glass (C) reduces heat buildup. Tempered glass (D) gives extra strength to patio doors and picture windows.

HOW TO BUY WINDOWS

If you're considering new windows for your home, here are some points to keep in mind as you shop for different products:

ENERGY RATINGS—Most manufacturers provide both the center-of-glass and the entire window energy ratings. Obviously, the entire window R-value is a better indicator of performance. Don't be confused if you see a U-value alongside the familiar R-value. These values are actually just different sides of the same coin. R-values measure resistance to heat transfer—the higher the better. U-values measure heat transfer— the lower the better.

SHADING COEFFICIENT—This rating tells how much solar energy a window captures. A single pane of clear glass has a shading coefficient of 1. A completely opaque window would be rated at 0. If reducing cooling costs is important in your area, pick a window that has a low shading coefficient. Tinted windows are good choices, but low-E window technology designed for warm climates can also produce low shading coefficients while providing clear light.

HANDLING LIGHT—Besides letting heat energy pass through, windows also allow light into our homes. Not all windows do this equally. Clear double-glazed windows allow about 77% of the visible light to pass through. Low-E glass allows about 70%, and a high-R window, around 62%. Some of the light is in the form of ultraviolet radiation that can fade carpets and furniture. Some windows cut UV radiation transmission to less than 1%.

AIR INFILTRATION—This is important in all climates. Windows should be well constructed and allow a minimum of air infiltra-tion. Some window designs are inherently tighter than others. Casement and awning windows are tighter than double-hung windows, for example. A rating of 0.02 or 0.03 is very tight; a rating of 0.5 is loose. These ratings apply to the window itself, not to the actual installation. Keep in mind that stopping leaks around the window once it's in the wall is the responsibility of the installer. A poor installation can negate the benefits you might expect to realize from an efficient window.

In addition to wood, several other materials are now used in the construction of window frames. Here are the benefits and drawbacks of the various materials:

WOOD—Though they have good insulating qualities and provide a better seal than metal frames, wood frames are often more expensive than other materials. Wood swells and contracts due to humidity fluctuations, and must be painted regularly.

ALUMINUM—Frames made of aluminum never need painting, but the choice of colors is limited. Aluminum is a poor insulator, and can be susceptible to condensation.

STEEL—Frames made of steel are very durable, but they have poor insulating value. Like aluminum, steel is subject to condensation. Steel frames must be painted.

VINYL-CLAD—Wood frames clad with vinyl have good insulating properties, are very durable, and never need to be painted. Vinyl can be brittle in bitter cold, however.

• Look for broken glass. In addition to being dangerous, cracked glass reduces the efficiency of the windows. Replacing single-pane glass is a fairly easy do-it-yourself project. Double- or triple-glazed window panes, however, must be special-ordered and should be installed by a professional. Cracked glass can be covered with clear packing tape to protect it until replacement is possible.

• Check the condition of the window frames. Sand and paint any bare wood, and patch any rotten wood as soon as you discover it. If you have vinyl or aluminum-clad windows, look for any cracks in the surfaces.

• Inspect the glazing that seals the glass panel in the window frame. Replace any cracked or missing glazing to prevent moisture from seriously damaging the window frame.

• Clean and lubricate all sliding surfaces and mechanical operating mechanisms. Use beeswax or soap to lubricate sliding wood windows, and greaseless spray lubricant for sliding vinyl windows. Use light spray oil to lubricate mechanical parts.

• Make sure sliding windows operate smoothly and haven't been painted in place. To free a sticky window, cut any paint film in the crack between window stop and sash, then place a block of wood along the window sash and tap it lightly with a hammer.

• Check the weatherstripping. Here's a simple test to see how snugly your windows fit: place a dollar bill under a window, close the window, and then try to slide the bill out. If it pulls out, you have a gap that should be filled with weatherstripping. Refer to the following pages for information on weatherstripping.

• Test the operation of double-hung windows. Many older double-hung windows operate with a system of pulleys, counterweights and sash cords located inside hollow pockets on both sides of the window frame. Inspect and replace the sash cords as necessary (*photos, below*).

HOW TO REPAIR SASH CORDS

Many older sash windows are balanced by counterweights hidden in the frame. Sometimes you'll find windows that have just one working sash cord. Some older houses have windows with both sash cords broken. In that case, it is easier to fix the problem than live with a faulty window that will not stay open.

1. Remove the lower window sash from the frame. On most double-hung windows, you'll need to remove the stop moldings before you can remove the sashes.

2. Pull the knotted or nailed cords from the holes in the sides of the window sashes, then unscrew or pry off the cover of the weight pocket found in the lower window channel. Remove the weights from the pockets, and untie or cut away the broken cords.

3. Tie the end of a new sash cord to a small nail, then feed the new sash cord over the pulley and down into weight pocket. Make sure the new cord is not twisted and that it runs smoothly over the pulley wheel.

4. Tie the end of the new cord to the weight, then insert it back into the pocket. Pull the cord taut and trim it to right length (about 3" longer than the length needed to reach the hole in the side of the window sash). Tie a tight knot; wedge it into the sash. Reattach the pocket cover, then install the sash and stop moldings.

Wood storm windows (left) require an investment of time and energy to install and remove every year, but they have a handsome payback. These storm windows are excellent insulators. Properly weatherstripped wooden storm windows provide a very tight seal against drafts.
TIP: Storing wood storm windows or screens by piling them against a wall can cause the frames to warp. Instead, build an elevated rack and use hooks to hang the windows by their frames.

Removing metal storm windows (below) is certainly easier than removing wood storm windows. Simply press in the release tabs in the lower rail and lift the sash toward you. Remember to align the tubular sash hangers (on the corners of the top rail) with the notches in the frame's side channels. The biggest problem plaguing metal storm windows is stickiness. The metal slides need to be lubricated in order to work without binding.

Storm Windows

Storm windows do just what their name implies: they give your house an extra layer of protection in bad weather. Long before there was energy-efficient window technology, storm windows roughly doubled the insulating value of single-glazed windows.

Back when most houses had wood storm windows, spring and fall were defined by the moments when storm windows came off and went on. On a crisp autumn day, whole neighborhoods featured storm window-toting homeowners clambering up and down their ladders. In the spring, the ladders came out again and the storm windows came down.

Some homes still have these windows, of course. And if they are well maintained, old-fashioned windows provide very good insulation and will last for decade after decade. They do require attention, however. Wood-frame storm windows need periodic painting, reglazing and weatherstripping. If you have these windows, periodically check to see that the hangers are tight. Also check to see if there are any gaps when the windows are mounted on your house.

Many older houses have replaced wood storm windows and screens with metal combination storm windows. Most newer houses in cold-weather climates were built with metal storm windows already in place. Metal storm windows need much less maintenance than their wood brethren, and they eliminate the seasonal installation and removal chores. But metal combination storm windows still need to be cleaned and lubricated to work smoothly. As with any window, try to eliminate any gaps where drafts can penetrate.

Weatherstripping

You probably wouldn't even notice a ¼-inch gap under your front door. But you would see its effects on your heating bill. Consider that with a 36-inch-wide door, a ¼-inch gap is equivalent to a 9-sq.-inch hole drawing cold air straight into your house.

Now imagine if you had similar gaps under your back door and around your windows. Each of these gaps is similar to having a baseball-size hole in your wall.

Besides making your house less drafty, weatherstripping pays off in a hurry. A few dollars spent now will save you dozens of dollars over coming winters.

In addition, weatherstripping also keeps out insects, dust, noise and moisture. Ideally, it should also make your doors and windows more soundproof when closed.

Convinced?

Testing how well your doors and windows are sealed is easy. On a windy day, hang a piece of toilet paper from a coat hanger and suspend it next to doors and windows. If it flutters, you've got a leak. A lighted candle or a smoky incense stick will indicate the same problems.

Weatherstripping Basics

The secret to energy-tight windows and doors is to block air movement and to create a sealed, dead-air space between the outside air and your interior.

Even if there is no air movement, you can lose heat if metal-framed windows or doors lack a thermal break to keep interior heat from conducting through the frame.

Another symptom of flawed weatherstripping is a buildup of condensation or frost on the inside of your windows. This indicates that moisture is building up in the space between the storm window and the regular window. Updating the interior weatherstripping should help to minimize the flow of moist, warm air into the gap. If that fails, drill a small hole in the corner of the exterior storm window frame to help ventilate the gap.

The primary heat loss in doors is around the edges, and nowhere more than under the door. Most thresholds take a lot of wear and tear. By installing a threshold and door sweep with replaceable gaskets, you can always have a good seal on your door.

Window weatherstripping is simple to apply. Self-adhesive compressible foam or rubber strips are available at all good hardware stores. More substantial products that seal the gap between top and bottom sashes are also available.

HIGH-TECH WINDOW FILM

It's paradoxical that despite all we invest in windows, most of us rush to draw the blinds to block out the summer sun. Window glass is obviously not a particularly good energy barrier. Not only is direct sunlight often too bright and too hot, but it carries too much UV radiation and produces glare. In fact, single-pane glass blocks less than 25% of the UV rays that damage skin and fade carpets, drapes and furnishings. It reflects roughly 10% of the light and heat that strikes it while allowing about 90% to pass through. The year-round numbers for double-glazed windows are only slightly better. Often what we need is a window that's a little more discriminating—one that lets in as much visible light as we want, while excluding some of sunlight's less desirable characteristics.

With the advent of add-on window films, we now have a product that addresses this need. However, not all window film works the same way. The value of any one film is directly related to how you intend to use it.

Window films were introduced in 1969 to address problems surrounding the control of sunlight in houses and businesses. Although fairly effective, these films received mixed reviews. Failings included fading film dyes, easily scratched surfaces and highly mirrored reflections. Poor installation also led to blisters, cracks and edge peeling.

Within certain limits, most of the problems with older films have been solved. Today's offerings are more attractive (some are virtually invisible) and they are more durable. Balancing performance and appearance, window films can now block up to 98% of UV radiation and up to 80% of normal heat gain. They can also provide a degree of privacy. In the winter, films can decrease emissivity, allowing you to keep more of the heat you pay for.

Window film, installed, can cost from $3 to $8 per square foot. Installed yourself, the cost can be as little as $1 per square foot. Department of Energy models predict a payback in energy savings within three to five years. Site studies show that 100 sq. ft. of window film can reduce the air-conditioning load of a building by as much as 12,000 BTU. Because the issue is really summer heat gain, the most dramatic savings occur in the Sun Belt states.

Composite
siding

Cedar
siding

Aluminum
siding

Panel
siding

Stucco

SIDING & TRIM

Realtors know how much the exterior surface of a house adds to its value. They know its style and condition have a major impact on potential buyers.

You, too, obviously want to keep the exterior of your house looking great. Who doesn't take pride in the appearance of their dwelling?

But the value of siding and trim is more than skin deep. These exterior surfaces protect your house against the elements. Without proper siding and trim, your house would become unlivable: rain and snow would seep in; cold drafts would swirl through; rodents and insects would make themselves at home; and rot would eventually destroy your framing.

The material used on exteriors varies widely. Standard materials include wood, masonry and manufactured sidings made out of vinyl or metal. Some of these materials have changed dramatically over the years, but one aspect remains the same: no matter what the material, all types of siding and trim need maintenance and repair.

Traditional wood lap siding, long popular in the U.S., needs regular upkeep, a task well within the realm of most homeowners. Wood shakes also require regular care and some easily performed repairs.

Masonry siding, such as brick veneer and stucco, rarely needs much attention, but when it does, it can often be repaired with a few simple-to-apply products.

Manufactured siding, once the butt of jokes, has gained respectability. Aluminum, vinyl and steel siding have become common in recent decades, and their quality has improved. As in the past, their selling point has been low maintenance. These products are now living up to their billing. Manufactured siding is also becoming easier to repair.

In this chapter we'll look at each of these materials and talk about how to preserve their life spans.

Wood shingles and shakes (page 61), normally cedar or redwood, give a rustic appearance. Missing or damaged shakes should be repaired immediately.

Brick (page 64) is the most durable siding, and is the easiest to maintain. Repairs can be made with do-it-yourself products.

Vinyl siding (page 65) is less prone to denting than metal siding and requires little maintenance during its life.

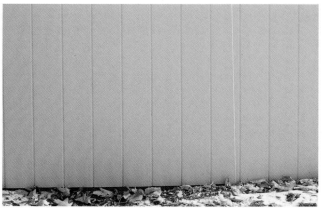

Wood siding (page 61) is easy to work with and simple to repair, but it needs to be painted or stained regularly.

Separated butt joints are not uncommon with wood lap siding. Small gaps (¼" or less) can be filled with caulk. Wider gaps indicate a more serious problem with moisture or shifting. Never seal the gaps along the bottom edges of siding.

Buckled siding occurs most often with vinyl or metal siding. The root of the problem can be traced to the points where the siding fits into trim and channels. If these expansion gaps are too small, the siding can buckle with temperature fluctuations.

Missing or cracked pieces of siding, like the cedar shingles shown here, need to be replaced quickly. Whenever one section of siding is damaged, carefully check surrounding areas to be certain the adjoining siding is secure.

Inspecting the Exterior

When you inspect your siding and trim, keep an eye peeled for areas where a problem may be brewing, such as next to the roof, in corners, above windows and doors and areas adjacent to the foundation. Look for rotting, cracking, stains, dents or missing pieces.

Even if you have low-maintenance siding, you may still have wood trim that needs periodic refinishing. Many homeowners tend to neglect woodwork in out-of-the-way areas. In some parts of the country, for example, the trim on roof dormers faces greater extremes of temperature and moisture, and deteriorates faster, than the trim on the lower wall.

Some manufactured siding comes with a warranty. If your siding is still covered, read the warranty document carefully. Doing any repair work yourself could invalidate the warranty. If you do have problems developing, make certain the manufacturer repairs the siding before the warranty expires.

Asbestos Shingles

Many homes built in the 1940s and 1950s were covered with milled asbestos cement shingles. These shingles often have a rough, heavily ridged surface. As long as the shingles are in good condition there is little to worry about. But airborne asbestos dust is a serious health hazard—it dramatically increases the risk of lung cancer—so removing asbestos shingles is a job to do carefully. Because asbestos is hazardous, its handling and disposal are regulated, and should be performed by trained professionals. If you must work with the shingles, wear an air filtration mask. Remember that asbestos fibers are too small to be captured by a vacuum.

Wood Siding

A builder's choice of siding materials has always depended upon available natural resources. In countries where there are now relatively few trees, such as England, houses are often built with masonry siding. In North America, where lumber is abundant, most houses are sided with wood.

Wood's advantages are many. It is easy to work with and is a good insulator (wood has an R-value of 1.25 per inch compared to aluminum's R-value of .0007). Wood resists denting and shrugs off most temperature changes. And compared to other siding materials, it is easy to repair should problems arise.

The disadvantage of wood is obvious: you have to keep it painted or stained. (More on that later.)

Most wood siding comes from softwood species, such as pine or fir. In some newer construction, manufactured composite board is used. Shakes and shingles are commonly hewn from cedar or redwood trees.

The durability of siding varies substantially depending upon the quality of lumber. Woodwork on turn-of-the-century houses is often very rot-resistant and tough. This siding was cut from massive old-growth trees, which produced lumber that had a dense cellular structure. Today's lumber comes almost entirely from younger trees, which produce less durable wood.

Many newer houses are sided with *composite* boards. Despite what the manufacturers claim about these products, many brands will not hold up as well as natural lumber. When scraping composite boards prior to painting, for example, you'll have to be careful not to gouge them.

Wood siding can be applied as horizontal strips, shakes or shingles, vertical strips or even large plywood panels. Whatever the appli-

Repairing cracks and splits in wood is not hard to do. Apply epoxy wood glue to both sides of the crack and then press the board back together. It helps to wedge a scrap piece of board against the bottom edge of the cracked siding until the glue has set. If the problem is close to the ground, prop a 2 × 4 against the scrap board. Then drive galvanized deck screws on either side of the crack to reinforce the board.

cation, the siding must shed water without letting any penetrate behind the boards.

Horizontal siding has been the most popular wood exterior in this country. This style sheds water very well and is easy to paint or stain. However, you need to watch out for cracks and splits in the siding. These can be repaired by gluing both sides of the crack and then squeezing the board tight (*photo, above*). Also make certain to caulk small gaps in the joints between board ends (*top photo, opposite page*).

Vertical siding is more common on houses built in mild, dry climates, where the penetrating effects of rain and snow are less marked. If you have this siding, you should also have a wide roof overhang to protect the gaps from rain. Otherwise, water can flow down the siding gaps, leading to rot and paint problems. Check the

edges for any damage, and make certain the narrow batten strips covering the gaps are secure.

Shakes and shingles, with few exceptions, are made of either cedar or redwood. Because these woods naturally resist decay, they are often left untreated and allowed to weather. Treating wood with preservatives will help maintain its original appearance.

Replacement Tip

Broken or damaged shakes or shingles are not uncommon. To replace the broken piece, split it with a hammer and chisel, then slip a hacksaw blade under the top board to cut off any nail heads remaining. Cut a replacement piece (leaving room for narrow expansion gaps on each side), slip it into place, and nail along the top edge of the exposed area on the patch. Cover the nail heads with caulk.

Wood Treatments

Wood that is freshly painted or stained looks great. But eventually the paint or stain will flake, peel or fade. Not only does this look shabby, but it exposes your wood to the elements. If you visit Boston, you'll see plenty of 200-year-old houses that are still standing tall, thanks to proper painting. On the other hand, you've probably seen abandoned farmhouses or barns that, once left to the elements, have crumbled to the ground in just a few decades.

Treating wood is a time-consuming process, but the good news is that the work you do can last a long time. When applied correctly, treatments can last eight years or longer, especially with regular maintenance.

Before you plan any work, take a tour of your house. If any exterior wood is bare, you've got problems, unless you have a rot-resistant wood, such as redwood, which can be left unfinished.

Paint that is chipping, cracking or alligatoring needs to be repaired.

Localized paint problems may be caused by moisture seeping through the walls from inside the house—the siding and trim outside of bathrooms are most susceptible. If paint problems stem from excess moisture, they will reappear quickly, no matter how well you prepare the surface. The only way to prevent future problems is to improve the ventilation indoors or install better vapor barriers in your walls.

Mildew will often form in cracks and humid areas that receive little sunlight. You can kill mildew by washing the affected area with bleach or a mixture of water and trisodium phosphate (TSP).

Most older houses have been painted in the past with lead paint. Lead is a genuine hazard to children.

To Strip or Not?

When it comes time to paint, you'll need to determine whether your walls need to be stripped or primed. A simple test can help you make this determination.

Locate a small, inconspicuous area on your house where the paint is in poor condition. Wash your test area with water and wait until it dries.

Cover the spot with a coat of paint and let the paint dry for 24 hours. Apply duct tape to the test area and then rip it off.

If the tape pulls away both the new and the old layers of paint, you'll need to strip off all the old paint before you repaint the house. If only the new layer pulls away, you can repaint directly over the old paint if you first apply a primer. If the tape pulls away no paint, you can go ahead and start applying paint without primer—after removing any obvious loose paint and cleaning dirty areas.

Blistering can result from poor preparation, a hasty application of paint or vapor seeping through walls. The blisters are caused by trapped moisture.

Peeling is associated with persistent moisture problems, generally from a leak or an inadequate vapor barrier. Localized peeling can result from a leaky roof, gutter system or even a leaky pipe.

Alligatoring is typically seen on old paint and surfaces. It can be caused by excessive layers of paint, inadequate surface preparation, or insufficient drying time for a primer.

*Finish sheens vary widely. **Gloss enamel**, a highly reflective finish, is desired where easy washability is important. Gloss paints tend to show irregularities, however. **Medium gloss or semigloss** paint produces a very washable surface with slightly less reflection. **Eggshell** enamel combines the soft finish of flat paint with the washability of enamel. **Flat latex** has a soft finish that hides surface irregularities.*

Paint & Stain

When shopping for paint or stain, don't save money by purchasing bargain-basement products. High-quality paint and stain will produce better results with less work and will last longer. They'll save you time and require less maintenance in the long run.

Paints are broken down into a number of categories. You'll obviously want paint intended for exterior use. Just as with interior projects, most painters follow a few simple rules when it comes to choosing between finishes. Trim is often painted in a high-gloss or semi-gloss finish, which is easy to wash, while siding is often covered with a low-gloss or flat finish. Some painters like to apply semi-gloss to siding and high-gloss to trim.

Oil paint uses an alkyd base to suspend the paint pigment. At one time, all paint used an oil base, and until recently it was better than latex in overall performance, especially when lead was an additive. In the last decade or so, latex paint has improved to the point where it is often just as durable as oil. Oil paint is still the best covering for high-traffic areas, such as doors and porch floors. The best stain-hiding primers tend to be oil-based. Oil enamel also has a higher gloss than latex enamel.

However, oil paint is not easy to work with. It produces a strong odor and is harder to apply. Oil paint takes several hours to dry, it produces a bigger mess, and clean-up takes longer because solvents are required to clean your brushes and rollers.

Latex paint has a water base. It is easy to apply and cleans up with soap and water. Latex paint erodes more slowly than oil paint, but because it creates a thinner surface film, it doesn't cover surface irregularities as well. For most jobs, when you have a choice, you'll appreciate using latex paint because it is much easier to work with.

Exterior stain is essentially a partially transparent paint. It often contains wood preservatives and may also contain pesticides and anti-fungal ingredients. Because stain won't hide dirt as paint does, wood must be well cleaned before staining. Never apply stain over painted wood.

Stain is very thin, so it can be difficult to apply without dripping and splattering. Make certain to cover areas below your work site. On lap siding, stain one board at a time to avoid creating lines.

Painting Safety

• *Keep paint and solvents away from children. If a child drinks any paint or solvent, seek treatment immediately—* DON'T INDUCE VOMITING.

• *Wear protective eyewear. If you splash paint in your eyes, flush them with large amounts of water and, if necessary, seek medical help.*

• *If using oil-based paints, stains or solvents, don't smoke.*

• *Remove paint chips and clean up thoroughly after scraping or sanding—older paint is likely to contain lead.*

Brick

If you have brick siding, you can plan on lots of summer days in the hammock watching your neighbors paint their wood-sided houses. Brick is also the most durable siding.

Still, brick needs maintenance. The most common repair is tuck-pointing—the process of replacing crumbling mortar joints with fresh mortar. Minor repairs are well within the realm of most home-owners, but consult a professional before attempting major repairs, such as replacing bricks or rebuilding a structure.

Small tuck-pointing jobs require only a few small hand tools: a masonry chisel, a hammer, a joint filler, a mortar hawk and a jointing tool. If you can paint a house, you should be qualified to tuck-point failing mortar.

Stucco

Traditional stucco consists of three coats of a mix containing Portland cement and sand. Stucco is either applied over wire mesh attached to sheathing, or troweled over concrete block. The final coat of stucco is tinted to provide color.

Properly installed, stucco is very durable. A small number of hairline cracks are inevitable—even on properly installed stucco. You can fill these cracks with a tinted masonry caulk or patching mortar. But major cracking, flaking and delamination point to more major problems. Such cases suggest that the stucco was applied incorrectly or that your house foundation and

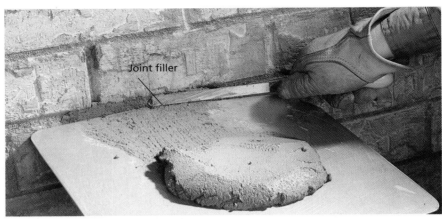
Joint filler

Once crumbling mortar is removed, apply new mortar in ¼"-thick layers, letting each application dry for 30 minutes before applying the next layer. Fill the joints until the mortar is flush with the brick face, then smooth and profile with a jointing tool.

framing is shifting. In this case, repairs must be made by a qualified professional.

Over the past twenty years, a synthetic stucco, known as *EIFS* (exterior insulated finish system) has come into wide use. Its formula replaces the Portland cement in traditional stucco with modern acrylic resins. The material is troweled over insulated sheathing with wire mesh fastened to it. This acrylic stucco provides better thermal insulation. However, some types of EIFS have recently come under attack for a host of problems. If you have synthetic stucco, it's a good idea to periodically inspect your framing members and door and window frames for signs of rot.

Stucco is best left unpainted, but if you choose to paint it, make sure to use a top-quality masonry paint. After major repairs, for example,

you may have no choice but to paint the stucco to hide the repaired areas.

Paint or Stucco?

When your stucco was applied, color was added to the final layer. It therefore does not need painting. But what happens if your stucco is badly stained or has ugly patch marks? Stucco traditionalists insist that the only cure is to add an additional thin layer of new stucco over the old material—a messy and time-consuming process. Nontraditionalists argue that stucco responds well to a quality flat latex exterior paint. Of course, painting has two drawbacks: once you paint, you'll forever have to repaint. And a layer of new stucco cannot be added to painted stucco.

REMOVING STAINS FROM BRICK & BLOCK

• **Paint stains and graffiti:** You have a number of options. Specialized graffiti and paint removing solutions are now available. Another choice is brushing on paint thinner. More tenacious stains may require a sandblaster or high-pressure water sprayer.

• **Egg splatter:** Dissolve oxalic acid crystals in water, following manufacturer's instructions, in a nonmetallic container. Brush onto surface.

• **Efflorescence:** Scrub surface with a stiff-bristled brush. Use a household cleaning solution where accumulation is heavy.

• **Iron stains:** Spray or brush a solution of oxalic acid crystals dissolved in water, following manufacturer's instructions. Apply directly to the stain.

• **Ivy:** Do not pull vines from the wall. Rather, cut them away from the surface, then let the remaining stems dry before you scrub them off with a stiff-bristled brush and household cleaning solution.

• **Smoke stains:** Scrub surface with household cleanser containing bleach, or use a mixture of ammonia and water.

Metal

Aluminum or steel siding requires very little maintenance. It is formed from aluminum or steel sheets and may be textured to look like wood siding. The factory-applied color coating may last twenty years or more before it fades and needs to be repainted.

Aluminum siding's chief drawback is that it is easily dented. Hail, baseballs or ladders can all wreak havoc on it. Newer aluminum siding is more dent-resistant and may use an enamel or vinyl finish that helps make touch-up painting unnecessary. No metal siding is immune from dents, however. If aluminum siding is improperly applied, it can buckle under extreme heat.

Steel siding looks like aluminum, but is not dented as easily. It is popular in the Midwest, where violent hailstorms are common. A drawback is that the steel will rust if scratched. These spots must be painted.

To keep your siding clean, you should wash off the siding at least once a year with a hose.

Damaged sections of metal siding can be cut out and replaced, but repairing metal siding can be troublesome if the manufacturer no longer stocks the right style. If you have scrap pieces left over from the original installation, make sure you hold on to them.

Vinyl

Vinyl siding requires even less maintenance than metal. It doesn't rust and it's much less likely to dent than metal siding.

Although vinyl siding is now the most widely used form of manufactured siding, it does have drawbacks. Vinyl siding expands and contracts with changes in the temperature. In fact, a 12-foot section of vinyl siding may expand or shrink more than ½ inch, depending on the weather.

The key to a good appearance

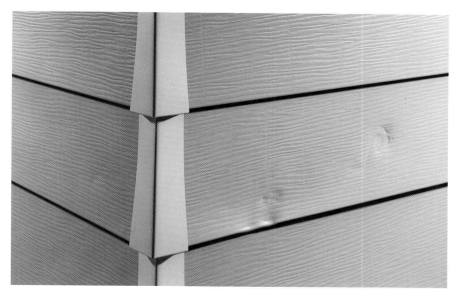

If minor surface damage occurs, it is often better to leave the siding alone—attempts at repair often look worse than the damage.

Nailing strip

Shown cut away for clarity

Vinyl and metal siding are attached to nailing strips. Properly installed siding will allow the material to expand and contract without buckling or exposing large gaps.

is correct installation. A sloppy job can result in buckled siding or unsightly and uneven gaps. If you see these flaws, try to have the installation contractor address the problem.

Another form of plastic siding is *polypropylene,* which can be molded to appear like cedar shingles, stone or brick.

With vinyl and polypropylene siding, you don't have to worry about painting. Color is added to the entire thickness, so these sidings are not harmed by scratches. To maintain them, you need only rinse them off with a hose once or twice a year.

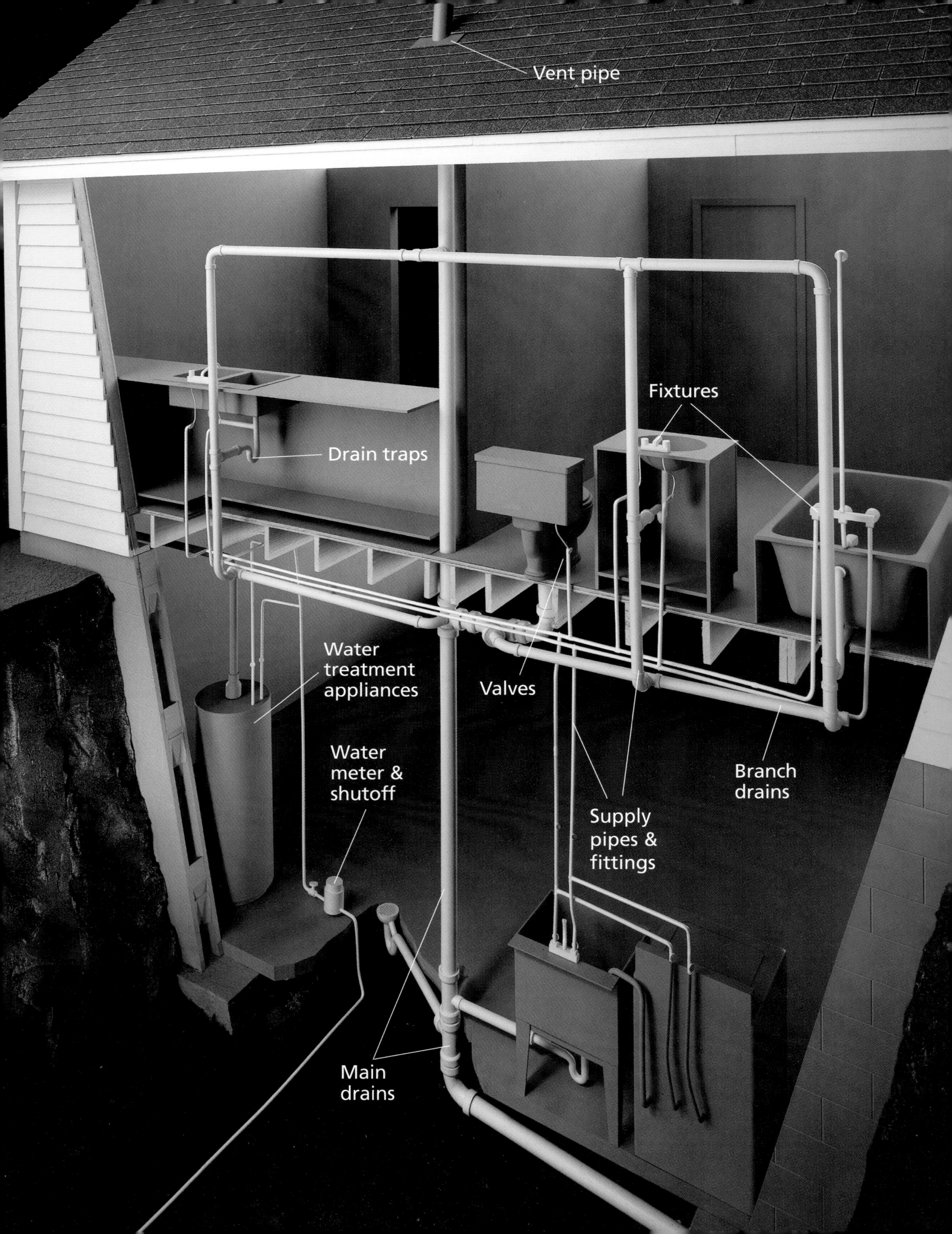

Vent pipe

Drain traps

Fixtures

Water treatment appliances

Valves

Water meter & shutoff

Branch drains

Supply pipes & fittings

Main drains

Plumbing

After the construction workers completed the exterior shell of your home, another group of contractors installed several important mechanical systems running inside the walls and below the floors. Though these systems are largely invisible, they are crucial to a properly functioning house.

The first of these systems to be installed was the plumbing. Behind the visible fixtures you see today—the tubs, sinks and faucets—lies a hidden arterial network of pressurized water supply pipes and gravity-assisted drain pipes. You may be able to see some parts of this network exposed in basements and utility rooms, but for the most part the plumbing system does its crucial work unnoticed.

If you're lucky, you rarely need to worry about your plumbing. Your toilet flushes and your sink drains smoothly; you have plenty of hot water and your shower has good water pressure.

But luck doesn't last forever. Many problems can occur in this system. Pipes can break, drains can plug, valves can leak. When trouble arises, it's helpful if you know how the system works. And it's very important that the system work properly, both for convenience and your family's health.

Basic Principles

The basics of a plumbing system are easy to understand. Water enters your house through a pressurized water line. After being split into hot and cold water lines, the water supply runs to each fixture in your home. Once used, fresh water become waste water, and it enters the drain-waste-vent (DWV) system. Gravity now takes over, pulling the waste water down a series of sloped, ever larger pipes toward the house sewer.

Water arrives under pressure; water leaves by gravity, taking with it dish soap, human waste and anything else put down the drain. It's a simple and elegant system. Until something goes wrong. Ironically, the same principles that allow your system to operate smoothly are what cause many of the problems. Under the stress of constant pressure, supply pipes corrode and eventually leak or burst. And the slow movement of waste through the DWV pipes can lead to clogs.

In this chapter you'll learn more about plumbing fundamentals, which will make it possible for you to follow the flow of water through your house. You'll also learn to identify parts of the system that could give you trouble in the future. While every house relies on the same plumbing principles—pressure in, gravity out—plumbing materials vary widely from house to house. Many systems are amalgams of different materials—especially in older homes, where repairs and updates may have been done in several phases. Identifying these materials and knowing their characteristics will help you when troubles eventually arise.

The Water Meter & Main Shutoff

Start your tour of the plumbing system with the main water supply shutoff valve. If a pipe bursts or another plumbing emergency arises, you'll need to locate this valve quickly in order to stop the water flow and keep water from damaging your house.

About 85 percent of all homes receive their water from a municipal supply. If you have municipal service, the shutoff is adjacent to the water meter, usually on the basement wall facing the street side of your house. If you don't have a basement, look in the crawl space or along the ground-floor wall next to the street.

The water meter and main shutoff valve for your water supply system are located at the point where the main supply pipe enters your home—usually in the basement, garage or other utility area.

WELLS

Fifteen percent of American households rely on private wells for their water. There are three different well designs in common use, and each design consists of three parts: the *well pipe*, the *pump* and the *storage tank*. Although wells are generally dependable, they can act up.

The *jet pump* is the most common design for a shallow well. It creates a vacuum to draw water up a well. Jet pumps are defined as either a single-drop pipe pump or a double-drop pipe pump. The single-drop jet pump is limited to wells roughly 30 feet deep—but less at higher elevations, where air pressure drops. A double-drop pump can lift water from 100 feet or more, because the surface impeller directs a portion of its water back down the second pipe (hence the term "double-drop"). The water passes through an ejector at the bottom, which creates more pressure and lift in the suction pipe. This type also needs a continuous prime to work: when the pump is turned on, the prime water is pushed through impellers and new water is pulled up behind the prime.

For a deeper well, a *submersible pump* can be suspended directly into the aquifer. The pump's electric motor is sealed and the impellers simply push water up the pipe and into your house. A submersible pump can reach very deep aquifers, and it is considered to be nearly problem-free. A submersible pump may perform without servicing for 20 to 25 years, but it has a major drawback: if the pump motor burns out, a truck-mounted derrick is required to retrieve it. Submersible pumps may also be used in shallow wells, but silt, sand, algae and other contaminants can shorten the pump's life.

Another type of pump, the *piston pump*, has rarely been installed since the 1950s, but many keep churning. This classic style is driven by a windmill—or by a hand-operated pitcher mechanism. The piston, submerged in the well shaft below water level, is connected to a rod that extends up the well casing.

No matter what kind of system you have, the components on the output side of the pump are all similar. A well pump is not intended to run continuously and doesn't start every time you open a tap.

Your well almost certainly features a galvanized steel pressure tank, with a pressure switch, pressure gauge and drain valve attached to the tank or mounted nearby. Whenever the system is activated, water is pumped up into the tank from the ground, compressing the air in the tank. When the air pressure reaches a determined threshold, the well pump shuts off. This air pressure provides the force needed to push the water from the tank into the fixtures. Once the water in the tank drops enough to reduce the air pressure to a predetermined level, the pump starts up again and begins to draw additional water.

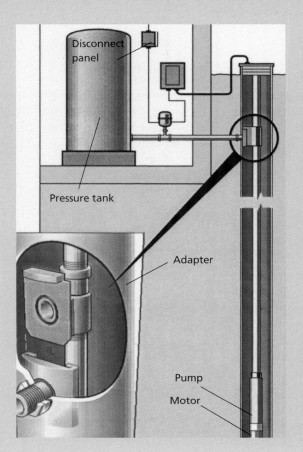

Disconnect panel

Pressure tank

Adapter

Pump

Motor

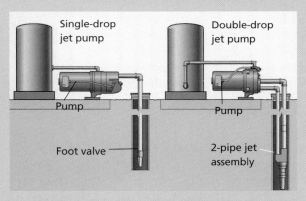

Single-drop jet pump

Double-drop jet pump

Pump

Pump

Foot valve

2-pipe jet assembly

In a shallow well jet pump, the impeller and jet assembly are above ground. In wells deeper than 30 ft., the jet assembly is located in the well shaft itself.

Left: *A submersible pump is suspended directly into the aquifer. The submerged motor is sealed, and the impellers force water up the pipe and into your house.*

The water meter, usually made of brass, is no larger than 6 inches in diameter. It will often have a clear top and a dial similar to your car's odometer. (Some areas now have sealed electronic meters. These allow the meter to be read off-site by utility workers.) If you have trouble finding the water meter, just follow the cold water inlet pipe from your water heater back to the source.

Most meters have shutoff valves on both sides (recently, many local plumbing codes require this). If you have a well (opposite page), you'll likely find the shutoff valve located on the outlet side of your water storage tank.

Main Water Supply Pipe

While at the water meter, study the pipe leading into your house. It can give you important information about your system. If the main supply pipe leading from the street to the meter is made of steel, you could be in for a sizable repair bill in the near future. Most steel main supply pipes were installed more than 25 years ago, and are nearing the end of their life span. The cost for upgrading the main supply line from the city water main is your responsibility.

If you find that the main supply pipe is copper, you can rest a bit easier. As real estate agents will tell you, the presence of "copper-to-the-street" indicates a relatively recent installation. In addition, copper pipe lasts a good deal longer than steel.

WATER PRESSURE

Normal pressure for water entering your house is 40 to 55 pounds per square inch (psi) but the pressure can be as low as 30 psi or as high as 80 psi.

Pressures lower than 30 psi can result in poor water flow from fixtures. Pressures higher than 60 psi could cause pipes to burst or "hammer." Some homes with high municipal pressure have a pressure-reducing valve near the main shutoff (right). Less can be done to change low water pressure. You can, however, clean valves and replace undersized or clogged pipes. A more dramatic measure is to install a pressure-boosting pump. If you have questions about your home's water pressure, check it with a pressure gauge connected to your hose bib or have a plumber check the pressure.

Another way to evaluate your system's water capacity is to measure how much water flows into your home in one minute. Doing so requires some plumbing knowledge, but it's not difficult:

1. Count the total number of plumbing fixtures in your home and calculate the total fixture units, using the values from the Unit Rating Chart (below).
2. Shut off your main water supply valve, then disconnect the pipe on the house side of the shutoff valve.
3. Construct a test spout of plastic pipe and position it so it directs water from the open water supply pipe into a large watertight tub.
4. Open the main valve and let the water run into the container for exactly fifteen seconds.

5. Measure the water by emptying it with a gallon jug. Multiply by four. You now have the gallons-per-minute rate of your main water supply.
6. Compare the rate with the Water Capacity Chart (below). If the number equals or is greater than the minimum capacity in the chart, your water pressure meets the needs of your home.

A pressure-reducing valve can reduce dangerously high water pressure. The pressure-reducing valve is attached on the house side of the water meter and main shutoff valve.

Unit Rating Chart

Fixture	Unit rating
Toilet	3
Vanity sink	1
Shower, tub	2
Dishwasher	2
Kitchen, utility sink	2
Clothes washer	2
Sillcock	3

Water Capacity Chart

Fixture Units	Minimum Gallons per Minute
10	8
15	11
20	14
25	17
30	20

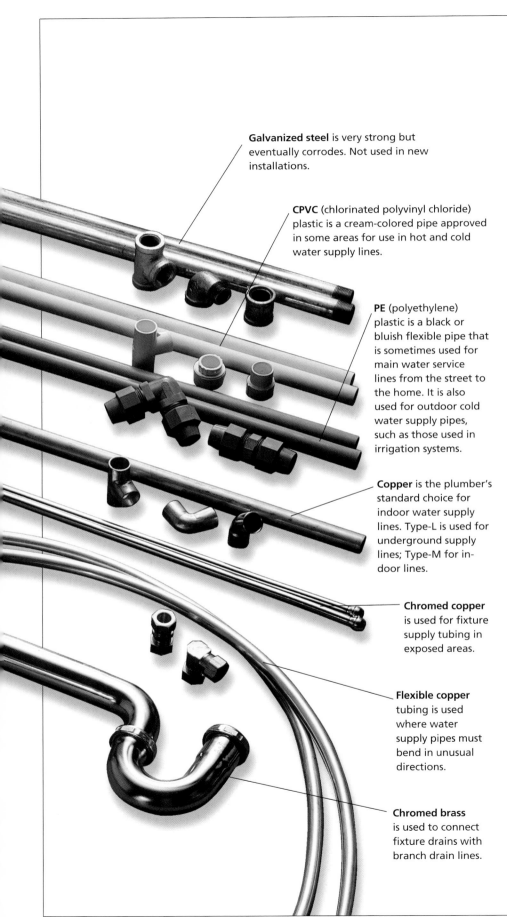

Galvanized steel is very strong but eventually corrodes. Not used in new installations.

CPVC (chlorinated polyvinyl chloride) plastic is a cream-colored pipe approved in some areas for use in hot and cold water supply lines.

PE (polyethylene) plastic is a black or bluish flexible pipe that is sometimes used for main water service lines from the street to the home. It is also used for outdoor cold water supply pipes, such as those used in irrigation systems.

Copper is the plumber's standard choice for indoor water supply lines. Type-L is used for underground supply lines; Type-M for indoor lines.

Chromed copper is used for fixture supply tubing in exposed areas.

Flexible copper tubing is used where water supply pipes must bend in unusual directions.

Chromed brass is used to connect fixture drains with branch drain lines.

Supply Pipes & Fittings

As you trace your water supply system from the main shutoff to the individual plumbing fixtures, you may notice several different types of pipes and fittings. Older houses can have a wider variety of piping, especially if the plumbing has been partially updated through the decades. Knowing what kind of piping you have is important for troubleshooting and repairs.

Your water supply system is pressurized, and the pipes must be able to withstand the pressure year after year. Water supply lines are typically steel, copper or plastic.

Galvanized steel was commonly used in homes until the 1960s. Now, however, it is rarely used, for simple reasons: it rusts, and it's much harder to install than copper or plastic. Steel is tough, however, so it is sometimes installed where pipes are exposed and could be subject to damage. (NOTE: Galvanized steel pipe is also called *iron* pipe, while another type of piping, called *black iron,* is still commonly used for gas piping. The two should never be mixed. Galvanized steel will react with gas, causing zinc to flake off and plug a water heater or furnace. And if black iron pipe is used in a water supply system, it will quickly be destroyed by rust.)

Copper is considered the best choice for water supply lines, and it is occasionally used in drain-waste-vent systems. Copper resists scale deposits better than plastic, and is much more corrosion-resistant than steel. Copper offers little resistance to water flow, which means that water pressure through copper is better than it is through a comparably sized steel pipe. Copper is light, and easy to handle and join. Copper's only drawback is that it is more expensive than other materials. This sometimes prevents budget-minded plumbing contractors from using it.

Plastic piping is used for water supply pipes in some areas, where local codes permit it. Plastic has its benefits: it is inexpensive, very easy to work with, and it doesn't corrode or rust. It also has insulating properties that minimize heat loss in hot water pipes and prevent sweating on cold water pipes.

Although plastic has gained wider acceptance in recent years, you might find that your local Building Code allows it for only certain uses, such as outdoor plumbing. In addition, a great many plumbers reject plastic water supply pipe as inferior to copper.

Plastic water supply pipe earned its poor and somewhat unfair reputation because early generations of plastic piping used to carry hot water sometimes deteriorated. Today, PVC, CPVC and PE pipes are acceptable for cold water use, but only CPVC and PB rated at 180°F and 100 psi, or greater, should be used for hot water lines.

One note: plastic is a material favored by do-it-yourselfers. If your house has plastic piping and you suspect an amateur installed it, have it inspected by a professional to determine if the job was up to Building Code specifications.

90° elbows are used to make right-angle bends in a pipe run. Drain-waste-vent (DWV) elbows are curved to prevent debris from being trapped in the bend.

Tee-fittings are used to connect branch lines in water supply and drain-waste-vent systems. A tee-fitting used in a DWV system is called a "waste-tee" or "sanitary tee."

Couplings are used to join two straight pipes. Special transition fittings are used to join two pipes that are made from different materials.

Reducers connect pipes of different diameters. Reducing tee-fittings and elbows are also available.

45° elbows are used to make gradual bends in a pipe run. Elbows are also available with 60° and 72° bends.

DIELECTRIC FITTINGS

If you attempt to repair pipes yourself, you need to be aware that joining different pipe materials can be tricky. A trait called *galvanic action* can lead to premature corrosion and clogging. Galvanic action causes molecules to transfer from one type of metal to another, dramatically shortening a pipe's life span. Specialized fittings are therefore required to join pipes of different materials. And pipes must be supported with brackets and straps of the same material. In addition, pipe fittings come in a wide number of variations. If you are not certain how to repair a pipe, either study good how-to books or call a plumber. A friendly clerk at your hardware store can also be a good source of information.

Dielectric fittings allow you to join dissimilar metals, like copper and brass.

Valves

Tracing your water supply lines from the water meter to the fixtures in your home, you'll discover that the various branch lines are controlled by a number of different types of valves. Your sink and tub faucets are the most visible of these valves, but other equally important valves control water flow through-out the house. Many of these valves allow you to shut off water to specific fixtures or appliances, instead of shutting off water to the whole house.

The valves in a copper or galvanized steel water supply system are made of brass, while plastic valves are used in plastic water supply systems. If your tour of the plumbing system reveals metal valves installed on plastic pipes, or plastic valves on metal pipes, replace these valves with ones that match the pipe material. Because metal and plastic expand and contract at different rates, mixing the materials may cause problems.

Each valve style is designed for a specific purpose and application. As you inspect each valve in your home, determine its type and make sure it is appropriate for its function. Inspect all valves carefully to make sure they work properly. Look for leaks, and make sure each valve operates smoothly and will fully stop the flow of water when closed. Faulty valves should be replaced before they cause expensive damage.

A gate valve receives its name from the inner gate that lowers to stop the flow of water when the wheel-style handle is tightened. Gate valves are designed to be either completely open or fully closed; they aren't suited to adjust the volume of flow. The valves located at your water meter should be gate valves. Because there are no rubber compression washers used, gate valves are nearly trouble-free.

A globe valve can be identified by a bulge at the base of the valve body. The handle is a rotating wheel. Because it contains inner partitions that impede the flow of water, a globe valve is generally unsuited for use as a main shutoff or branch line shutoff. It can be used, however, where water volume is not an issue, such as when controlling water supply to a single fixture or appliance. Most globe valves feature neoprene compression washers that will gradually age and need to be replaced.

A shutoff valve is required by plumbing code for each hot and cold water supply tube feeding a plumbing fixture. If you discover fixtures without shutoffs, it's a good idea to install shutoff valves.

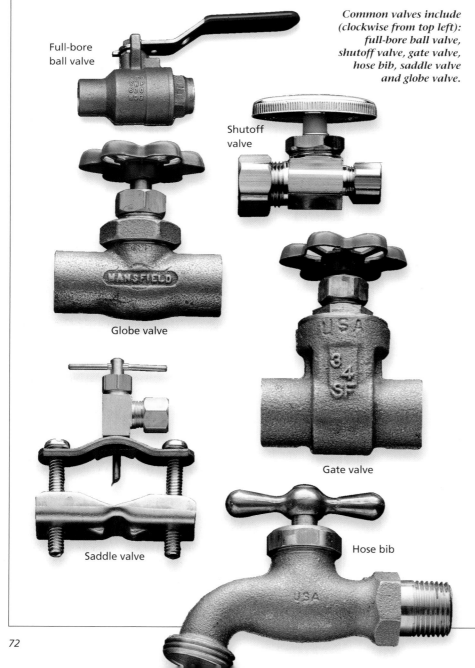

Common valves include (clockwise from top left): full-bore ball valve, shutoff valve, gate valve, hose bib, saddle valve and globe valve.

Full-bore ball valve

Shutoff valve

Globe valve

Gate valve

Saddle valve

Hose bib

Shutoff valves allow you to quickly turn off the water when problems arise or when a fixture needs to be replaced or repaired.

Fixture shutoffs are designed to be either fully open or completely shut; a partially closed shutoff will often leak. Homeowners often replace "leaky" shutoffs, when simply opening the valve fully could have solved the problem.

A saddle valve is clamped onto a water supply pipe, and has a metal spike that pierces the pipe. Saddle valves are often used to provide water for refrigerator icemakers, water filters and other low-volume appliances. Saddle valves have a high failure rate. Make sure to inspect all valves regularly and replace them promptly when they begin to fail.

Hose bibs are simple compression faucets often found on utility sinks and exterior sillcocks. They have a threaded spout to accept a garden hose. Because sillcocks use rubber washers, they may gradually develop leaks. Replace the inner washers when this happens.

If you live in a region with cold winters, exterior hose bibs should have a frostproof design to ensure that pipes don't freeze and burst.

Most Building Codes require that hose bib valves have a vacuum breaker to prevent contaminated water from being drawn back into the fresh water supply if water pressure drops suddenly. If your house is more than a few years old, it's likely that all hose bibs will need to be either replaced or equipped with anti-syphon devices.

A full-bore ball valve is generally used where water may need to be turned off very quickly. A quick quarter-turn of the handle, which is often a toggle lever, closes the valve completely. Branch line shutoffs should use full-bore ball valves, since they don't restrict the flow of water when open. Like gate valves, full-bore ball valves are very dependable.

Vacuum breaker

Exterior hose bibs should be equipped with a vacuum breaker feature.

WATER FILTERS

Water picks up trace amounts of the substances it touches along its route to your plumbing fixtures. The minerals, bacteria and chemicals in water give it its color and taste. Some of these additions are not healthy.

As a way to reduce undesirable contaminants, millions of homeowners have installed home water filters—and not just homeowners with their own wells. More than half of the people buying water filters today receive their water from municipal water systems.

If you have a private well, test the water once a year for traces of bacteria, nitrates and by-products of sewage and fertilizers. If you receive your water from a municipal line, you might consider getting your water tested if any of the following situations apply:

• A family member has a chronic health problem.

• You notice a change in the taste, color or odor of your water.

• Your plumbing has lead supply pipes or lead solder.

• Tests show you have high levels of radon in the air.

To locate a good testing laboratory, call your local health department. Or, check your phone book for an independent, state-certified testing laboratory.

Once you've learned the nature of the contaminants in your water, you'll need to select a proper filter. Different water filters remove different contaminants. A carbon filter, for example, will help remove lead, but it won't remove bacteria.

Most homes rely on point-of-use systems, which filter just water used for drinking, instead of point-of-entry systems, which filter all water entering a house. Here are some of the most common systems:

SEDIMENT FILTERS. These screen out large impurities, and are often used as prefilters in a combined system. They work well for clearing cloudy water.

DISTILLATION FILTERS. After these filters turn water into vapor with a heating element, the recondensed water that results is free of bacteria, radium and other compounds. These filters can cost as little as $100 for a countertop model to more than $4,500 for a whole-house distiller.

DISINFECTING UNITS. These systems target bacteria. In one type, ultraviolet light kills bacteria. Other designs rely on chlorination and ozonation, which generates surplus oxygen in the water.

CARBON FILTERS. Faucet-mounted types with activated charcoal filters remove unpleasant odors. Other types have solid-block filters that remove heavy metals, such as lead or mercury. All types should be replaced periodically to prevent the growth of bacteria.

REVERSE OSMOSIS. These systems use pressure to force water through a semipermeable membrane. Reverse osmosis is effective at removing most contaminants, but it will not remove harmful bacteria. Once the water is filtered, it goes to a holding tank where it's stored until needed. The main drawback of reverse-osmosis systems is that for every five gallons used, only one or two gallons are potable. The rest flushes the membrane and carries away contaminants.

Carbon filter detail

Often installed on a countertop, carbon filters collect impurities through absorption.

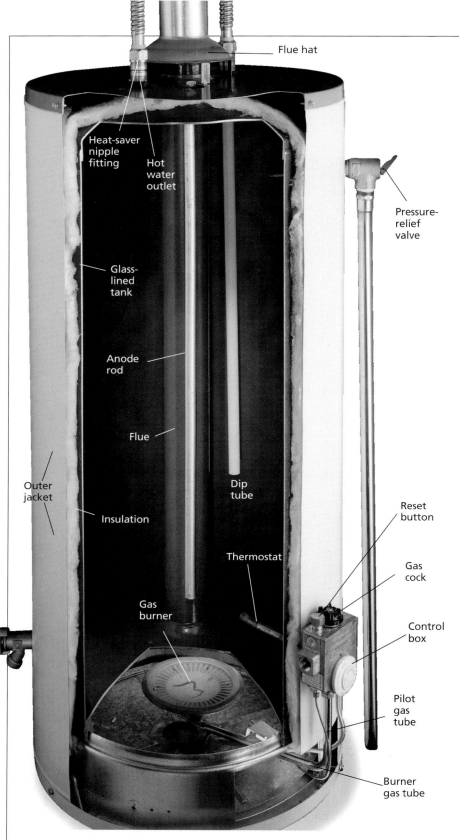

Flue hat

Heat-saver
nipple
fitting

Hot
water
outlet

Pressure-
relief
valve

Glass-
lined
tank

Anode
rod

Flue

Dip
tube

Outer
jacket

Insulation

Reset
button

Gas
cock

Thermostat

Control
box

Gas
burner

Pilot
gas
tube

Burner
gas tube

HOW A GAS WATER HEATER WORKS: Hot water leaves the tank through the hot water outlet as fresh cold water enters through the dip tube. As the water temperature drops, the thermostat opens the gas valve and the gas burner ignites. Exhaust gases heat the water as they are vented up through the flue. When water temperature reaches the preset threshold, the thermostat shuts off the gas, extinguishing the burner. The anode rod protects the tank lining from rust by attracting corrosive elements in the water. The pressure-relief valve guards against ruptures caused by heat buildup in the tank.

Water Treatment Appliances

On their journey to the plumbing fixtures, your water supply pipes may pass through one or more water treatment appliances. Your system undoubtedly has a water heater, but it may also have a water softener and water filter.

Water Heaters

Your water heater will either be a gas-powered or electric appliance. Both types are thermostatically controlled to maintain constant temperatures inside the tank.

Begin your inspection at the top of the water heater. If you see a flue hat and duct leading to a chimney or outside vent, you have a gas-powered heater. Examine the pipes delivering cold water into the tank and transporting hot water out. These pipes may be fitted with special heat-saver nipples that help conserve heat in the tank. (Older water heaters retrofitted with these nipples can also save substantial energy.)

The typical hot water heater consists of a glass-lined steel tank, a layer of insulation and a sheet-metal jacket. Near the top of the tank, you should see a pressure-relief valve, possibly fitted with a long downspout. This valve should be periodically tested (*see sidebar*). If your heater does not have this feature, you'd be wise to have a plumber remedy this situation.

Now inspect the control box and thermostat control, located near the bottom of the tank. One way to reduce wear and tear on your water heater is to turn the thermostat down. A heater that runs at 160°F puts more stress on a tank and costs more to operate than a heater set at 140°F.

Also near the bottom of the tank you should find a hose bib that can be used to drain the tank. It's a good idea to periodically flush the tank (*see sidebar*). If such a flushing consistently produces a lot of sediment, it's a good indication that the water heater is nearing the end of its useful life. Another sign is an audible gurgling or rumbling sound, which is caused by bubbles percolating through a thick layer of sediment at the bottom.

If you have a gas water heater, remove the cover to the burner chamber and inspect the burner element. If the burner flame is yellow in color, it may mean that the burner needs to be cleaned.

The life span of a water heater often depends on how long the steel tank lasts. Don't be surprised if your heater needs to be replaced after ten or fifteen years.

A possible way to extend the life of your water heater by up to five years is to replace the *anode rod*, if it can be removed easily. An anode rod is a magnesium or aluminum element suspended in the water. It retards tank corrosion by drawing corrosive elements in the water. Instead of your tank corroding, the anode rod decays. Inexpensive water heaters have one rod, while extended-life heaters may feature dual rods.

Water Softeners

Your home may also have a water softener, probably located near the water heater. If the water entering the home contains too many dissolved minerals, it is said to be *hard*. These minerals can foul the water's taste, clog pipes and appliances with buildup, and contribute to soap scum. Water softeners can reduce these problems by substituting sodium for the offending calcium, magnesium or iron.

Some experts believe that water softeners are installed more often than needed, and in the wrong place. The chemical process used to soften water raises the sodium level in drinking water—a bad thing for people on low-sodium diets.

If you do have a softener—or plan to install one—make sure it is not connected so it treats your cold water drinking faucets or outdoor hose bibs. Softened water will kill grass quickly.

Instead, a water softener should treat only the water headed for the water heater. In this way, you'll have soft water where you need it most: in your clothes washer and dishwasher, and at fixtures where you mix hot and cold water, such as in your tub or shower.

MAINTENANCE TIPS FOR WATER HEATERS

Lower the temperature setting to 140°F. A lower temperature setting reduces damage to the tank caused by overheating, and also reduces energy use. If you are concerned about children or elderly family members, you may want to set the thermostat as low as 130°F.

Test the pressure-relief valve annually. Lift up on the lever and let it snap back into place; the valve should release a burst of water. If the valve doesn't work—or if the heater doesn't have a pressure-relief valve, have a plumber install one.

Flush the water heater once each year by draining several gallons of water from the tank. Flushing removes sediment buildup that causes corrosion and reduces the efficiency of the heater.

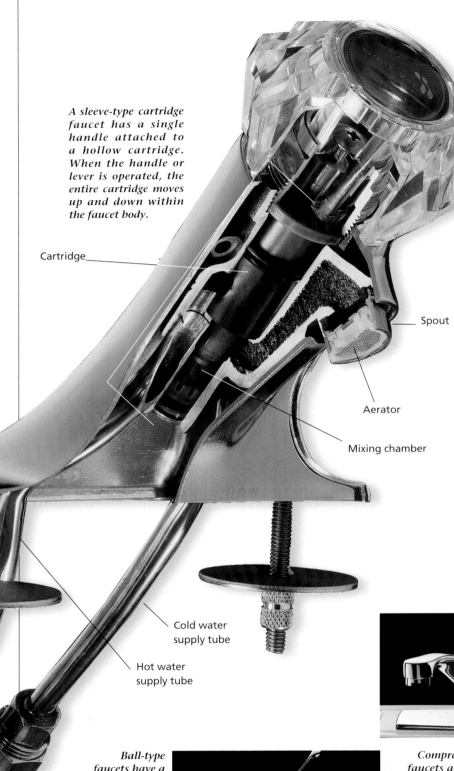

A sleeve-type cartridge faucet has a single handle attached to a hollow cartridge. When the handle or lever is operated, the entire cartridge moves up and down within the faucet body.

Cartridge

Spout

Aerator

Mixing chamber

Cold water supply tube

Hot water supply tube

Fixtures

After inspecting the beginnings of your plumbing system, turn your attention to the more visible elements. The fresh water carried by your supply system is delivered to you for use at the plumbing fixtures—your sinks, faucets, tubs, showers and toilets. Plumbing fixtures also represent the point where the water supply system meets the drain-waste-vent system.

Basic plumbing fixtures have not changed much in design for decades, but they have become much more efficient. A toilet once used five or more gallons during every flush. Now toilets are required to flush just 1.6 gallons. Shower heads today must flow no more than 1.2 gallons per minute, far less than they used to. Some faucets share similar efficiencies.

The materials used in plumbing fixtures have also changed for the better. Tubs, for example, have made a transition from fragile porcelain and oppressively heavy cast iron to sturdy lightweight fiberglass.

Plumbing fixtures must stand up to constant use, and despite their advances they still suffer from many of the same problems that plagued them in decades past.

Disc-type cartridge faucets have a single-lever handle with a limited range of motion and a "heavy" feel. The inner cartridge does not rise and fall as the lever is operated.

Ball-type faucets have a single handle which rotates smoothly in all directions.

Compression faucets always have two handles. When you close the faucet, you will feel the neoprene washers being squeezed.

Faucets

You probably have several different styles of faucets in your home. Each faucet design has its own virtues and drawbacks, but all faucets can develop leaks. When leaks occur it's usually because inner components—washers, O-rings, seals or cartridges—have become worn or cracked. These parts are designed to be replaced, and you can find new parts at any full-service hardware store or home center.

If you take a faucet apart, work carefully and keep track of how the parts fit together. Begin by identifying the type and make of faucet. Before starting any actual work on a fixture, be sure to turn off the water supply.

Most important, fix a leak as soon as possible. Even a small leak can waste thousands of gallons if left unchecked long enough. If left unrepaired, a leak can also cut a channel in the metal faucet seat, which may require that the entire faucet be replaced.

Though they may take many different appearances, your sink, tub and shower, and utility faucets will almost certainly fit into one of the following categories. Knowing which types you own will help you anticipate problems and make timely repairs.

Compression faucet design, also known as a *stem-and-seat* faucet, was the standard for any faucet installed more than 30 years ago. Some compression faucets are still sold today. Most double-handle faucets use this design, in which a neoprene washer attached to a valve stem compresses against a metal valve seat inside the faucet. If you notice that the movement of the handles resembles that of a jar lid being opened and closed, then your faucet is probably one with a compression design.

Compression faucets can remain in service for many years, but they will periodically develop leaks, and

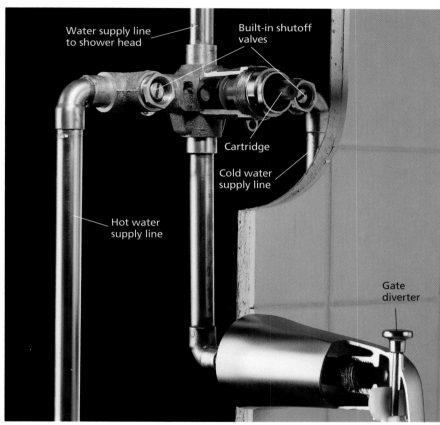

Tub and shower faucets may look different, but they operate using the same principles as a sink faucet (opposite page): a compression stem, a sleeve-type cartridge or a disc-type cartridge. In the example shown here, a sleeve-type cartridge mixes hot and cold water and sends it to the tub spout and up to the shower head. A gate diverter on the tub spout halts water flow when the shower is in use.

finding replacement parts can be difficult for older models. If you have a compression faucet, it's likely you'll want to replace it one day.

Ball-type faucet was the first design to omit the compression washer. A ball-type faucet has a single-lever handle. Inside, a hollow metal or plastic ball controls the hot-cold water mix and volume. These faucets are extremely durable, and replacement parts are readily available. You may want to replace a ball-type faucet when you grow tired of the look, but it's unlikely the faucet will fail.

Cartridge faucet represents a newer generation of washerless

faucets. A cartridge faucet uses an insert that contains all mechanical parts. The handle screw is hidden under an index cap on the collar. Most are single handle with one cartridge that mixes and controls the water flow, though some styles use two handles and separate hot and cold cartridges. Older cartridge designs use a sleeve-type cartridge, while later models may feature a disc-type cartridge. Fixing a sleeve-type faucet is often a matter of popping in a new cartridge every ten to fifteen years; a disc-type faucet may never need any attention whatsoever.

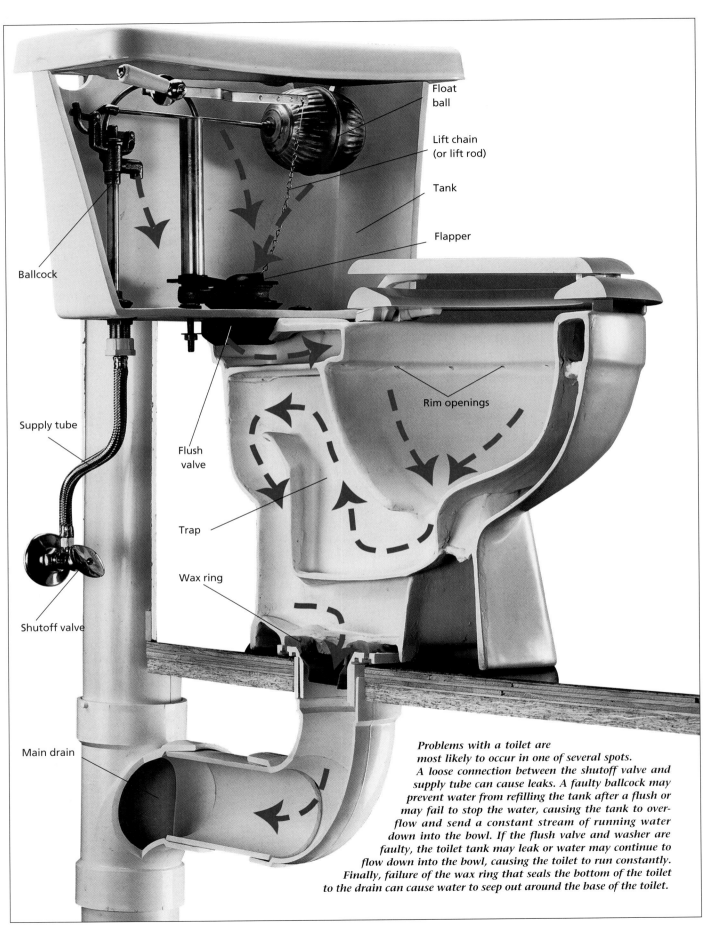

Float ball

Lift chain (or lift rod)

Tank

Flapper

Ballcock

Supply tube

Flush valve

Rim openings

Trap

Shutoff valve

Wax ring

Main drain

Problems with a toilet are most likely to occur in one of several spots. A loose connection between the shutoff valve and supply tube can cause leaks. A faulty ballcock may prevent water from refilling the tank after a flush or may fail to stop the water, causing the tank to over-flow and send a constant stream of running water down into the bowl. If the flush valve and washer are faulty, the toilet tank may leak or water may continue to flow down into the bowl, causing the toilet to run constantly. Finally, failure of the wax ring that seals the bottom of the toilet to the drain can cause water to seep out around the base of the toilet.

Toilets

Your toilet sees heavier use than other plumbing fixtures, yet its operation remains a mystery to most people. Studying a toilet in operation can help you understand where and why problems occur.

Begin your inspection with the *supply tube*, which carries water to the tank. Does it have a *shutoff valve*? If your toilet overflows, closing that valve will be your first concern. (If the toilet doesn't have a shutoff valve, consider installing one right away.)

Next, remove the tank cover and identify the *ballcock* that controls the flow of water into the tank. All ballcocks can be adjusted to alter the water level. Push the handle and watch how a flush occurs. When you trip the handle, the *lift chain* (or lift rod) raises a *flapper* or *tank ball*, allowing water to flow through the *flush valve* opening and into the *toilet bowl*.

Flowing through the *rim openings* as well as down the back of the bowl, water pushes the waste through the *trap* and creates the suction that pulls the waste down into the *main drain*.

As the water level falls in the tank, a float ball or float cup drops, opening the ballcock valve to introduce fresh water into the tank.

As the flush ends, you should see the flapper reseat itself firmly, sealing the flush valve. As the float ball or float cup rises in the tank, it shuts off the ballcock and stops the flow of water.

Inspect the floor around the base of the toilet. The transition from the toilet to the main drain is sealed with a *wax ring*. Check for seepage, discolorations or sponginess within the flooring material—these are indications of leaks in the wax ring or cracks in the toilet tank. Moisture can permanently damage the subfloor, so leaks should be corrected quickly.

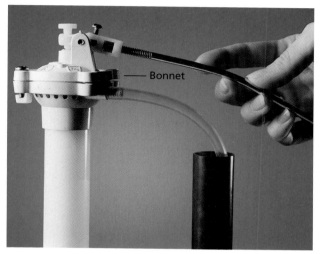

— Bonnet

Diaphragm ballcock, usually plastic, has a wide bonnet and a brass float arm. The bonnet contains a rubber diaphragm. As water rises in the tank after a flush, the float ball applies pressure to the float arm, closing the ballcock valve. The water level in the tank can be adjusted by bending the float arm up or down.

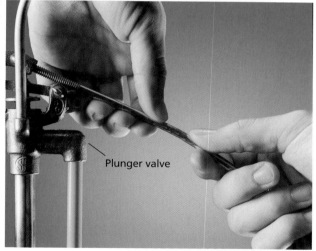

Plunger valve

Plunger-valve ballcock is made of brass. Water flow is controlled by a plunger attached to the float arm and ball. As the water rises, the float arm forces the plunger down against a valve seat, stopping the flow of water. This traditional style is an enduring favorite for good reason: it's durable and easy to adjust or repair. The water level in the tank can be adjusted by bending the float arm up or down.

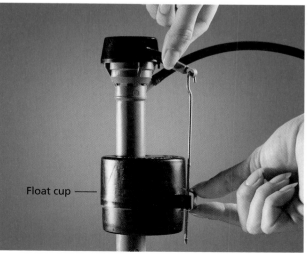

Float cup —

Float cup ballcock is made of plastic and designed for easy adjustment. As the water level rises in the tank, the float cup pushes a lever that closes a rubber seal inside the ballcock. Water level in the tank is controlled by adjusting the position of the float cup along the pull rod.

Drain Traps

After water is used at a sink, tub, shower or other fixture, it enters the drain-waste-vent system through a *drain trap*. The easiest place to see a drain trap is probably under a bathroom or kitchen sink, but every fixture in your home has one. Take a look at a drain trap from the side (*photo, below*). It should resemble the letter P, with the bend pointing toward the floor. This trap bend is designed to hold water, which is flushed away and replenished with new water each time you use the fixture.

Many homeowners (and sometimes children) have been thrilled to discover the holding action of a drain trap when some cherished piece of jewelry or a toy has been accidentally dropped down a drain. But beyond this occasional conve-nience, a drain trap serves a serious and important purpose. The standing water in the trap seals the drain line and prevents sewer gases from backing up into your home. Even in quantities too small for you to smell, sewer gas can cause health problems, such as respiratory diffi-culties and headaches.

Plumbing codes require that all drain traps have threaded connec-tions so they can be removed for cleaning or repair. Traps with one bend pointing up and another pointing down are called S-traps. Because the vertical movement of water through an S-trap can create a sucking action that can empty the trap, this configuration is now forbidden by codes. If you have S-traps or one-piece traps that cannot be disassembled, you may want to consider replacing them with up-to-date chrome or plastic P-traps.

Fixture Traps

It's wise to inspect each drain trap in your house. Check for cor-rosion in chromed brass traps, and look for deterioration, stains and other signs of leakage near the trap. If you find signs of trouble, check the pipes and connections—they should be tight and free of corro-sion. Also make sure the sink is properly sealed against the drain opening. Each sink has a strainer assembly that connects the sink to the trap and drain line. Leaks sometimes occur between the strainer body and the lip of the drain opening.

Also sniff for the odor of sewer gas. Though it's not unusual to get an occasional whiff of sewer gas from a drain, if this happens frequently, you may want to have a plumber investigate the problem.

Run water into the drain trap

The familiar P-trap holds water in a bend to seal the drain pipe and prevent sewer gases from rising into your home. All exposed drain traps must have threaded fittings that allow them to be disassembled and cleaned.

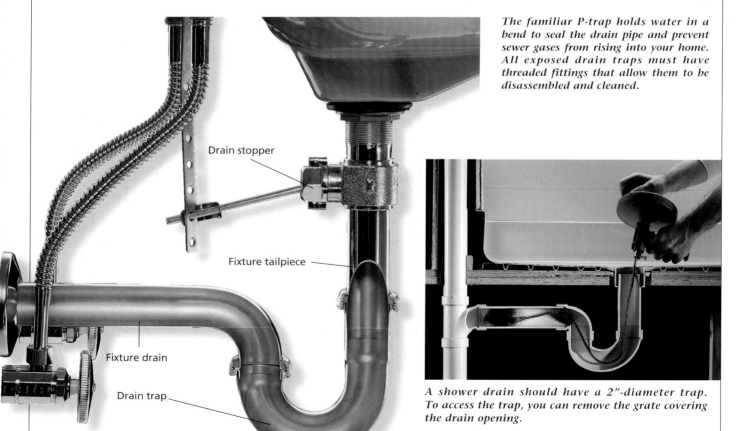

Drain stopper

Fixture tailpiece

Fixture drain

Drain trap

A shower drain should have a 2"-diameter trap. To access the trap, you can remove the grate covering the drain opening.

and listen to the sound of the drain. If you hear loud gurgling, it may mean that your drain is poorly vented—a problem that should be addressed by a plumbing contractor.

Also make sure the drain traps are the right size for the fixture they serve:

• Vanity sinks may be served by 1¼-inch-diameter drain traps.

• Bathtubs, kitchen sinks, dishwashers, clothes washers and utility sinks should be served by 1½-inch-diameter drain traps.

• Showers and floor drains in concrete slabs should be served by 2-inch-diameter drain traps.

Floor Drains

After evaluating each fixture trap, locate and inspect all floor drains in your home. Basements and utility rooms generally have at least one floor drain. Since these drains rarely carry water, the water in their traps can evaporate, allowing sewer gases to rise into your home. If your floor drain is a newer model, it may have a hollow ball that fits into the drain opening. This ball fits snugly enough to prevent sewer gases from entering your home; when water flows into the drain, the ball floats up, allowing water to pass.

If your floor drain has no float ball, a tennis ball works just as well.

Main Drain Trap

As a last guardian against sewer gases, your drain system should have a U-shaped main drain trap located near the point where the main drain leaves your home and runs to the city sewer system or to a septic tank. In some cases, this trap is found in a shallow pit under a metal or wood cover. If your floor drains back up, the main trap is a likely place to look for clogs. This trap fitting also provides a place to auger out the main drain, should it become clogged with tree roots or another obstruction.

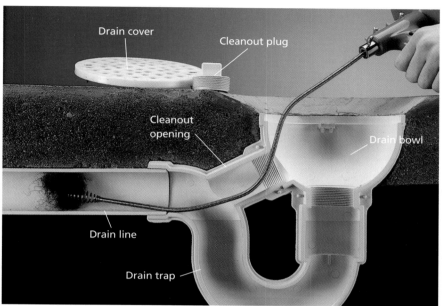

A floor drain often has a cleanout opening that allows you to auger the drain line while bypassing the drain trap.

The main drain in your home may have a U-shaped trap that protects your entire home. Look for hubbed fittings on the floor of your basement, near the wall facing the street.

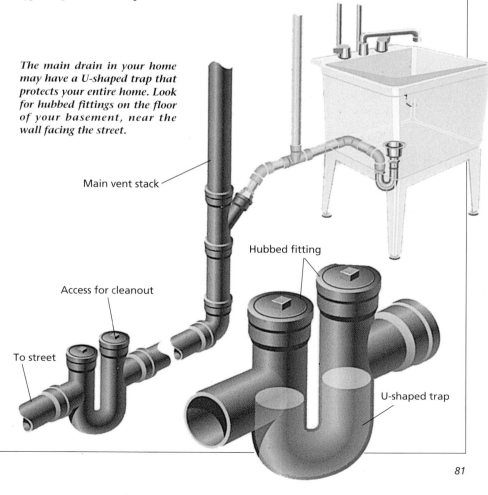

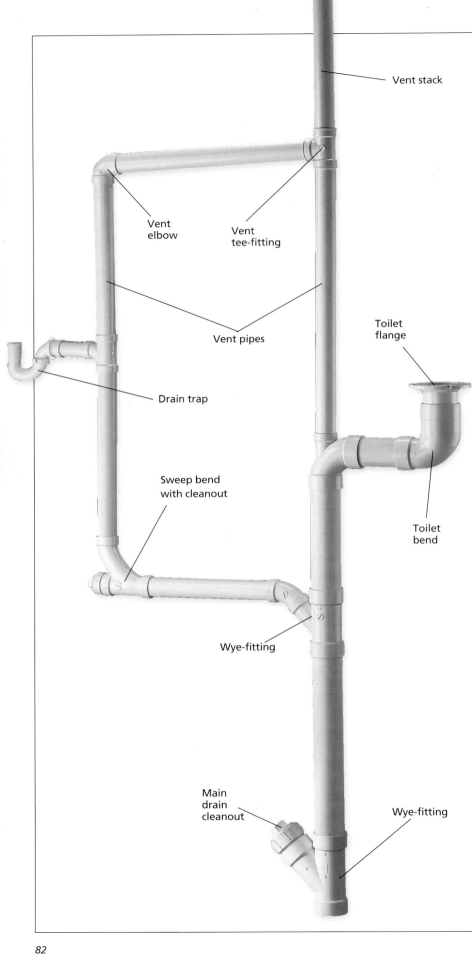

Vent stack

Vent
elbow

Vent
tee-fitting

Vent pipes

Toilet
flange

Drain trap

Sweep bend
with cleanout

Toilet
bend

Wye-fitting

Main
drain
cleanout

Wye-fitting

The Drain-Waste-Vent System

From the drain traps, waste water flows from your plumbing fixtures into a system of drain-waste-vent (DWV) pipes, which are largely hidden from view inside the walls and floors of your home. These pipes carry waste out of the house, into the sewer system or septic tank.

As you inspect the DWV system, pay particular attention to the various cleanout fittings in the pipes. Because waste water flows slowly in DWV pipes, under no pressure, these pipes are susceptible to clogs. Knowing exactly where all the cleanout fittings are located can make life much easier when a clogged drain line causes waste water to back up into your plumbing fixtures.

In order for waste water to flow freely down the drain piping, the DWV system needs air. To provide that air, the drain pipes are joined to a vent system connected to the outdoors, usually through one or more vent stacks that extend up through your roof. If a plumbing system is not vented adequately, fixtures don't work smoothly—toilets don't flush completely; drains gurgle, choke and overflow. More important, inadequately vented lines can pull water from traps, allowing sewer gas into your home.

In addition, the horizontal branch drain pipes must be angled slightly downward, about ⅛ inch per linear foot, to ensure the pipes drain completely without sucking water from the traps.

This model of a DWV system shows how the pipes and fittings for the drain and vent systems are connected. Make sure you know where the drain traps, wye-fittings, and other cleanout fittings are located, and make sure these fittings can be readily opened.

Pipe Materials

DWV piping is much larger than that used in water supply lines, ranging from 1¼ to 4 inches in diameter. You can easily spot vent pipes on your roof; and the main soil stack, with cleanout access, will be evident in your basement or utility room.

***Metal** DWV pipes are standard in any house more than 30 years old. Cast iron and galvanized steel are now considered obsolete, except in specific usages such as underground lines where strength and root protection is needed. While a cast-iron stack and main drain may last almost indefinitely, galvanized steel drain pipes, which have thinner walls, will eventually rust through and leak. If your drain system features galvanized steel drain pipes, you can expect to repair or replace them someday.*

***Plastic** pipes are now the standard for new DWV installations. Since drain-waste-vent pipes do not require heat resistance, inexpensive PVC or ABS pipes are acceptable. CPVC, often used as water supply pipe, can also be used in DWV applications.*

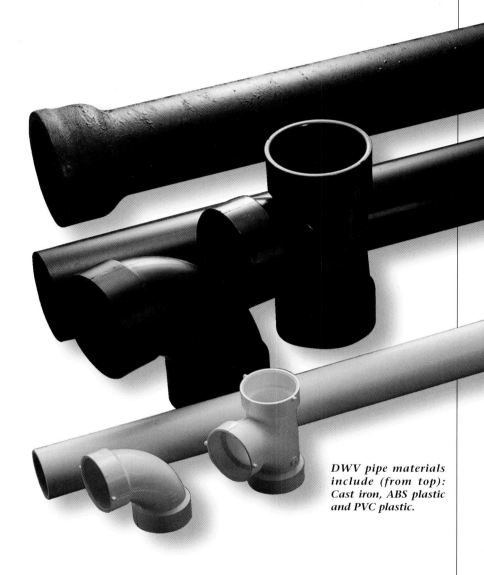

DWV pipe materials include (from top): Cast iron, ABS plastic and PVC plastic.

DWV fittings come in two basic shapes, which can help you identify the function of the pipes. Pipes joined with fittings that have gradual, sweeping bends (below left) are drain pipes. Those with sharp bends (below right) are vent pipes.

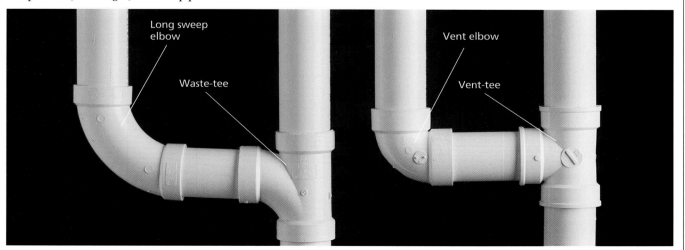

Long sweep elbow

Waste-tee

Vent elbow

Vent-tee

Branch Drains

Branch drain lines—another vital element within the DWV system—carry waste water from your fixtures to the main waste and vent stack. Branch lines typically serve several fixtures, and codes include specific rules to limit the load carried by a given size of drain pipe.

To begin with, plumbing codes assign a unit of measure called a *drain fixture unit rating* to each type of fixture typically found in a house.

• Vanity sinks and floor drains are assigned 1 fixture unit.

• Showers, tubs, clothes washers, dishwashers and most other fixtures are assigned 2 fixture units.

• Kitchen sinks with attached food disposers are assigned 3 fixture units.

Codes then specify the number of units that can be carried by a given pipe size. If your inspection shows that a horizontal branch drain is carrying a load too large for its size, watch these lines to see if they habitually run slow or back up. At some point you may want to have these branch drains upgraded to meet code requirements.

• 1¼-inch pipe can carry only 1 fixture unit.

• 1½-inch pipe can carry 3 fixture units.

• 2-inch pipe can carry up to 6 fixture units.

• 2½-inch pipe can carry a maximum of 12 fixture units.

• 3-inch pipe can carry 20 fixture units.

Code also assigns a degree of slope for branch drain lines. Horizontal drain pipes less than 3 inches in diameter should slope ¼ inch per foot toward the main drain. Drain pipes that are 3 inches or more in diameter should slope ⅛ inch per foot.

Every horizontal branch drain run should have a cleanout at the end (*photo, above*). These cleanouts make branch lines easier to service if they become clogged.

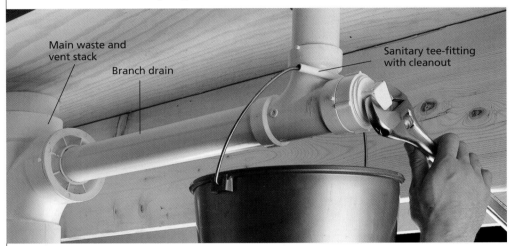

Main waste and vent stack

Branch drain

Sanitary tee-fitting with cleanout

Branch drain lines (above) feed into the main waste and vent stack. Frequently serving several fixture drain lines, branch drain lines usually have a cleanout plug at the end of their horizontal run. This cleanout plug can be removed to clear clogs in the line.

Main drain and cleanout for the main stack is usually located near a basement wall, facing the street. If the fitting is frozen in place, you can use a hammer and cold chisel to knock it loose.

Main Drains

When waste water finally reaches the main waste and vent stack, it begins its horizontal journey out of your home—into the municipal sewer network or into a septic tank.

Look for a floor cleanout fitting near the point where the main drain passes through your foundation wall. Should tree roots or other material obstruct the main drain, you can auger it out through this fitting. Plumbers recommend that the main drain be augered every two years or so to forestall more serious problems. If the main drain collapses, excavating your yard to gain access to the pipe is very expensive.

Vent Stack

Finally, you should periodically check the top of the DWV stack extending up through your roof. This opening provides fresh air to your entire drain system. Make sure this vent is unobstructed. If birds, animals or snow and ice cover this vent, your plumbing cannot work correctly.

Sewer/Septic System

If your DWV system is connected to municipal sewer service, your visual tour ends at the street. However, if you are among the 15% of homeowners not served by municipal service, your household waste probably drains into a septic field.

Most septic systems consist of an underground tank and a network of pipes fanning out from the tank. When sewage reaches the tank, the solid wastes settle to the bottom, where they are consumed by microorganisms. As the tank fills, the water flows out of the tank through porous drain pipes that distribute the water into the soil. The water is filtered clean as it drains down through thick layers of soil and rock on its return to the water table.

Used correctly, a septic system requires only that residual wastes be pumped out every few years.

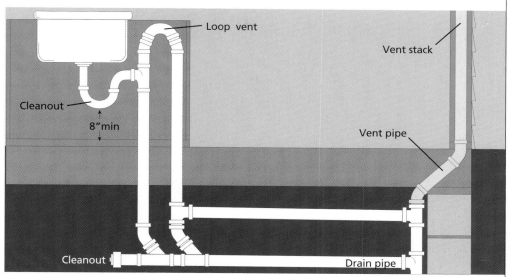

A loop vent makes it possible to vent a sink when there is no adjacent wall to house the vent pipe. If you have an island sink in your kitchen, make sure it is vented in a manner that meets code requirements. In this configuration, a loop of pipe arches up against the countertop—away from the drain—before dropping through the floor. The vent pipe then runs horizontally to an existing vent pipe.

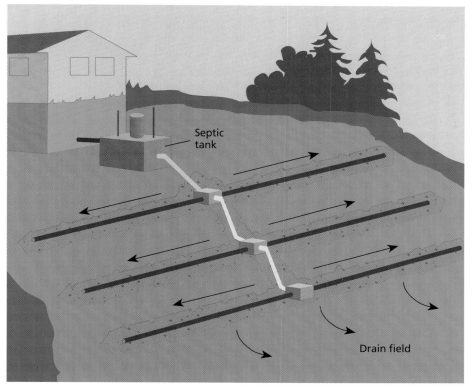

In a typical septic system, waste water leaves the house to enter a septic tank, where solids settle to the bottom. Water at the top of the tank flows onward to a series of porous pipes that distribute the water to the soil, where it is gradually filtered pure as it moves through many feet of soil on its way back to the water table.

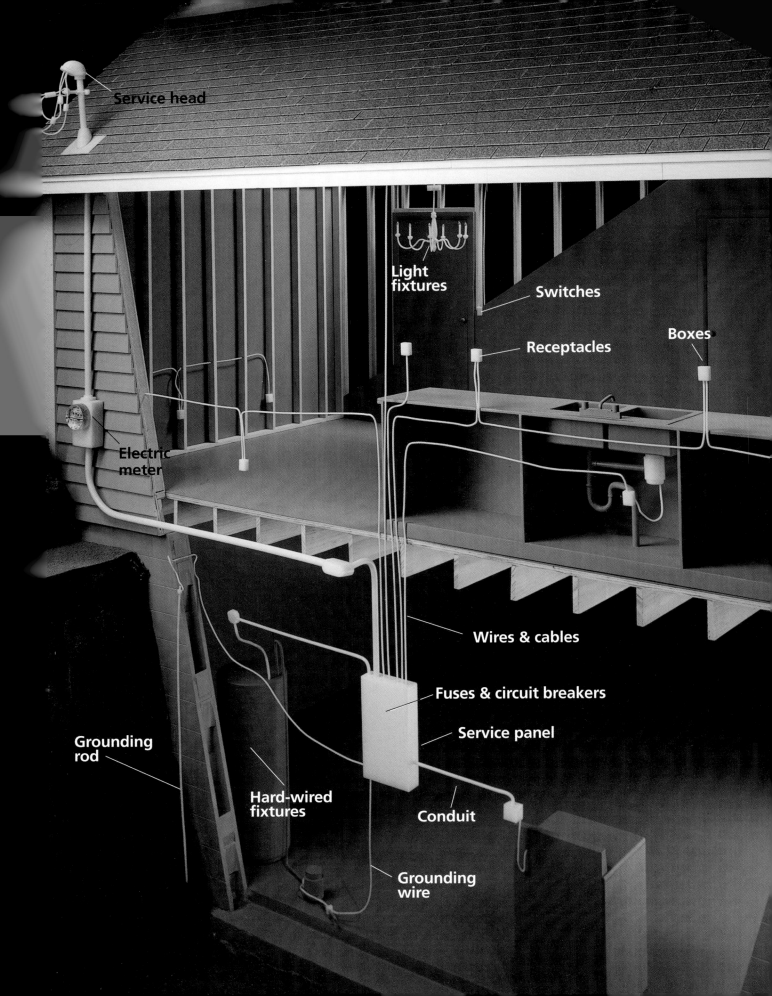

Service head

Light fixtures

Switches

Receptacles

Boxes

Electric meter

Wires & cables

Grounding rod

Fuses & circuit breakers

Service panel

Hard-wired fixtures

Conduit

Grounding wire

WIRING

Plenty of homeowners are apprehensive about electricity. Even die-hard do-it-yourselfers sometimes find themselves uneasy confronting their electrical system.

But there is nothing magical about electricity. There is no voodoo in your home wiring.

Instead, electricity always follows the laws of physics.

If you know how electricity works, you're going to know how to have a safer, better functioning house. On one level, this knowledge will help you lose any apprehension you have about electricity. And on another nuts-and-bolts level, you'll simply know if your wiring can handle the draw of a new window air conditioner.

In addition, homeowners who understand their electrical system are able to distinguish the differences between problems that can be fixed with a minor repair and those best left to a licensed electrician.

The electrical flow inside your house mirrors the flow of water through your plumbing system. Just as water arrives under pressure, electrical current flows through hot wires that are also pressurized by voltage. Electricity is available for use at lights, outlets and appliances much like water flows through plumbing fixtures. And, finally, just as your waste-water leaves by gravity, electrical current flows back to its source through "unpressurized" neutral wires, which are said to be at zero voltage.

That's the simplified version. Let's take a look at the specifics of your electrical system.

The Service Head

Begin your tour of the electrical system by standing in your yard. Power companies either string local power lines overhead and attach them to a service head on your house, or they bury power lines.

If your house is supplied by overhead wires, it should have a service mast attached to the roof or the siding. The mast anchors your electrical service wires and keeps moisture from entering your house.

When you have overhead lines, count how many wires are going into your service mast. It's very likely you have three wires. Two are power lines, each carrying 120 volts of current, and the third is a neutral wire. Each 120-volt line, combined with the neutral wire, provides the standard 120-volt power found at most outlets and switches. For power-intensive appliances, like water heaters or clothes dryers, the two 120-volt lines are combined to produce a 240-volt circuit.

Buried wires enter straight into the basement of your house, or climb a foundation wall to where your service panel is located. Either way, the wires will be inside conduit.

If your home was built before 1950, at one time you probably

GLOSSARY OF ELECTRICAL TERMS

AMPERE (or Amp): Refers to the rate at which electrical power flows to a device.

CABLE: Two or more wires grouped together and covered with a sheath.

CIRCUIT: A continuous loop of electrical current flowing along wires or cables.

CIRCUIT BREAKER: An electromagnetic switch that interrupts an electrical circuit in the event of an overload or short circuit. Unlike a fuse, it can be reset.

CONDUCTOR: Any material that allows electrical current to flow through it.

CONDUIT: A metal or plastic tube designed to protect wires.

CONTINUITY: An uninterrupted electrical pathway through a circuit or electrical device.

FUSE: A safety device that interrupts electrical circuits during overloads or short circuits.

GROUNDING WIRE: A wire used in an electrical circuit to conduct current to the earth in the event of a short circuit.

HOT WIRE: Any wire that carries voltage. In an electrical circuit, it usually is covered with black or red insulation.

NEUTRAL WIRE: A wire that returns current at zero voltage to the source of electrical power. Wire is normally white or light gray.

OHMS: A measure of electrical resistance. One volt will force 1 amp through a conductor having a resistance of 1 ohm.

SHORT CIRCUIT: Improper contact between two current-carrying wires or between a hot wire and a grounded conductor.

UL: An abbreviation of Underwriters Laboratories Inc., an organization that tests electrical devices and products for safety.

VOLTAGE (or volt): A measurement of electricity in terms of pressure.

WATTAGE (or watt): A measurement of electrical power in terms of energy consumed. Watts can be calculated by multiplying volts times amps.

BASICS OF ELECTRICITY

The electrical current flowing through your toaster or light fixture is made up of electrons–the negatively charged particles of the atom that are in constant orbit around the atom's nucleus. When we harness electricity, we are really harnessing the power inherent in the motion of electrons.

The enormous spinning generators in power plants produce alternating current. As the armature turns in a generator, electrons are pushed in one direction by the magnetic pole on the generator, and then pulled back by the opposite magnetic pole. These hugely powerful magnetic fields cause trillions upon trillions of electrons to stream through power lines, first in one direction, then back, over and over again. In the U.S, Canada and most of Mexico, the frequency of this alternating current is 60 cycles per second, properly referred to as 60 hertz (60 Hz). In many other foreign countries, the alternating current runs at 50 Hz.

Power plants typically generate power at about 15,000 volts. Some smaller plants produce only a few thousand watts, or a few kilowatts, while huge power plants have their outputs measured in millions of watts, or megawatts.

Before power is shipped on high-voltage power lines, the current is stepped up by a transformer. The higher voltage allows power companies to ship the energy more efficiently. The lines on those large metal towers carry from 220,000 volts to more than 750,000 volts. The enormous voltage can interfere with your car radio and produce an audible humming sound.

When high-voltage lines connect with local lines, the voltage is stepped down again, normally to less than 12,000 volts. Additional utility pole transformers, located within neighborhoods, reduce the high-voltage current that flows through power lines. These transformers reduce 10,000-volt current to the normal 120-volt and 240-volt current used in the home. A transformer holds two coils of wire windings connected to a metal core. How much the voltage is altered depends upon how many turns of wiring

This familiar type of utility pole transformer reduces high-voltage utility current to 120-volt current for distribution to individual homes. If you are considering upgrading your electrical service, it's possible that your electric company will need to upgrade the neighborhood transformer, if it is already operating at maximum capacity.

are wrapped around each coil. The voltage is proportional to the ratio of windings. Thus, a transformer reducing 12,000-volt current to 120-volt current has an incoming coil with 100 times the windings as the number of outgoing coil windings.

Inside your house, your electric meter and service panel measure and regulate the flow of electrons, just as water is regulated in your plumbing system. Three common electrical terms are amps, volts and watts. Here's what they mean:

Amps, or amperes, refer to how many electrons are flowing past a certain point for a fixed time. One amp represents the flow of roughly six billion billion electrons in one second.

Volts refer to the pressure behind the amps. Voltage is very analogous to water pressure. The higher the voltage, the higher the pressure. The water coming out of a common garden hose will merely soak you; water under much higher pressure will blast paint off rocks. Similarly, whereas a 12-volt system will give you a mild jolt, a 120-volt system can kill you. And just as water pressure varies, so does electrical pressure. Your home is wired for pressures of 120 volts and 240 volts, but the voltage varies slightly, just as water pressure varies when all your neighbors water their lawns at the same time. Your 120-volt circuits could be receiving from 114 to 126 volts, which will vary throughout the day.

Watts measure the power being used by an electrical device. The equation is amps × volts = watts. For example, a hair dryer drawing 10 amps of power at 120 volts uses 1,200 watts. A dryer drawing 30 amps at 240 volts uses 7,200 watts. Conversely, you can easily determine that a hair dryer rated at 1,200 watts running on 120 volts draws 10 amps. A 60-watt light bulb on a 120-volt system requires .5 amps. And so on.

Once you know this simple equation, you will be able to map your home's electrical circuits and determine whether any part of your electrical system is overburdened.

had just two wires running to the service head. One was a 120-volt line and the other was the grounded neutral wire. With no second 120-volt line, this wiring system couldn't provide 240-volt circuits. Because they cannot supply the amount of power a modern home requires, most two-wire services have been updated to three-wire services. If you do still have a two-wire service, you should upgrade to a three-wire service. When it comes time to sell, for example, you'll find that most home loan programs won't give a mortgage for a house that has a two-wire service.

Whatever the number of wires you have, and regardless of whether your electrical service is suspended or buried, your service wires should run through metal or plastic conduit to your electric meter and service panel. *These wires are always live, unless turned off by your electric company!* Never attempt repairs or inspections of service wires, and keep metal ladders away. Any work on this portion of your electrical service should be done only by a certified electrician.

The Electric Meter

All electricity that enters your home is measured by your electric meter. If you know how to read the meter, you can verify if your electric bill is accurate, and you can determine how much energy you save with different energy-saving techniques.

Your electric meter measures every watt of power you consume. It is usually attached to the side of the house, and it is connected to your service head. Tampering with your meter is both dangerous and illegal. The wiring inside the meter is always hot, and the meter is the property of your electric company.

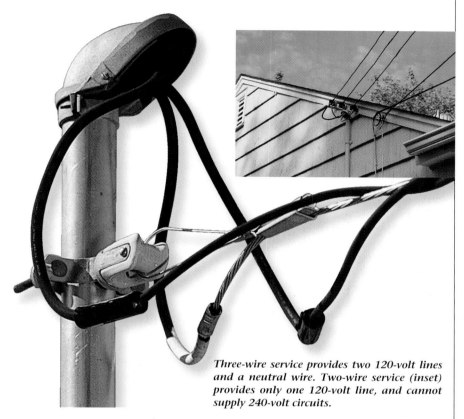

Three-wire service provides two 120-volt lines and a neutral wire. Two-wire service (inset) provides only one 120-volt line, and cannot supply 240-volt circuits.

Most electrical meters have five dials; some older models have four dials. From left to right, the dials move in opposite directions. To read your meter, read from left to right. When the pointer sits between two numbers, note the lower number. If the pointer aims directly at a number, look at the next dial and see if it has reached or passed 0. If it has, note the number on the left. If the pointer to the right has not yet reached zero, record the next lowest number on the left dial. The full five-digit (or four-digit) number reveals how many kilowatts you have consumed. Recheck the dial after a month and you will see how many kilowatts you used during the period.

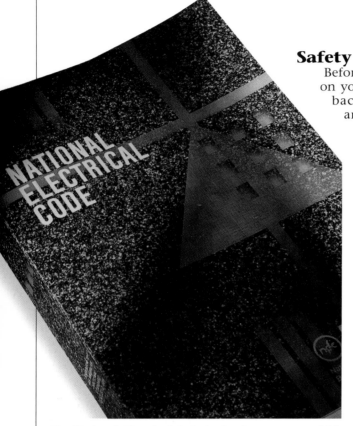

The National Electrical Code is the document on which most municipalities base their local Electrical Codes. It is updated every few years.

Safety

Before you go any further on your electrical tour, step back for a few minutes and consider issues of safety. The secret of living safely with electricity is to respect it. Make certain the power is off before you work on any part of your electrical system. Shut off power to the proper circuit or turn off the master switch at the service entry panel. Then, check to be sure the power is off by testing for current with a circuit tester. Be methodical, and use common sense. If you ever have doubts as to whether a line is live, test the line or call a licensed electrician. Restore power only after the work has been completed.

The NEC

Electricians in the United States work according to standards defined in the National Electrical Code. The code book itself is dense and highly technical. It is not written for the layman. If you have questions, check your library or bookstore for a condensed version or one of the in-depth guides based upon the Code, such as "Practical Electrical Wiring," by Herbert P. Richter and W. Creighton Schwan.

Following code is extremely important to your family's safety and to the safety of future residents. How important is the NEC? The first electrical code in the U.S. was authored in 1881 as a way to reduce an epidemic of electrical fires.

UL Listing

In the United States, electrical components are tested by Under-

Safety Guidelines

•Use only fiberglass or wood ladders when working near the electrical service head.

•Never attempt to repair or replace your main service panel or service entrance head. These are jobs for licensed electricians only and require that the power company shuts off power to your house.

•Do not touch metal pipes, faucets or fixtures while working with electricity. The metal could provide a grounding path, allowing electricity to flow through your body.

•Close the service panel door and post a warning sign on it while you are working on electrical projects.

•Never install the wrong size fuse or breaker in the main service panel. Do not install a fuse or breaker that has a higher amperage rating than the circuit wire.

•Make a map of your household electrical circuits. This will help guide you to the circuits you need to turn off during repairs or inspections and will help you pinpoint problems.

•Keep a flashlight near your main service panel.

•Do not drill walls or ceilings without first shutting off power to the circuits that may be hidden behind them. Use only double-insulated power tools.

•Wear rubber-soled shoes or boots while working on or inspecting your electrical system. On damp floors, stand on dry wooden boards or a rubber mat.

• Never alter the prongs of a plug to fit a receptacle.

•Use only UL Listed electrical parts or devices. These have been tested for safety by Underwriters Laboratories.

•Use extension cords only for temporary connections. Never place them under rugs, or fasten them to walls, baseboards or other surfaces.

•Use GFCI receptacles in bathroom outlets and other areas specified by local codes.

•Protect children by installing receptacle caps or childproof receptacle covers.

•Remember, always make certain the power is off before working on your electrical system. Never rush.

writers Laboratories Inc. (A few other laboratories also test components, but Underwriters is by far the largest.) This independent agency subjects components to rigorous tests. If a device fails, UL will not "List" it. If a product is not UL Listed, do not buy it. Listed material carries the distinctive UL stamp.

The cost of electrical material is relatively small. Wire costs only a few cents per foot, and receptacles and boxes cost only a few dollars. Don't try to skimp and save a few cents by buying substandard material. Local electrical inspectors can reject products that are not UL Listed—and for good reason: non-listed devices may fail and cause fires.

Permits

If you plan to change your house's wiring, or add new wiring, you need to apply for a local permit. That also holds true if you are adding a major electrical appliance, like central air conditioning.

Local inspectors will make two visits. The first inspection will be conducted before walls or flooring is installed. The second inspection takes place when all work is finished. If you have any questions, call your local codes office.

Electric Shock

Should the worst happen, you need to be ready to act. Electrocution is always a risk where there is electricity. When a person comes into contact with an electric short circuit, their muscles may become rigid, making it impossible for them to break free. The longer a person is shocked, the greater likelihood they will be killed. You must act quickly. To knock the person

free from the short circuit, use a poor-conducting object (a wooden broomstick, a towel, a wooden chair). If nothing is nearby, use a flying tackle to break them loose as a last-ditch effort. Be certain not to grab onto the person, or you too may be electrocuted. Next, call immediately for an ambulance. If the person is not breathing, perform CPR.

VOLTAGE TESTERS

A voltage tester, also called a circuit tester, has a small bulb that glows when power passes through it. With this simple tool you'll be able to make certain power is off to a circuit, determine if an outlet is properly grounded, and find which wire is carrying live voltage.

To determine if a receptacle works, insert the probes of the voltage tester into each plug slot. If the tester lights, the outlet is energized. If the tester does not light, the receptacle is faulty or the fuse or circuit breaker has blown. To see if the problem is limited to the receptacle, test other receptacles on the same circuit. If they don't work, the problem is in the circuit.

DETERMINING IF A RECEPTACLE HAS POWER:

1: After turning off power at the main service panel, place one probe of the voltage tester into each slot of the receptacle. If the tester glows, power is still flowing. You must test both halves of a duplex outlet. And remember, this is only a preliminary test. You must confirm the power is off by removing the coverplate and testing for power at the receptacle wires.

Use a voltage tester to see if you have power in an outlet. The voltage tester will light up when power is flowing through the circuit. Make sure the circuit is dead before you work on any electrical device.

2: Remove the receptacle coverplate. Loosen the mounting screws and carefully pull the receptacle from its box, taking care not to touch any wires. Touch one probe of the tester to a brass screw terminal and one probe to a silver screw terminal. The tester should not glow. If wires are connected to both sets of terminals, test both sets.

IDENTIFYING HOT WIRES:

Identifying live wires is not always easy. In older wiring, a receptacle may be connected to two black wires. Or, the white and black wires may be reversed due to shoddy work by an electrician or previous homeowner. To find out which wire is hot, turn off the power, remove the receptacle, and separate all wires so they do not touch each other or anything else. Turn on the power. Carefully touch one probe of the tester to the bare grounding wire or the grounded metal box and the other probe to the ends of each wire. When the tester glows, you have identified the hot wire. Make sure to test all wires. Note all hot wires, then turn off the power and label the hot wire with black or red tape.

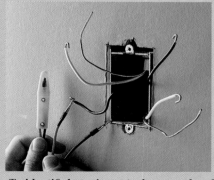

To identify hot wires, touch one probe of the circuit tester to the bare copper grounding wire (or to the metal box, if it is grounded), then touch the other probe to the bare end of each wire. When the light glows, you have a hot wire.

The Service Panel

After passing through the electrical meter, your service wires terminate in your service panel. The service panel distributes electrical current to your house's individual circuits. Here you should find the two hot feeder wires (or single hot feeder wire in a two-wire system) attached to the main breaker switch, which is in turn connected to the bus bar. The bus bar is a metal strip that connects the service feeder wires to your circuits. Hot feeder wires should be encased in black casing. The white wire, or neutral wire, is attached to the neutral bus bar. A thick ground wire will also be connected to the neutral bus bar and the ground wire will exit the service panel and connect to your metal water pipes or a grounding rod buried nearby, or both.

The appearance of a service panel can vary tremendously. Older panels generally use fuses; newer models rely on circuit breakers. Some very old houses that have never had an electrical update may

NOTE: *Removing the cover on your service panel will help you see how it works. This is not dangerous, provided you don't touch any wires or metal components inside the panel. But a novice should do no hands-on work inside a service panel. If you have any problems with your service panel, contact a licensed electrician.*

Two hot service wires provide 120 volts of power to the main circuit breaker. These wires are always hot. Each hot service wire is connected to a metal bus bar that runs through the panel to provide power to the circuit breakers.

Main circuit breaker protects the hot service wires from overloads, and transfers power to two hot bus bars. Shut this breaker OFF before removing the cover to look inside the panel.

Double-pole breaker connects to both hot bus bars to provide 240-volt power for electric clothes dryer, range and other large appliances.

Neutral service wire carries current back to the power source after it has passed through the home.

120-volt circuit wires

Grounding bus bar has terminals for linking circuit wires to the main grounding conductor.

Feeder circuit to subpanel

Two hot bus bars run through the center of the service panel, supplying power to the individual circuit breakers. Each carries 120 volts of power.

120/240-volt circuit

Grounding conductor

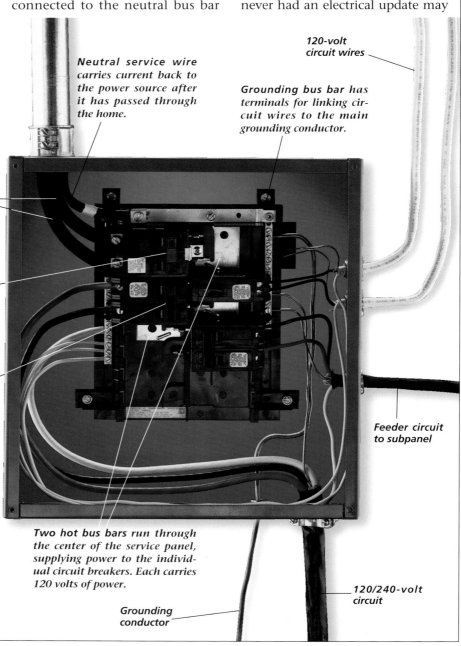

Grounding clamp

Your electrical service panel may be grounded to a clamp on a water pipe.

have a 30-amp service with only two circuits, both protected by fuses. New houses can have 200-amp service with 30 or more circuits, all with circuit breakers. You can determine the size of the service by reading the amperage rating printed on the main fuse block or main circuit breaker, located at the top of the main service panel.

It's always a good idea to keep the space around your service panel clean and uncluttered. Never store or pile anything against your service panel. Nor should you allow children to play near the panel.

Plus, always keep a flashlight next to the service panel in case you need to do any trouble-shooting when power goes out.

Tip

Use extra caution around your service panel. The wires leading into the panel are always electrified.

The 60-amp fuse panel (left), often installed between 1950 and 1965, is regarded as adequate for a small, 1100-square-foot house that has no more than one 240-volt appliance. The 100-amp circuit breaker panel (right), was generally installed in houses during the 1960s and later. To shut off power to a fuse box circuit, carefully unscrew the plug fuse, touching only the insulated rim. To shut off power to the entire house, hold the handle of the main fuse block and pull sharply. To shut off power to an individual circuit in a circuit breaker panel, flip the lever on the appropriate circuit breaker to the OFF position. To shut off power to the entire house, turn the main circuit breaker to the OFF position.

SUBPANELS

In addition to the main service panel, your electrical system may have one or more subpanels that control some of the circuits in the home. A subpanel is used to add circuits when the main service panel does not have enough open slots for the new circuits. The subpanel normally resembles the main service panel, with its own circuit breakers or fuses, but it is usually smaller. The subpanel can be found near the main panel, or located near the area served by the new circuit, such as in the garage or attic.

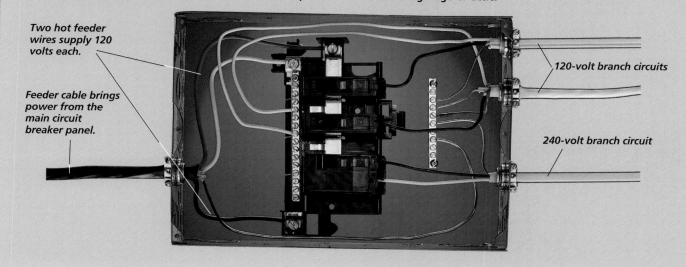

Two hot feeder wires supply 120 volts each.

Feeder cable brings power from the main circuit breaker panel.

120-volt branch circuits

240-volt branch circuit

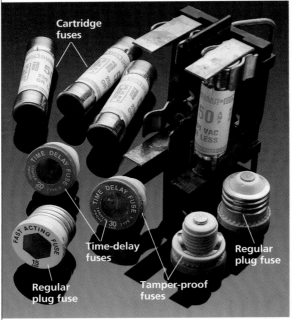

Cartridge fuses

Time-delay fuses

Regular plug fuse

Regular plug fuse

Tamper-proof fuses

Regular plug fuse

Fuses (left) are used in older service panels. Plug fuses normally control 120-volt circuits rated for 15, 20 or 30 amps. Time-delay fuses absorb a temporary heavy power load—such as that which may occur when a large motor starts up—without blowing. Cartridge fuses control 240-volt circuits and range from 30 to 100 amps.

Circuit breakers (below) are used in newer service panels. Single-pole breakers for 120-volt service are rated for 15 or 20 amps. Double-pole breakers rated for 20 to 50 amps control 240-volt circuits. GFCI (ground-fault circuit-interrupter) breakers provide shock protection for the entire circuit.

Fuses & Circuit Breakers

Inside your service panel you'll find your circuit breakers or fuses. Although these simple-looking devices are easy to ignore, the breakers or fuses are crucial safeguards that protect your electrical system from overloads and short circuits. A nonexistent or poor-quality fuse or circuit breaker can cause a fire.

It is a legendary story, but probably based on fact: A homeowner with a fuse box blows a fuse. When the fuse is replaced, it blows again. Frustrated, the homeowner slips a copper penny into the fuse holder. Voilà! The lights work again, the toaster toasts, the heater glows. The homeowner goes to bed.

The next morning, a fire inspector sifts through the remains of the house. He finds a scorched fuse box holding the trace of a melted penny. The inspector rules the fire an accident—caused by an overloaded circuit.

Fuse Panels

Most service panels installed before the mid-1960s rely on fuses. Screw-in fuses protect 120-volt circuits that power lights and receptacles. Cartridge fuses protect 240-volt appliance circuits and the main shutoff at the service panel. Inside each fuse is a metal alloy ribbon. If the circuit carries too much power, either from a short circuit or overload, the alloy ribbon melts and stops the flow of power before your circuit wiring melts or ignites. A fuse *must always* match the amperage rating of the circuit wiring. Some misguided homeowners, frustrated by frequent blown fuses, install the wrong fuse. They are playing a very dangerous game. Instead of risking blown fuses, these homeowners risk starting a fire.

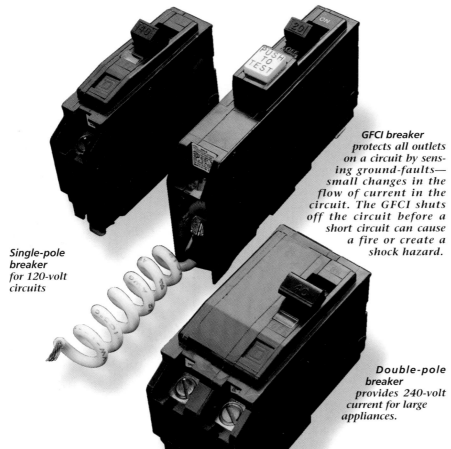

Single-pole breaker for 120-volt circuits

GFCI breaker protects all outlets on a circuit by sensing ground-faults—small changes in the flow of current in the circuit. The GFCI shuts off the circuit before a short circuit can cause a fire or create a shock hazard.

Double-pole breaker provides 240-volt current for large appliances.

Circuit Breaker Panels

In most service panels installed after 1965, circuit breakers protect the individual circuits. Single-pole breakers protect 120-volt circuits, and double-pole breakers protect 240-volt circuits. Amperage ratings for circuit breakers range from 15 to 100 amps.

Inside each circuit breaker is a permanent metal strip that bends when voltage passes through it. If a circuit is overloaded, the metal strip inside the breaker bends enough to trip a switch that stops the flow of power.

Circuit breakers, which can be reset after they trip, obviously have an advantage over one-time-use fuses, but circuit breakers can wear out. If the power demand is small, yet a circuit breaker repeatedly trips, the mechanism inside the breaker could be worn. A worn circuit breaker should be replaced.

Overloads

When a fuse blows or a circuit breaker trips, it is usually because there are too many devices drawing power through the circuit. Unplug some of the appliances and install a new fuse or reset the circuit breaker. If this solves the problem, move the appliances to another, less used, circuit. If the fuse blows or the circuit trips immediately again, suspect a short circuit in the system.

Grounding

If a short circuit occurs in your home, all that current wants to go somewhere. The safest place to "dump" that dangerous current is deep in the ground around your house, which is why your home has a grounding system. Remember that electricity follows the path of least resistance. Your grounding system is designed so that it provides less resistance to wayward current than a human body.

The method by which your house is grounded depends upon local codes. Many houses are grounded through their metal water pipes. Some houses have a copper grounding rod driven into the ground, usually near a basement wall. And many newer houses rely on both systems.

All grounding systems start in the service panel. There, a grounding wire is attached to the panel bus bar, and then to the water pipes or grounding rod. Therefore, any surge in current will follow the ground and bleed off into the surrounding soil instead of causing damage elsewhere.

In a water pipe system, grounding clamps must bridge your water meter and any sections of plastic piping that have been installed during a repair.

MAPPING CIRCUITS

Mapping your electrical circuits will help you pinpoint any electrical problems and tell you how much power you can safely draw. A circuit map shows all the lights, appliances, switches and receptacles connected to each circuit. Start by making a sketch of each room in your house on graph paper. Include the hallways, basement and attic. Also make a sketch of the exterior parts of your property that are wired for electricity. On each sketch, indicate the location of all light fixtures, receptacles, switches, appliances, heaters, fans, air conditioners, thermostats and doorbells. At the main service panel, number each circuit breaker or fuse with a piece of tape. Turn off all the breakers or loosen all the fuses, but leave the main shutoff on. Then turn on one circuit at a time (note the amperage rating of the circuit printed on the breaker lever or on the fuse rim). Now turn on all switches, lights and appliances in the house, and identify those that are powered by the electrified circuit. Mark them with the corresponding number of the circuit. Do the same with receptacles using a circuit tester. Go through your entire house, circuit by circuit, until finished. (To check the furnace, turn the thermostat to its highest setting. When the circuit is hot, the furnace will go on. Set the thermostat to the lowest setting to turn on a central air conditioner. Check the water heater by setting its thermostat to the highest setting. And don't forget to check the doorbell.)

Once you have done all that, complete your map. Indicate the circuit number, the voltage and the amperage rating of each receptacle, switch, light fixture and appliance. Tape a condensed index of your map to the door of your service panel. This should provide a brief summary of all the devices that are powered by each circuit. Also tape the completed circuit map, protected by a plastic sheath, to the service panel. Try to use waterproof ink for the map and the index.

A circuit map can help you identify electrical problems and balance loads on the system.

Circuit Basics

"Let the circle be unbroken." What applies to church hymns applies to your electrical system. An electrical circuit is simply a continuous loop. Electricity flows through the service panel to light fixtures, appliances, receptacles and switches and then returns to the service panel. Current enters on hot wires and returns along neutral wires. Hot wires are usually colored black or red, while neutral wires are usually white or light gray.

Most circuits also have a grounding wire, which will serve as a pathway for current if the circuit overloads or shorts. The grounding wire helps reduce the risk of deadly shock. Most grounding wires are made of either bare copper wire or insulated green wire. The service panel also has thick grounding wire connected to either a metal water pipe or a grounding rod buried in the ground outside, or both.

A circuit is rated to carry a certain amount of power. If you attempt to draw too many amps through the wiring of a circuit, you're likely to overheat the wiring. The heat, of course, comes from the resistance inherent in wiring. Remember that electricity responds like water: just as too much water forced through too small a pipe will create too much pressure, too much electricity forced through too small a wire will cause too much heat. To prevent this, a circuit is protected by fuses or circuit breakers.

Each household circuit starts and ends at your service panel, where it rejoins the main circuit. Current leaving the house on the neutral service wire returns to the utility pole transformer, where it joins your municipal power circuit.

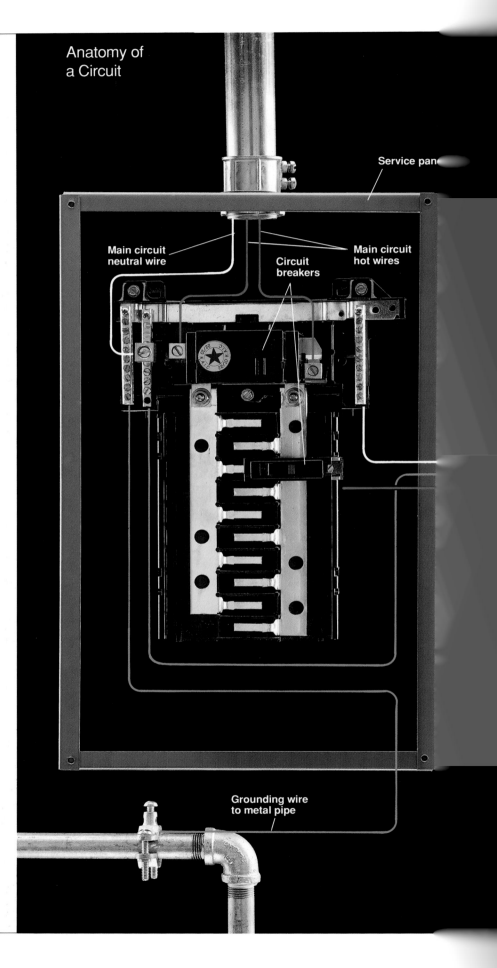

Anatomy of a Circuit

Service panel

Main circuit neutral wire

Main circuit hot wires

Circuit breakers

Grounding wire to metal pipe

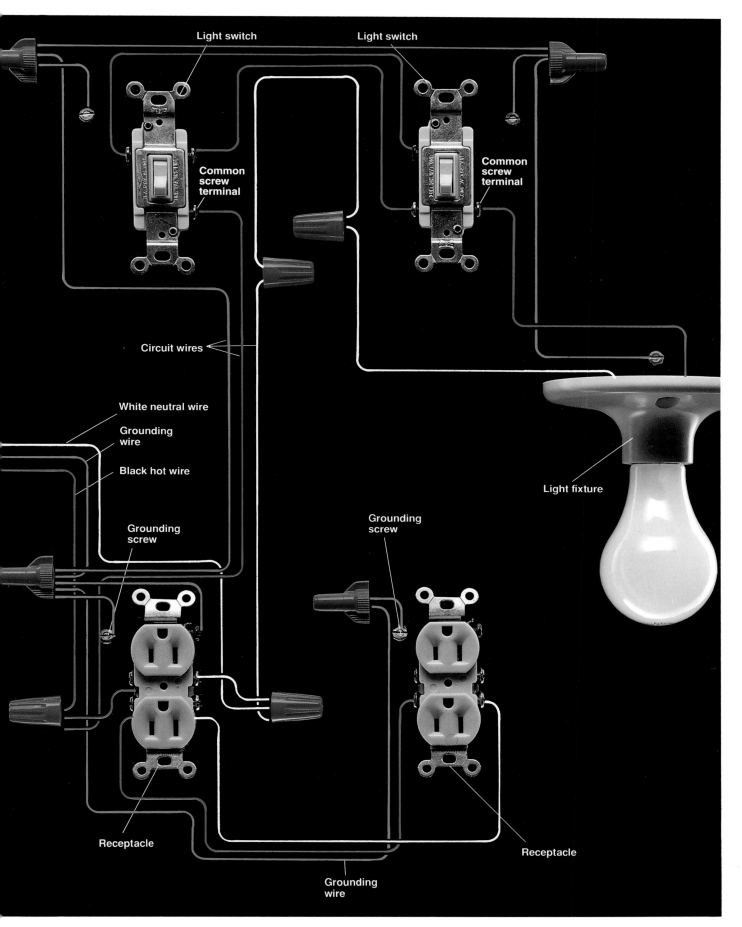

Light switch

Light switch

Common screw terminal

Common screw terminal

Circuit wires

White neutral wire

Grounding wire

Black hot wire

Grounding screw

Grounding screw

Light fixture

Receptacle

Receptacle

Grounding wire

Specification plate

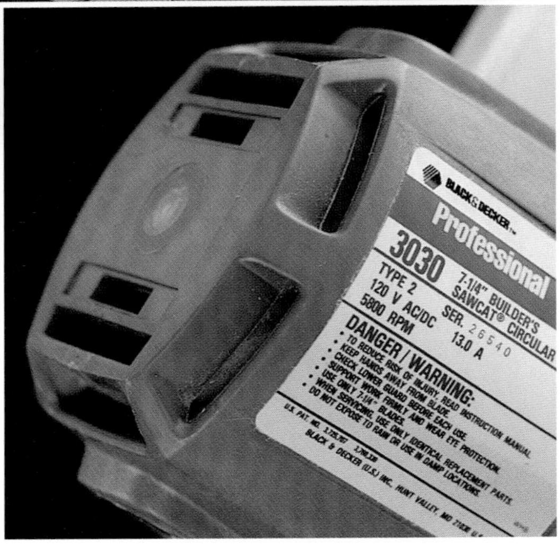

Each appliance has a specification plate (above) that includes amperage and wattage ratings. This plate may be inside the door, or on the back of the appliance.

Amperage ratings on tools or appliances can be used to find how much wattage they draw. Multiply the amperage by the voltage of the circuit. For example, this 13-amp, 120-volt motor is rated for 1560 watts.

Circuit Capacity Chart

Amps × Volts	Total Capacity	Safe Capacity
15 A × 120 V =	1800 watts	1440 watts
20 A × 120 V =	2400 watts	1920 watts
25 A × 120 V =	3000 watts	2400 watts
30 A × 120 V =	3600 watts	2880 watts
20 A × 240 V =	4800 watts	3840 watts
30 A × 240 V =	7200 watts	5760 watts

Total capacity is not the same as safe capacity. Use the chart at left to determine how much power you can safely draw through your home's electrical circuits.

Evaluating Electrical Loads

Your electrical circuits are designed to carry only so much electrical power, and no more. The demand of lights, tools and appliances must not exceed the capacity of a circuit.

You've probably heard the story, or seen it yourself: A homeowner installs a new window air conditioner. Everything works fine during the day. That night, however, the circuit breaker repeatedly trips. The next day everything is fine. The homeowner thinks the wiring must be faulty, but, after analyzing the system, discovers that one of the circuits was overloaded by installing the new air conditioner. The problem reveals itself only at night, when the lights come on.

Now clued in, this homeowner maps out all the circuits, and plugs the air conditioner into a different circuit that can absorb the electrical draw of the machine.

A circuit map will help you evaluate the electrical demands on each circuit and help you determine where you can place additional appliances or lights. It could tip you off that your electrical system needs to be updated.

The circuits in your house have a safe capacity—the amount of power the circuit wires can carry without tripping circuit breakers or blowing fuses. *The safe capacity is less than the total capacity.* A 20-amp, 120-volt circuit has a total capacity of 2400 watts, but a safe capacity of 1920 watts. The electrical draw on each circuit must not exceed the safe capacity. Finding the safe capacity and determining the demand is fairly easy. First, you need to determine the amperage and voltage rating of the circuit. The amperage rating is printed on the circuit breaker, or on the rim of the fuse. The type of circuit breaker or fuse indicates whether the circuit is 120 volts or 240 volts.

Safe capacity can be calculated by multiplying the amperage rating by the voltage, then reducing that figure by 20%.

Next, compare the safe capacity of the circuit to the total power demand. Determining the draw of electrical devices is simple. Wattage ratings are stamped on light bulbs, and appliance wattage ratings are often listed on the manufacturer's label. (Or, you can use the accompanying *Appliance Rating Table*, shown below). If an appliance only has an amperage rating, multiply the amperage by the voltage of the circuit to determine the wattage. For example, a 13-amp, 120-volt power tool is rated at 1560 watts.

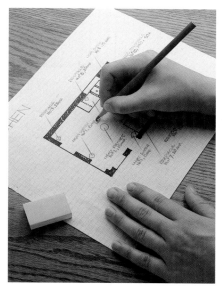
A circuit map will help you evaluate the capacities of your circuits.

Keep track of all power demands. To find the total circuit demand, add the wattage ratings for all the electrical devices on the circuit. If you are unsure about the wattage rating of a particular tool or appliance, use the highest number shown on the accompanying table to make calculations.

If the demand on the circuit exceeds the safe capacity, move some of the devices to another circuit that can handle the added draw.

Now you can understand why municipal power grids can have blackouts or brownouts during extremely hot days: with everyone drawing heavy power loads to run their home air-conditioning, the municipal grid can overheat — just as your circuits overheat when you draw too much power.

Appliance Rating Table

Appliance	Amps	Watts	Appliance	Amps	Watts
AC (central)	21 (240 V)	5040	Hair dryer	5 to 10	600 to 1200
AC (window)	6 to 13	720 to 1560	Heater (portable)	7 to 12	840 to 1440
Blender	2 to 4	240 to 480	Microwave oven	4 to 7	480 to 840
Broiler	12.5	1500	Range (240-V)	16 to 32	3840 to 7680
Can opener	1.2	144	Refrigerator	2 to 4	240 to 480
Circular saw	10 to 12	1200 to 1440	Router	8	960
Clothes dryer	16.5 to 34	3960 to 8160	Sander (portable)	2 to 5	240 to 600
Clothes iron	9	1080	Saw (table)	7 to 10	840 to 1200
Coffee maker	4 to 8	480 to 960	Sewing machine	1	120
Computer	4 to 7	480 to 84	Stereo	2.5 to 4	300 to 480
Dishwasher	8.5 to 12.5	1020 to 1500	Television (B&W)	2	240
Drill (portable)	2 to 4	240 to 480	Television (color)	2.5	300
Fan (ceiling)	3.5	420	Toaster	9	1080
Fan (portable)	2	240	Trash compactor	4 to 8	480 to 960
Freezer	2 to 4	240 to 480	Vacuum cleaner	6 to 11	720 to 1320
Frying pan	9	1080	Waffle iron	7.5	900
Furnace, gas	6.5 to 13	780 to 1560	Washing machine	12.5	1500
Garbage disposer	3.5 to 7.5	420 to 900	Water heater	10.5 to 21	2520 to 5040

These approximate amp and wattage ratings for common tools, appliances and fixtures can be used to estimate the total electrical load on an electrical circuit. To estimate the wattage for appliances not shown in this table, simply multiply the amp rating of the appliance times the voltage of the circuit. For example, a plug-in heater rated for 10 amps has a load of 1,200 watts (10 amps times 120 volts).

Wire

From the circuit breakers or fuses in your main service panel, a network of wires and cables brings power to each receptacle, light fixture and electrical appliance in your home. Unless you are repairing or replacing an appliance or device, these wires remain hidden.

The appearance of the wiring in a home can vary dramatically, depending on the age of the system.

• Wiring installed in the early part of this century, until about 1940, was covered with a layer of rubberized cloth fabric called "loom," but it had no sheath for additional protection. This wiring was commonly strung along porcelain insulators, which gave it the name of "knob and tube" wiring.

• Starting in the 1920s, some wiring was manufactured in flexible metal cable. This "Greenfield" or "BX" wiring proved much better than the knob and tube wiring because it shielded the wires from damage. The armored cable on Greenfield wiring lacked a grounding wire; the metal coils of the cable provided the ground.

• Metal conduit has been installed in many homes since the 1940s. Like Greenfield cable, the metal conduit shell protected wiring and provided a ground. Metal conduit is still recommended by code in some installations, such as exposed wiring in a basement or garage, but modern conduit will use a ground wire.

• Early NM (nonmetallic) cable was installed from 1930 to about 1965. Early NM, which has no ground wire, has flexible rubberized fabric protecting the wires. Electricians loved it because they did not have to snake individual wires through conduit.

• Modern NM (nonmetallic) cable, which includes a bare grounding wire, was introduced in 1965. The wire insulation and the outer sheathing is made of plastic vinyl; the gauge of the wire is printed on the sheathing. A "12-2" cable, for example, has two 12-gauge insulated conducting wires. Today almost all home wiring is NM, except where otherwise prohibited by code.

Telephone cable

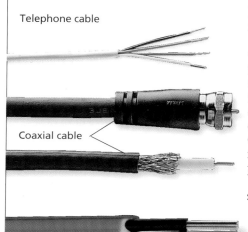

Coaxial cable

UF (underground feeder) cable

NM (nonmetallic) sheathed cable

Early NM (nonmetallic) sheathed cable

Metal conduit

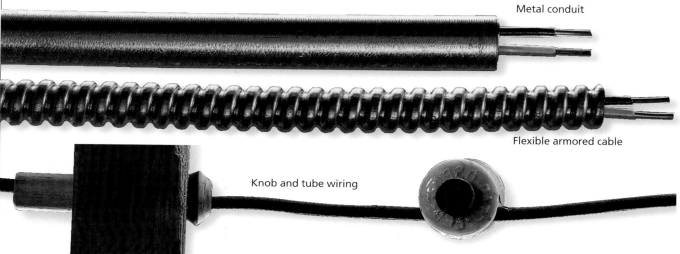

Flexible armored cable

Knob and tube wiring

• UF (underground feeder) cable is designed to be installed in damp conditions. Its wires are embedded in solid-core vinyl sheathing. Like NM cable, it too contains a bare copper grounding wire.

Inside the protective sheathing and insulation, the metal wire used to carry current is usually made of copper. In some houses, however, the wire conductors are aluminum—sometimes clad with copper or nickel. Aluminum or clad-aluminum wires have special safety concerns (below).

Wires in home circuitry can range from thick, #6 gauge cables, used for large appliances, to very thin #22 gauge wires, used only for low-voltage applications, like doorbells.

Wires must be large enough for the amperage rating of the circuit. A wire that is too small and is overloaded can become hot enough to melt its insulation and start a fire. The "ampacity" of wire refers to how much current it can safely carry.

Ampacity varies according to the size of wire and the material used.

Wire Ampacity Chart

Wire gauge	Ampacity	Maximum wattage	Typical Use
#14	15 amps	1440 (120 V)	Light fixtures, outlets
		2880 (240 V)	Room air conditioner, large tools
#12	20 amps	1920 (120 V)	Light fixtures, outlets, room air conditioner, appliances
		3840 (240 V)	Room air conditioner, large tools
#10	30 amps	2880 (120 V)	Commercial equipment
		5760 (240 V)	Clothes dryer
#8	40 amps	7680 (240 V)	Electric range, central air conditioning
#6	55 amps	10560 (240 V)	Central air conditioning, electric furnace

The chart shown above shows the ampacity of copper wire. Check your home to make certain the gauges of the circuit wires match the circuit ratings, stamped on the circuit breaker or fuse. If not, have an electrician correct the situation immediately. In addition, make sure the total wattage load likely to be placed on the circuit at any one time does not exceed the ratings shown in the third column. The Electrical Code states that the wattage load should never exceed 80% of the full wattage capacity of the circuit. A 15-amp 120-volt circuit, for example, has a maximum capacity of 1800 watts (15 × 120), but the load placed on it should be no more than 1440 (80% of 1800). Although the wires can safely carry the maximum wattage load, these high loads may eventually cause a circuit breaker to malfunction.

ALUMINUM WIRE

If you find aluminum wire in your home, you need to take special precautions. Aluminum wire is identified by its silver color and by the AL stamp on the cable sheathing. Two variations, copper-clad aluminum wire and nickel-clad aluminum wire, have a thin coating of copper or nickel bonded to a solid aluminum core.

During the 1960s and early 1970s, aluminum wire was installed in many houses, but by the early 1970s, all-aluminum wire was found to be a safety hazard if connected to devices with brass or copper screw terminals. The problem arose because aluminum expands and contracts at a different rate than copper or brass, and can gradually work loose from connections.

For a short while, switches and receptacles with an Underwriters Laboratories (UL) wire compatibility rating of AL-CU were used with both aluminum and copper wiring. Unfortunately, these AL-CU devices also proved to be hazardous when connected to aluminum wire

and copper-clad or nickel-clad aluminum wire.

Since 1971, switches and receptacles designed for use with aluminum wiring were introduced with the marking CO/ALR. Today this is the only approved device for aluminum wiring.

IMPORTANT: If you have aluminum wiring, you need to replace any switch or receptacle that does not bear the CO/ALR rating stamp. Aluminum wire or clad-aluminum wire is considered safe if proper installation methods are followed, and if the wires are connected to special switches and receptacles designed to be used with aluminum wire. A switch or receptacle that has no wire compatibility rating printed on the mounting strap is designed for use with copper wires only. (If you have copper-clad or nickel-clad aluminum wiring, see an electrician or consult a detailed description of the National Electrical Code for more information.)

But all parts of the system must be up to Code to be safe. If you have any doubts, have a qualified electrical inspector review your system.

Aluminum wiring can be identified by the AL stamp on the cable sheathing.

Electrical Boxes

Wherever circuit wires are spliced or joined to an electrical device, the wire connections must be made inside a plastic or metal electrical box that meets the requirements of the Electrical Code. Electrical boxes are designed to protect wiring from dust and debris and to shield framing members and other nearby material from electrical sparks in the event of a short circuit. If you find exposed wire connections or cable splices anywhere in your home, immediately call an electrician to remedy the situation.

Electrical boxes come in several shapes and depths. Each box must be roomy enough so that the screw terminal and twist connections can be made without crimping or damaging the circuit wires. Undersized boxes should be replaced with larger boxes. The Electrical Code also requires that all electrical boxes be securely mounted in walls and ceilings, and that they be accessible. Electrical boxes must never be covered with drywall, paneling or wallcovering.

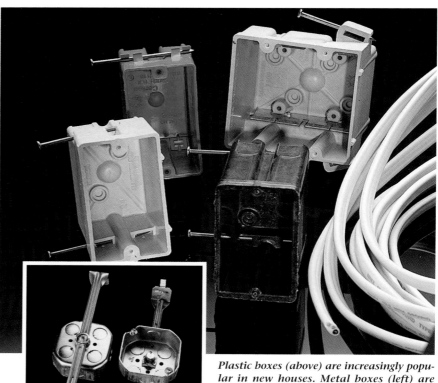

Plastic boxes (above) are increasingly popular in new houses. Metal boxes (left) are used for exposed indoor wiring or where strength is an issue, such as when a box must support a heavy ceiling light fixture. Always make certain your boxes are not too small or too shallow for the connections they must hold.

WIRING CONNECTIONS

Electricians are familiar with opening up an electrical box and finding wires twisted together and secured with a wad of decaying electrical tape. Such connections almost promise a future short circuit. Wire connections should instead be made with twist connectors, which have metal threads that grip the bare ends of the wires. When installed, the connectors should completely cover the bare portion of the wire ends. Twist connectors also connect pigtails—short sections of wiring used to connect two or more wires to a single screw terminal or to extend circuit wiring that is too short.

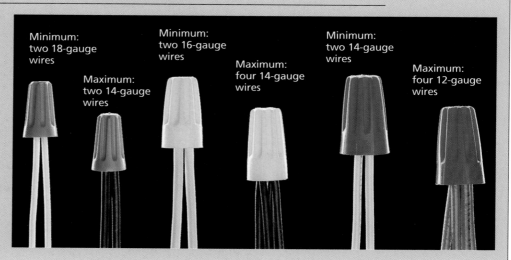

Minimum: two 18-gauge wires

Maximum: two 14-gauge wires

Minimum: two 16-gauge wires

Maximum: four 14-gauge wires

Minimum: two 14-gauge wires

Maximum: four 12-gauge wires

Electrical Box Chart

Box shape	Maximum number and size of wires in box (not counting pigtails and grounding wires)	
	14-gauge wires	12-gauge wires
Rectangular		
2" × 3" × 2½"-deep	3	3
2" × 3" × 3½"-deep	5	4
Square		
4"× 4" × 1½"-deep	6	5
4"× 4" × 2⅛"-deep	9	7
Octagonal		
1½"-deep:	4	3
2⅛"-deep:	7	6

An electrical box must be large enough so that wires aren't crimped or damaged. Use this chart as your guide. The National Electrical Code also says that all electrical boxes must be accessible. If you find boxes covered with drywall,

Box Types

Box type	Typical Uses
Plastic	Protected indoor wiring; used with NM cable, not used with metal conduit. Not suited for heavy light fixtures and fans.
Metal	Exposed indoor wiring; used with metal conduit. Protected indoor wiring; used with NM cable or metal conduit installations.
Cast aluminum	Outdoor wiring; used with metal conduit.
PVC Plastic	Outdoor wiring; used with PVC conduit. Exposed indoor wiring; used with PVC conduit.

paneling or wallcoverings, talk to an electrician about the problem. What box is right for a specific location? The chart above gives guidelines. Pay close attention if your home was rewired by a do-it-yourselfer or a less-than-vigilant electrician.

EVALUATING WIRING

If the wiring in your home is more than 30 years old, it may have some age-related problems. By inspecting electrical boxes and outlets, you can find many of these problems. Make sure to turn the power off before making this inspection.
• Sometimes the exposed connections on wires become dirty. These can be cleaned by using fine sandpaper.
• Scorch marks near screw terminals on outlets and switches often mean you have loose wires. The wire connections need to be cleaned with fine sandpaper and the receptacle needs to be replaced if it is damaged.

• Nicks and scratches in bare wires interfere with the flow of electricity. This can cause the wires to overheat.
• Cracked or damaged insulation is a serious problem. For a temporary fix, wrap the insulation with electrical tape until the wiring can be replaced.
• Dirt or dust buildup in electrical boxes can lead to a short circuit. Sometimes the deposits can add up slowly over the years; other times, remodeling projects can sift dust into boxes. Simply vacuum out the debris. Always make sure power is off before cleaning or repairing any electrical wiring.

Cracked insulation on wires poses a shock hazard and fire risk. Wiring in this condition should be replaced as soon as possible.

Switches

The scene has been repeated in countless horror movies: the mad scientist, grinning wildly in a darkened laboratory, gets ready to pull a huge electrical switch that will bring his creation to life.

You do the same thing, albeit with less drama, every time you turn on a light switch. Switches all work on the same principal. Opening them (turning a switch "off") is the equivalent of disconnecting a wire. Closing a switch (turning it "on") reconnects the wire.

Common wall switches today work with nearly flawless performance, if they are properly installed and replaced when worn. And switches do wear out. Household wall switches are turned off and on an average of more than 1,000 times each year. A heavily

used switch might be used 4,000 times or more in a year. This kind of use can loosen wire connections and wear out a switch's internal mechanism. Some signs that could point to a worn or loose switch include levers that do not stay in position, flickering lights, burned fuses or tripped circuit breakers and buzzing coming from the switch.

Basic Switch Types

Wall switches are available in three general categories.

Single-pole switches are used to control a light fixture from one location.

Three-way switches control lights from two different locations, such as at either end of a long hallway. These switches are always installed in pairs.

Four-way switches are used in combination with a pair of three-way switches to control lights from three or more locations. Although rare in most households, four-way switches are sometimes found in very large rooms.

Identifying a switch is easy. Just count the screw terminals. Single-pole switches have two screw terminals, three-way switches have three terminals and four-way switches have four terminals.

Some switches also include a grounding screw terminal, which is usually colored green. These switches are not required by most local codes, but some electricians prefer to install them in basements, kitchens and bathrooms, where they can provide additional protection against electrical shock. The circuit grounding wires are

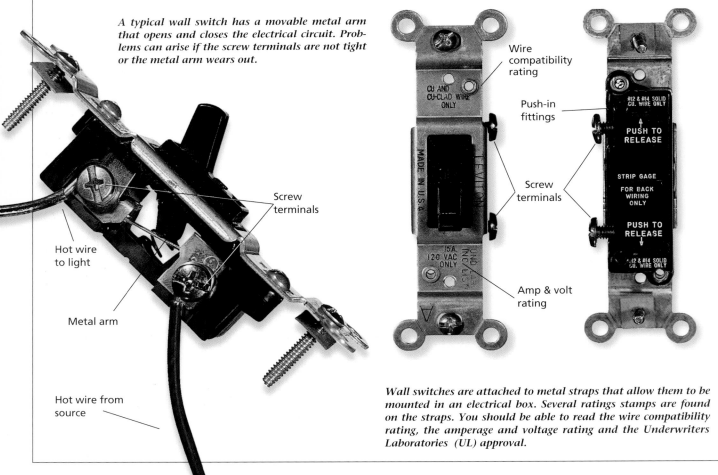

A typical wall switch has a movable metal arm that opens and closes the electrical circuit. Problems can arise if the screw terminals are not tight or the metal arm wears out.

Screw terminals

Hot wire to light

Metal arm

Hot wire from source

Wire compatibility rating

Push-in fittings

Screw terminals

Amp & volt rating

Wall switches are attached to metal straps that allow them to be mounted in an electrical box. Several ratings stamps are found on the straps. You should be able to read the wire compatibility rating, the amperage and voltage rating and the Underwriters Laboratories (UL) approval.

pigtailed to the grounding screw on this switch.

Specialty Switches

Speciality switches can be substituted for most ordinary wall switches, which means you can have a timer on your bathroom vent fan switch, a dimmer on your bedroom light switch or a pilot-light switch in your child's room.

Pilot-light switches have built-in bulbs that glow when the switch is turned on. These are handy in situations where the appliance or light fixture cannot be seen from the switch location. A pilot-light switch, because it requires a neutral wire connection, cannot be fitted to a switch box with a single two-wire cable.

Dimmer switches let you vary the brightness of a light fixture.

Dimmer switches can replace any single-pole switch, as long as the switch box is large enough. Dimmer switches take up more space than normal switches and they generate a small amount of heat. Make sure to buy the right type of dimmer for your fixture; those for incandescent fixtures are different than those for fluorescents.

Timer switches have an electrically powered control dial that allows you to turn lights on and off automatically once a day. Like a pilot-light switch, a timer switch requires a neutral wire connection. And, of course, the dial on this switch must be reset after a power failure.

Time-delay switches feature a spring-driven timer set by hand. These switches are often attached to heat lamps, exhaust vent fans

and space heaters. They can be installed without a neutral wire.

Electronic switches can provide added convenience and home security. They are also easy to install. Electronic switches include motion-sensor security switches, which turn on fixtures when a wide-angle infrared beam detects motion over a large area; automatic switches, which allow people to turn on switches simply by passing a hand near their narrow infrared beams; and programmable switches, which rely on digital controls to turn lights off and on throughout the day. An advantage of electronic switches is they don't require a neutral wire connection, and can thus be connected to a simple two-wire cable.

MAKING PROPER CONNECTIONS

Switches and receptacles commonly have both screw terminals and push-in fittings. To connect a wire to a screw terminal (*left*), form a C-shaped loop in the end of each wire. Hook each wire around the terminal so it forms a clockwise loop. The insulation should just touch the screw head. To connect wires to a push-in fitting (*center*), remove insulation by using the strip gauge found on the back of the switch. Then firmly push

the bare copper ends into the fittings (push-in fittings should never be used with aluminum wires). Make certain no bare copper is exposed. Few electricians use push-in fittings. They instead prefer the extra security of a well-tightened screw.

Twist connectors are used to connect a fixture with wires leads (such as a light fixture) to circuit wires. They can also be used to join circuit wires together at a junction box.

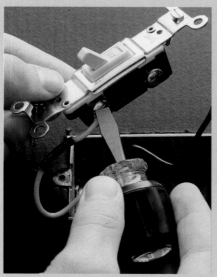

Screw terminal connection is preferred by professional electricians.

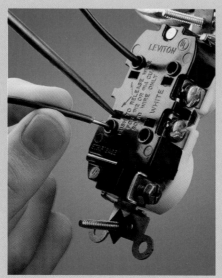

Push-in connection is easy to make, but is not as secure as a screw connection.

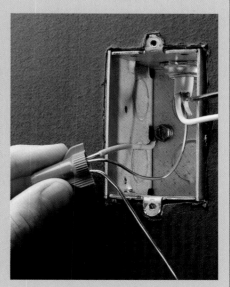

Twist connections are used to join wires at a junction box.

Receptacles

If you're like many people, the only time you pay much attention to receptacles is when you're looking to plug in your portable drill or vacuum cleaner.

Household receptacles, also called *outlets*, have no moving parts and can therefore last for decades. Older houses often have their original outlets still in place. Nevertheless, outlets that receive a lot of use can have worn-out metal contacts. When an outlet ages, its contacts can grasp the prongs of a plug too feebly to provide a good electrical connection.

Age can also cause the wiring inside the outlet to work its way loose, because of vibration or the constant heating and cooling of the wires. If an outlet is damaged, it should be replaced. However, if an outlet coverplate merely suffers from cosmetic damage, replace just the coverplate—not the receptacle.

Receptacle Types

When you examine an outlet, you may find it stamped with a voltage rating other than 120 or 240 volts. Standard single-pole outlets have gradually seen their voltage ratings creep upward from 110 volts to 125 volts. And double-pole outlet ratings have taken a similar climb, from 220 volts to 250 volts. Don't get worried. For purposes of replacement, a 110-volt outlet and a 125-volt outlet are considered to be identical. The same goes with outlets rated at 220 volts, 240 volts or 250 volts. Just make certain the outlet has the same amperage rating as the circuit.

Older outlets may look different from modern outlets, but many remain in good working order. But if and when you do replace a two-slot unpolarized outlet (no distinction between hot and neutral slots), make sure to install a polarized three-slot outlet. When no grounding is available, install a ground-fault-circuit-interrupter (GFCI) outlet.

With older outlets, you may find modern plugs don't fit. Never alter the prongs of the plugs as a remedy. Instead, either plug the appliance into a newer nearby outlet or, better yet, replace the unusable outlet with a new outlet.

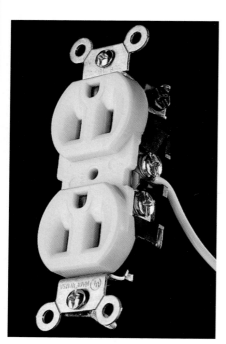

The modern three-slot duplex receptacle has two outlets. Each half has a long (neutral) slot, a short (hot) slot and a U-shaped grounding hole.

A 120/240-volt outlet has a different shape than the standard 120-volt outlet. The exact shape depends on the amperage rating. The outlet shown here is for a 50-amp range.

Older 120-volt outlets often have only two slots, with no grounding hole. If the outlet is polarized (one long neutral slot, one shorter "hot" slot), this type of outlet is safe, provided it's in good working order.

Three-prong adapters are discouraged by electrical inspectors. If you need to plug in appliances with a grounding prong, it's best to install newer, three-slot receptacles.

A 20-amp, 120-volt receptacle features a special T-shaped slot. It is installed for use with large appliances or portable tools that require 20 amps of current.

GFCI OUTLETS

Bathrooms, kitchens, basements, garages and outdoor receptacles—any location where there is direct access to the ground or to water—should have GFCI outlets. Like a circuit breaker, a GFCI trips and stops power flow if there is an imbalance ("ground fault") between the hot and neutral wires. A GFCI outlet, however, trips within .025 second to current imbalances as small as 5 milliamps (.0005 amp). A normal 15-amp circuit breaker, by contrast, requires an imbalance 3,000 times greater before it trips. This means that a GFCI can virtually prevent shock injuries to people in normal health—a claim no circuit breaker can make.

GFCI receptacles can also be installed to protect outlets that are not grounded. In most cases, it's easy to replace a standard receptacle with a GFCI outlet. A GFCI has a bigger body than a standard receptacle, however, which means that a crowded electrical box may need to be replaced with a larger box to make room for the GFCI.

Because GFCI outlets are so sensitive, they are most effective when they protect a single location. GFCI receptacles can be wired to protect several outlets or switches, but the more receptacles any GFCI protects, the more susceptible it is to *phantom tripping* caused by normal fluctuations in current flow.

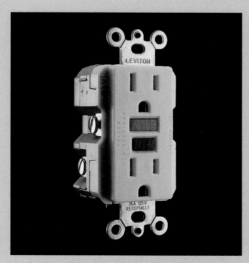

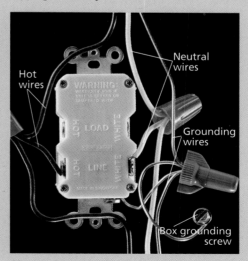

A duplex GFCI receptacle should be checked monthly simply by pressing the "test" button. If the receptacle is working properly, the circuit will be broken immediately.

Shown from the back, a GFCI receptacle wired for single-location protection has hot and neutral wires connected only to the screw terminals marked LINE.

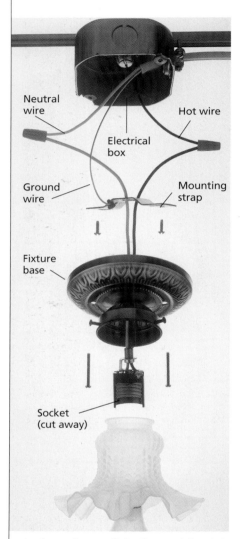

Neutral
wire

Hot wire

Electrical
box

Ground
wire

Mounting
strap

Fixture
base

Socket
(cut away)

Light Fixtures

Flip on a light switch and you get light, right? If a bulb blows, simply screw in any available bulb, right? Not quite.

If you're savvy, you'll know as much as you can about lights. Some basic knowledge will help you save money and have a safer house. It might even make you look better.

Incandescent bulbs are found in most fixtures. They produce light when current, passing through a thin metal filament, heats the filament until it glows.

Incandescent lights are popular for obvious reasons: They illuminate instantly, they are easy to replace and they are inexpensive to install. Plus, incandescent lights bring out warm "reddish" colors that enhance skin tones. Incandescent bulbs traditionally have a tungsten element, but halogen and low-voltage xenon bulbs are also available for specialized situations, such as track lighting.

A common and dangerous mis-

take is to install a light bulb with a wattage rating that is too high for the fixture. A 100-watt bulb installed in a 60-watt fixture can overheat the fixture. This can melt wiring, cause a short circuit or start a fire. *Never overload a fixture's wattage rating.* If you need more light, change the fixture or add another fixture.

Also make certain nothing flammable is put near a light bulb. A standard tungsten filament heats to about 4,000°F, and halogen lamps run even hotter. Any building insulation should be at least 3 inches from a recessed ceiling light, unless the fixture is specifically rated for contact with insulation.

Most of the time, problems with light fixtures are caused by loose, burned-out or defective bulbs. But wiring can crack or melt in a fixture—especially if a higher wattage bulb was mistakenly installed.

Fluorescent lights have illuminated factories and stores for years, and recent advances have made them more popular for home use.

The fluorescent tubes contain

An incandescent light fixture (above) is simple in function. The black (hot) wire delivers power to a small tab located at the bottom of the metal socket. Current flows through a filament inside the bulb, causing it to heat up and glow, then flows through the threaded portion of the socket and back to the neutral wire. Fixtures must be attached to a sturdy electrical box that is properly installed.

A recessed light fixture (right) requires additional care to make certain it is installed correctly. Unless the fixture is rated for contact with insulation, a recessed light must be at least 3" from the insulation. Also, make certain the reflector fits correctly and is not damaged.

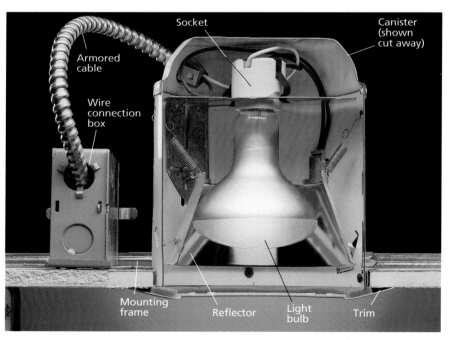

Socket

Canister
(shown
cut away)

Armored
cable

Wire
connection
box

Mounting
frame

Reflector

Light
bulb

Trim

short cathodes of tungsten at both ends and a mixture of gas (usually argon or argon with another gas). A tiny bit of mercury is also in the tube, which vaporizes when power is turned on and the argon heats. Electric current then follows the path of the vaporized mercury, which in turn creates invisible ultraviolet light. Visible light is produced when a chemical coating inside the tube is exposed to the ultraviolet light and becomes fluorescent.

Fluorescent fixtures require a special transformer, called a ballast, which regulates flow of current to the tube. If a ballast wears out, it may leak a black, oily substance and cause the fixture to hum loudly. Replace such a fixture.

If the sockets on a fluorescent fixture crack, they can be replaced with new sockets, available from any reputable hardware store. When fluorescent tubes need replacement, never break them; they contain small amounts of mercury. Check with your local authorities for disposal guidelines.

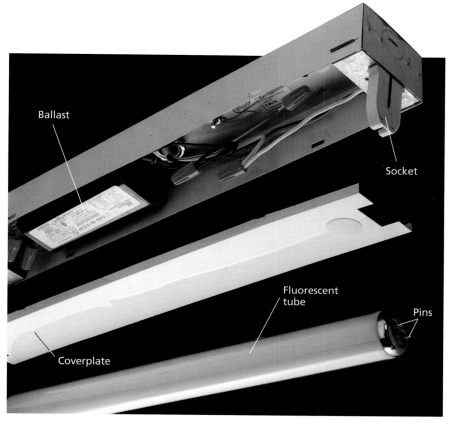

A fluorescent light fixture has several components. The ballast, a special transformer that regulates the flow of 120-volt current, sits inside the fixture. The fluorescent tube attaches to the sockets via pins, which conduct electricity into the gas-filled tube. The resulting light is softened by a plastic diffuser cover.

LIGHT BULBS

Light bulbs have not changed much in appearance since Thomas Edison began producing them in 1879, but their durability and efficiency have taken great leaps forward. Today a 60-watt light bulb has an average life of at least 1,000 hours. This same modern bulb produces 870 lumens, or about 14.5 lumens per watt (Edison's first lamps were only 1/10th as efficient).

Incandescent bulbs have some interesting characteristics.

• Bulbs with higher wattage produce proportionally more light than lower-wattage bulbs. A 25-watt light bulb produces 235 lumens; a 100-watt bulb, 1,750 lumens. The 100-watt bulb produces nearly 7.5 times more light than the 25-watt bulb, despite using only 4 times more electricity. In other words, a fixture using a single 100-watt bulb will provide much more light than a fixture using four 25-watt bulbs.

• Bulbs with smaller wattages tend to last longer. A 25-watt bulb will last on average more than 3 times longer than a 100-watt bulb.

• A typical light bulb costs much more to operate than it does to buy. A 100-watt light bulb that lasts, on average, 750 hours will consume 75 kilowatt hours (KWh). If electricity costs 8 cents per kWh, the bulb will use $6 of power over its life span.

Fluorescent lights are relatively trouble-free, and can use much less energy than incandescent bulbs. A fluorescent tube can last several years, and it produces two to four times as much candlepower per watt as an incandescent light. Fluorescent lights have several noteworthy drawbacks, however. A traditional fluorescent lamp that is never turned off may indeed last about 25,000 hours. But a fluorescent lamp turned on and off constantly may have a life of only 1,000 hours because the cathodes wear out during start-ups. Another drawback? Many fluorescent lamps produce a cooler blue-white color, which can give skin a washed-out look. Finally, fluorescent lamps flicker a moment before they start.

Nevertheless, new technology helps cure some of these shortcomings. Some newer bulbs are color corrected to match the color of incandescent bulbs. New electronic ballasts make three-way fluorescent lights possible. The new ballasts also reduce the buzzing often associated with traditional magnetic ballasts. Adapters make it possible to screw a fluorescent light into a regular light socket. A 10/20/35-watt three-way fluorescent produces roughly the same lumens as a 50/100/150-watt three-way incandescent bulb. Although fluorescent bulbs and their adaptors cost much more to buy initially, they can save a great deal down the road. One manufacturer claims its 10/20/35-watt fluorescent lamp can save more than $100 over the life of the bulb.

Hard-Wired Fixtures & Appliances

Everyone knows that ceiling light fixtures are wired directly into your electrical circuitry. But you may be surprised how many more devices are hard-wired. You may have more than you realize, including ceiling fans, dryers, hot water heaters, baseboard heaters, dishwashers and central air conditioners. Many of these appliances require their own dedicated circuit—a point to consider if you are thinking of remodeling.

Electric Range

An electric range is best connected to an outlet, but you may find that yours is hard-wired. Electric ranges vary widely in how much power they use—some require as little as 3,000 watts while others need as much as 12,000 watts—but they all require a dedicated 120/240-volt circuit. The range's clock and timer run on 120 volts, while the heating elements draw 240 volts. If your stove is hard-wired, have the wiring in the connecting conduit inspected. Often this wiring will overheat, due to its proximity to the hot stove. If the wiring is damaged, have it replaced by an electrician.

Water Heater

Your electric water heater requires its own dedicated 30-amp, 240-volt circuit. The cable leading to the heater's wire connection box should be protected with a flexible or rigid conduit; if not, have this work done by an electrician. Most water heaters are rated between 3,500 and 4,500 watts. If the nameplate on the heater lists several wattage ratings, use the one labeled "total connected wattage" when determining the heater's electrical loads.

Baseboard Heater

As a general rule, 240-volt electric baseboard heaters are rated for about 250 watts for each linear foot. Circuit connections are made in an access box attached to each heater. Unlike regular furnaces—which have a low-voltage thermostat—baseboard heaters are connected to a 240-volt "line-voltage" thermostat. Electric baseboard room heaters require dedicated circuits—large houses will require several circuits.

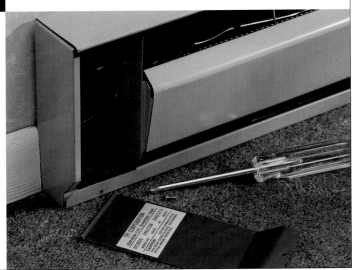

Dishwasher

A dishwasher installed permanently under a countertop requires a dedicated 15-amp, 120-volt circuit. Built-in dishwashers usually draw from 1,000 watts to 1,500 watts; portable dishwashers draw less power. Portable units are regarded as part of a small-appliance circuit and are not added in when determining your home's electrical load.

Ceiling Fan

Ceiling fans require less than an amp of electricity—most run on about 75 watts or less, so they are unlikely to overtax your electrical circuit. But because they can weigh up to 30 pounds, ceiling fans need to be attached to a sturdy box secured to a ceiling joist. A properly installed metal octagonal box can support a ceiling fixture of up to 35 pounds. Make certain an existing fan is properly braced.

Central Air Conditioner

A central air conditioner requires its own dedicated 240-volt circuit. A large air conditioner will be one of your home's biggest consumers of electricity. It will likely draw from 2,300 watts to 5,500 watts, depending upon the model. The exact power demand will be printed on a nameplate near the electrical panel hookup. Air conditioners, because they can run almost constantly in hot weather, will put a sizable dent in your utility budget.

Low-Voltage Wiring

When visitors ring your doorbell, they are activating a low-voltage system. These systems run on only about a tenth the voltage of normal household current—and their wires carry only a few milliamps of electricity, which is dramatically less amperage than what flows through your normal household wiring.

The doorbell is low voltage for a very good reason. Imagine a doorbell running on 120 volts. A wire comes loose, and the circuit is ready to short. Your neighbor stands outside your house in a pouring rain and pushes the doorbell button and...

Get the picture? Doorbells running on low voltage will give you just a tiny shock if the system shorts. Plus, low-voltage systems operate more efficiently and wiring them is much easier.

Your house likely has three electrical devices that run on low-voltage current: the doorbell, the thermostat and the telephone (which is supplied by its own power grid). Additionally, quite a few homeowners are installing low-voltage lighting systems.

Doorbells

Doorbells are simple devices. The doorbell switch, when pushed, activates a magnetic coil in the chime box, causing plungers to strike the tuning bars (which are connected to the chimes). Problems are pretty much limited to the button, loose wires, a broken or dirty bell clapper or a faulty transformer. Because the button is exposed to the elements, it is often the culprit on a malfunctioning doorbell. Sometimes, the clapper can become gummed up. Cleaning it is relatively easy—just don't let the wires fall back into the walls.

Low-Voltage Lights

Today, low-voltage kits allow you to line your sidewalk with guidelights or string miniature lights under the treads of a staircase. Low voltage contains a rela-

Low-voltage lighting can illuminate a wide area without adding a huge cost to your electric bill.

tively weak bite, so any short circuits are much less worrisome than 120-volt current. As a result, they do not have to be grounded or buried deep underground.

If you have a low-voltage lighting transformer, check the power rating. Most run less than 300 watts. Make certain your lighting system isn't overtaxing the transformer. If that happens, wires will overheat or lights won't work. Be certain that an outdoor transformer is weatherproof and connected to household wiring with exterior conduit.

Thermostats

The thermostat for your whole-house heating/air-conditioning system is a low-voltage system. The thermostat is powered by a transformer that reduces 120-volt current to about 24 volts. A low-voltage thermostat is very durable, but it can fail if its wire connections become loose or dirty, if parts become corroded or if the transformer breaks down.

The transformer on a low-voltage thermostat is located either inside a furnace access panel or

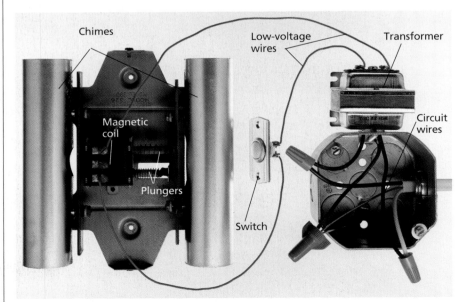

A doorbell system is powered by a small transformer, which reduces 120-volt current to 20 volts or less. When the doorbell is pushed, the switch activates a magnetic coil inside the chime unit, causing a plunger to strike a musical tuning bar.

connected to an electrical junction box. Thin wires (18- to 22-gauge) carry current to the thermostat and return signals to the furnace. Thermostats have from two to six wires connected to them, depending upon the system.

As you might imagine, thermostat technology has improved over the years. Many homeowners choose to replace standard one-temperature thermostats with programmable thermostats. These "set-back" thermostats can allow you to turn down heat at night or during the middle of the day. These programmable thermostats can cut energy consumption by up to 35 percent.

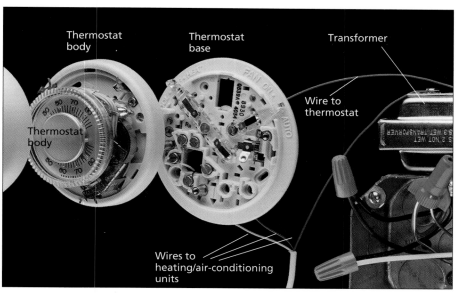

A low-voltage thermostat has a transformer mounted to the electrical junction box or inside a furnace access panel. Very-narrow-gauge wires conduct current to the thermostat, which monitors room temperature.

HOW A THERMOSTAT WORKS

A thermostat is so simple and reliable that it's easily taken for granted. Without it, you'd have to shut the furnace off or on whenever the room became too hot or too cold. A thermostat performs two distinct functions: it reacts to changes in ambient temperature and it sends a message to your furnace.

Most thermostats rely on a bimetal coil to sense temperature changes. The bimetal element is produced when two different metals, each with different rates of expansion and contraction, are bonded together. When this bimetal element is heated, it bends or curls. By determining how much the bimetal element bends at various temperatures, engineers can devise very accurate switches that activate only when certain temperatures have been reached.

Bimetal thermostats fall into one of two types. Thermostats with mercury switches have a small vial of mercury attached to a bimetal strip. Inside the vial, on one end, are two low-voltage contacts. When the bimetal bends, the vial tips and the

Programmable thermostats allow you to reduce your heating and cooling bills without affecting your family's comfort.

mercury flows from one end of the vial to the end where the contacts are located. The mercury then closes the electrical circuit. Thermostats with magnetic switches have a magnet attached to the bimetal strip. Near the strip is a pair of contacts that are not touching. But when the bimetal strip bends, it brings the magnet closer to the contacts, which brings the contacts together and closes the electrical circuit.

In both cases, the completed circuit then activates a relay switch on the furnace or air conditioner, which causes the appliance to turn on, until the bimetal strip—reacting to the change in temperature—opens the electrical circuit in the thermostat. These thermostats, which contain a battery in case of power failure, make it possible for you to fine-tune your interior temperatures around the clock. Most also have a setting that reduces strain on your furnace or air conditioner when you leave for any extended period. Best of all, these programmable units quickly recoup their purchase costs.

Telephone Lines

The phone lines coming into your house may look like thin power lines, but they don't pack anywhere near the same electric punch. Telephone lines are charged with roughly 48 volts of current, at very low amperage (only 20 to 35 milliamps). The phone lines carry roughly as much power as your doorbell wires. In other words, the phone lines contain enough power to tingle your hands, but nothing more serious than that.

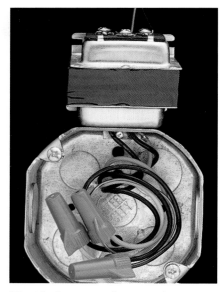

The telephone transformer activates your ringer. Without the transformer, you'd have an open telephone line, but your ringer would never work. If you have problems with the transformer, call your phone company—it belongs to them.

Phone technology has changed dramatically in recent years, and so has the way we use our phones. Just a decade-and-a-half ago a homeowner wanting to install a new phone had to call Ma Bell with the phone's ringer equivalency number and the FCC registration code. Now, of course,

people just plug in a new phone and go on with their lives.

Some things have not changed, though. Phone companies have jurisdiction over the phone lines and transformer located on your property. If you need to move the transformer, call your local phone company. If your external phone lines are damaged, that's a job for the phone company.

Past the transformer, home phone wiring is fair game. You can alter, connect or upgrade phone lines as you wish. All phone wiring should comply with the National Electrical Code, so it should not be placed in conduits or pipes containing other electrical wiring. Also, telephone wire should not be placed near bare power lines or lightning rods, antennas, transformers or heating pipes.

With the widespread advent of computer modems, many households have multiple phone lines. There is no distinction—yet—in the type of everyday residential phone lines that carry computer data versus voice data.

Cordless telephones are another popular technology. Their drawback is that during power outages, cordless phones go dead, because they normally rely on outside electrical power. Meanwhile, older-fashioned corded phones will work when the electricity is off (provided the phone lines are still working). If you live in a rugged area where power outages are a fact of life, consider having at least one regular corded phone for an emergency backup.

A common problem with phones is line static. If your phone lines inside your house run longer than 250 feet—possible if your wiring follows a circuitous route through a large house, or if you extend a phone line to a distant garage or barn—you will start to encounter line resistance and volt-

Modern cordless phones are handy, but don't plan on calling for help during a power outage. These phones, unlike older corded models, require an outside power source. If your electricity is out, so are your cordless phones.

age loss. This leads to a loss of clarity on the line. The same thing can happen if you put too many phones on one line. Most phone companies suggest installing no more than four phones per line.

In homes where the phone lines have not been updated for a quarter century, you might find 4-prong jacks still attached to the wall. Most 4-prong jacks probably have modular converters "piggybacked" to them, which allow modern phone plugs to fit. It is not difficult to remove the bulky 4-prong jack and install a smaller modular jack. A consumer electronics store has more information.

Security Systems

Residences account for about two out of three burglaries in the U.S. Several million occur yearly, with roughly one in six households taking a hit. Losses average more than $1,300 per household.

Forcible entry occurs in 70% of these cases, and most of the action takes place from 6 p.m. to midnight when the weather is warm. Doors account for the most popular means of access at 63%. Windows place a distant second, just one in four. When an attached garage is handy, its portals are used 8% of the time.

Police and other experts caution that there's no perfect security system, only levels of deterrence. The more, the better. Most criminals prefer the path of least resistance. Some of the most effective deterrents are the easiest to implement: outdoor lights, door deadbolts, window locks and indoor light timers.

Electronic security systems add another layer of deterrence. There are now more than 7 million security systems in the U.S and there is no lack of home security products and alarm systems on the market. Choices abound.

Systems that only activate internal or external alarms depend on being heard—and heeded—and then on someone alerting the police or fire department. These devices might shoo away an intruder, but there is no guarantee the cavalry is going to come.

Some home security systems do have the ability to make calls automatically to designated numbers that are stored in memory. But again, there is no guarantee the people who are on the phone list will be home. It's one reason why police prefer monitored systems. Police estimate that home security systems have generated about 14 million false alarms. Some munici-palities, in response, have started levying fines for false alarms. Others have taken the extreme measure of suspending response to repeat offenders.

Lately, security-equipment makers have attempted to remedy these ills, mostly through improvements in sensor and communications technology, user controls and installation know-how.

For example, sensor technology has become much more sensitive. Perimeter sensors for glass breakage come in two flavors. One is an acoustic transducer that "hears" the break. The other measures flexing in the material. Either can be fooled and emit a false alarm, but newer sensors incorporate both.

Motion sensors boast similar upgrading. To make them less error prone, new motion-detector systems combine infrared and microwave technologies. Infrared works best in focused line-of-sight applications, while microwaves can blanket a room. By combining and comparing both inputs, the processor in a security system can make an intelligent analysis. Man? Mouse?

These systems, however, command relatively high prices. Often they are financed with a loan, whether they are a retrofit or part of new construction.

Of course, homeowners need to determine whether the expense of an alarm system is justified. The average burglary nets about $1,300 in goods. Some high-end security systems cost much more than that to install and operate.

Here's something to ponder. A private consulting company recently sent a questionnaire to hundreds of convicted felons. These prisoners, all incarcerated for property crimes, responded that the best deterrent is an alarm system linked directly to a police station. After that is a system monitored by private security patrols.

And the next most effective deterrent? A dog.

Some of the more popular security products now available include (clockwise from left): do-it-yourself low-frequency intruder alarm, motion sensor security light, and a dead-bolt lockset.

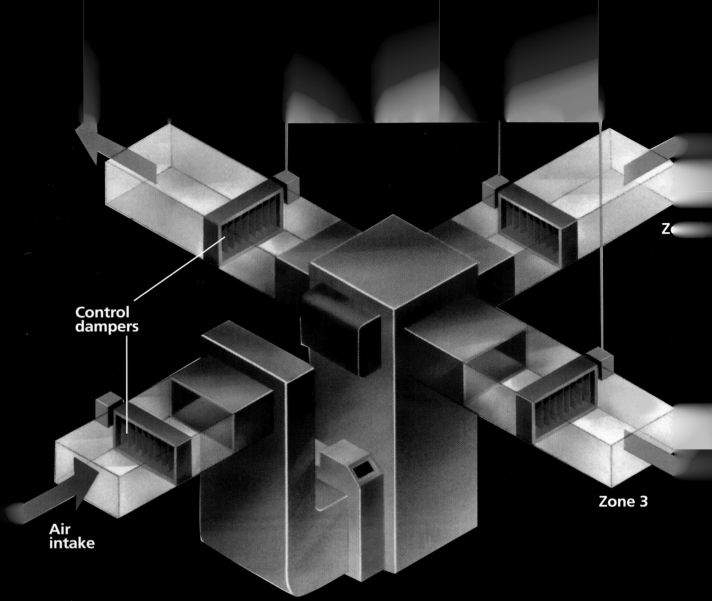

Control dampers

Air intake

Zone 3

Z...

ARE YOU IN CONTROL?

Even in a modestly sized house, it is both economical and convenient to be able to control the amount of heated or cooled air sent to different areas. You may prefer that your main living area is set at a comfortable 68°F, for example, while a back room or upstairs area is cooler at various times.

To accomplish this, a heating and cooling system often is composed of two or more independent zones, each controlled by its own thermostat. In a forced-circulation system—either hot water or forced air—each zone thermostat controls a circulator that sends heated water or air through its own dedicated circuit of pipes or ducts.

The location of a thermostat is an important aspect in keeping temperatures consistent throughout the house. Thermostats should not be located near heating and cooling registers, or in front of doors or other drafty areas.

When purchasing a thermostat, keep in mind that more is not necessarily better in this case. The more setbacks and other features a unit has, the more complicated it can be to program. Most people find that two setbacks per day is enough.

If your thermostat is an older model, it probably collects a fair amount of dust on its electrical contacts. To clean them, snap off the cover and run an index card or similar material through them. Blow or brush away dust on other elements as well.

A hot water system uses a boiler and may be divided into several zones, each controlled by a separate thermostat and pipe loop from the boiler.

HEATING, VENTILATION & AIR CONDITIONING

Your central heating, ventilation and air-conditioning (HVAC) system serves as your home's climate control system. It was installed about the same time as the plumbing and electrical systems. Though its components are generally hidden, the HVAC system is nonetheless a leading contributor to your house's overall comfort and safety levels. If designed and functioning properly, the HVAC system holds indoor temperatures fairly constant—no matter what the outdoor conditions might be.

On the following pages, you'll learn how to identify the type of HVAC system you have, how to evaluate it, and what problems to look for. Aside from your mortgage, heating and cooling may be the biggest continuing expense related to your house. So in addition to giving you a sense of how an HVAC system does its job and why it's so essential, this chapter will examine ways to make it more efficient and help you decide if replacing an older system is warranted.

The operation of the HVAC system is affected by basic structural elements of your home. The HVAC system is only as efficient as the walls and roof that keep the outdoor environment at bay. See the chapters on roofing (pages 30 to 39) and insulation (pages 40 to 47) for information on these systems.

Air Quality

Beginning in the early 1970s, when energy prices soared, the emphasis among HVAC contractors was making heating and air conditioning systems as efficient as possible. The answer was super-high-efficiency furnaces and elaborate house sealing methods. But while people have been very efficient in insulating and sealing their homes to conserve energy, they've done little to ensure a constant flow of fresh air in the home. As a result, the air in many modern, airtight homes is thought to contain 10 times as many pollutants as an old, drafty house. Some medical experts associate the rise in childhood asthma to indoor molds that occur in airtight homes with insufficient ventilation to remove moisture.

As you inspect and evaluate your HVAC system, keep an eye open for signs of poor air quality.

HOW DOES YOUR FURNACE RATE?

The U.S. Department of Energy standards rate the fuel consumption of each home heating unit made, using a rating called the Annual Fuel Utilization Efficiency (AFUE). The AFUE indicates how much heat the system extracts from the fuel provided in a single season. New furnaces are required to have at least a 78.2 percent AFUE. To find the AFUE rating, look for a yellow "Energy Guide" label on the appliance. For a contractor-supplied furnace, you'll need to ask the HVAC contractor what AFUE rating is listed.

Remember that the AFUE is a rating of the furnace unit itself; it doesn't provide an accurate measure of your entire system. A forced-air system with long runs of uninsulated duct work, for example, may lose up to 30 percent of the heat generated by a super-high-efficiency furnace.

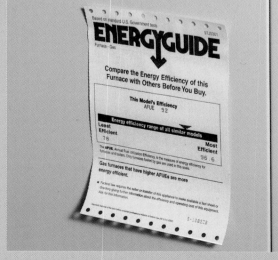

In newer furnaces, the Annual Fuel Utilization Efficiency sticker is glued to the side of the appliance.

Heating Basics

In an ideal world, a structure could be heated to the perfect temperature once and then left alone. But here on Earth, where yearly temperatures may vary 150°F or more from summer to winter, we have had to devise ways to generate a steady supply of heat in the face of continually fluctuating temperatures.

Maybe it's been a while since you've paid much attention to your furnace or boiler. Out of sight and out of mind; it's easy to take these appliances for granted. But learning some basic facts can help you get the most out of your system, and can help you determine if a system needs to be repaired or replaced.

Although the appearance and technology of heating systems varies widely, they all operate on a simple principle. Heat is generated at a central source, is dispersed to designated areas through some medium (air, steam or water) traveling through a channel (pipes or ducts). At the termination point, registers or radiators release the heat into living spaces. Return lines bring cool air, water or vapor back to the furnace or boiler for reheating.

An appliance that supplies heat to an air transfer system is a *furnace*. One that heats water or makes steam is called a *boiler*. Another type of appliance, known as a *heat pump*, acts as both an air conditioner and a furnace, using refrigerant to direct heat into or out of your home.

Your furnace or boiler may be installed in the basement, in a closet or utility room on the main floor or in the attic. Heat pump units are usually outside the house.

Furnaces, boilers and heat pumps have varied expected life spans. Yours may have been designed to last 15 years or 40. The durability of the appliance depends on the quality of its materials and construction—and on how well it has been maintained.

When evaluating your heating unit, you'll want to be aware of two ratings numbers, the AFUE (Annual Fuel Utilization Efficiency) and COP (Co-efficiency of Performance). These ratings are important barometers of your heating equipment's efficiency. The COP measures the efficiency of electric heating equipment. A COP of 1.0 indicates 100 percent heating efficiency, meaning that the heat energy produced is exactly equal to the energy the appliance consumes. Heat pump equipment can have a COP of over 1.0 because it draws energy from an external source that isn't measured.

Heating appliances are rated by size, based on the number of BTUs they can provide per hour. A BTU (British Thermal Unit) is a measure of quantity for heat. One BTU is the amount of heat it takes to raise one pound of water one degree

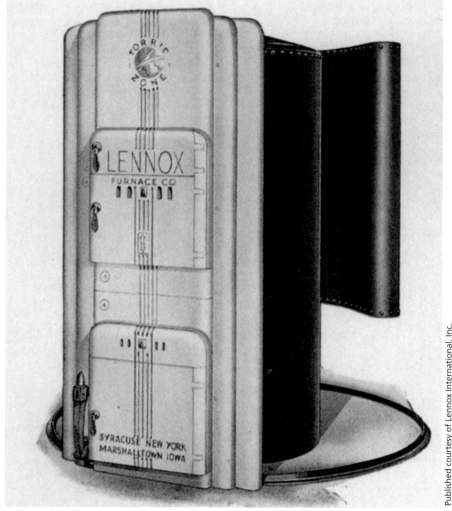

Many very old furnaces are still running trouble-free, though they are not as fuel-efficient as modern furnaces. The oil-fired furnace unit shown here dates back to 1944.

Published courtesy of Lennox International, Inc.

Fahrenheit, from 59°F to 60°F.

The house's size, the number and placement of windows, the amount of insulation, outdoor weather and other factors should be considered when determining the BTUs required to heat a house. "Manual J," published by the Air Conditioning Contractors of America (ACCA), is a handy reference for determining if your heating system is sufficient for the load it carries.

Remember, though, that bigger is not always better when it comes to a furnace or boiler. A unit that is too large not only robs your basement of extra space but it tends to use more energy because it turns on and off more often.

Heating Fuel Options

The relative popularity of different fuels depends on the availability and the cost of each in your region of the country. Natural gas, oil and electricity are the most common choices, although propane, wood and coal also are used to fuel heating appliances.

Natural gas-fired appliances are connected directly to the gas utility pipelines. Natural gas or propane is primarily methane, which burns more cleanly than oil. It's colorless and odorless in its natural state, so utility companies add a distinctive odor to it so you can readily detect even small leaks. Like oil-fired systems, propane gas-fired appliances are tied to storage tanks rather than a pipeline.

Oil-fired heating systems draw the oil from refillable tanks. The tanks may be in the basement, crawl space or outside the house, connected to the boiler or furnace by a pipe. If the oil tank is inside, it should be at least seven feet away from the heating appliance.

Electric furnaces cost less than other furnaces, and are cheaper to install, but they can cost up to three times as much as other fuels for the same amount of heat. Electric furnaces produce heat cleanly because there is no combustion in the unit. Compared to oil- and gas-burning furnaces, they're nearly maintenance-free.

Tip

Newer furnaces and boilers use electronic ignition, but older models use a pilot light to ignite the main burner. Many homeowners let the pilot light burn all year long, mistakenly believing that this keeps dampness out of the system and prevents rust. In reality, natural gas releases hydrogen oxide—water—as it burns. The moisture released by the burning pilot light condenses on the cool surfaces of the heat exchanger and can cause rust. Extinguishing the pilot light at the end of the heating season saves on the cost of gas and also extends the life of your furnace.

HEATING COMPARISON CHART

If you're considering a new heating system, this chart will help you evaluate alternatives. Follow this procedure:

First, call your local utility suppliers and ask them for current energy costs, per unit. Then, mark these actual costs on each heating-system column. Finally, look for the column with the lowest mark; this will indicate the most energy-efficient system for you. Remember that fuel costs vary by region and may change over time.

Suppose, for example, that heating oil in your area costs $.90 per gallon,

natural gas $.54 per therm, and electricity costs $.07 per kilowatt hour. When this example is plotted on the chart, you can clearly see that a natural gas furnace will be noticeably cheaper to run than a fuel oil furnace, and far less expensive than electric heat.

Of course, you'll also want to consider the cost of the furnace unit itself and other necessary hardware when deciding on the best system to install. And it's also a good idea to check with an energy expert for advice on how fuel prices might change over the next 20 years or so.

Heating oil $/gallon	Natural gas $/therm	Direct electric ¢/KWH	Electric furnace ¢/KWH	Heat pump ¢/KWH	Propane gas $/gallon
2.10	1.70		6.5	12.5	
2.00	1.60	7.0		12.0	1.50
1.90	1.50		6.0	11.5	1.40
1.80		6.5		11.0	
1.70	1.40		5.5	10.5	1.30
1.60	1.30	6.0		10.0	1.20
1.50	1.20		5.0	9.5	
1.40		5.5		9.0	1.10
1.30	1.10		4.5	8.5	1.00
1.20	1.00	5.0		8.0	
1.10	.90		4.0	7.5	.90
1.00	.80	4.5		7.0	.80
.90	.70		3.5	6.5	
.80		4.0		6.0	.70
.70	.60		3.0	5.5	.60
.60	.50	3.5		5.0	.50
			2.5	4.5	
		3.0		4.0	
			2.0		
		2.5			
		2.0			

Hot-Air Systems

The most popular type of central heating system is the hot-air furnace. A hot-air system injects heated air directly into various rooms and transports cool air back to the heating appliance using a network of hot- and cold-air ducts. If you have such a system, you may already know and appreciate the fact that hot-air systems are efficient and relatively easy to maintain.

While the outcomes are the same, there are variations in how hot-air systems work.

Gravity-based systems include older hot-air furnaces that have no mechanical blowers. Air movement is driven simply by the physics of hot air rising and cool air descending. Gravity air systems can be identified by the fact that the heat registers are generally installed on interior walls, and by the large cold-air return registers installed in the flooring.

Gravity air systems do not provide the instant heat that forced air systems offer. But because they are so simple in function, gravity air furnaces are exceptionally long-lived. Thousands of 40- to 50-year old gravity air furnaces are still happily functioning. The burners should be inspected and cleaned periodically.

Forced-air systems. Most new homes, and many updated older houses, now use forced-air systems, in which a motor-driven fan pushes air from the furnace to the rooms in the home. These systems provide more predictable heating, and are easily adapted to moving cool air from a central air conditioning unit. Forced-air furnaces usually are equipped with filters to remove dust and pollen, and many are also fitted with humidifiers that can be used to increase air moisture levels during dry conditions.

Warm-air registers are usually installed on exterior walls, with cold-air returns installed on interior walls. Some systems, like those in which the furnace is installed in a utility room on the main floor, don't have return ducts but draw air from their surroundings.

Gas valve
Burners
Heat exchanger
Fan blower

Published courtesy of Carrier Corporation

At left: Forced-air furnaces are the most common of all heating systems. While more efficient to operate, their higher number of mechanical parts, like blower motors, means that they need to be periodically serviced.

Maintaining Your Furnace

- *Have a professional inspect and clean your furnace and ductwork every other year.*
- *Using a strong light, occasionally inspect the exhaust pipe that runs from your furnace to the chimney. Look for any dents, loose or open joints, or rusted areas, and replace pipes as needed.*
- *Check the air filter every month and replace it if it looks clogged.*
- *Inspect the tension on blower belts. They should have about one inch of play, measured midway between the motor and fan pulleys. To adjust the tension, loosen the motor-mount bolt, moving the motor as necessary and then retightening.*
- *If you hear a squealing noise, tighten the fan belt and oil the motor bearings as recommended by the unit's manufacturer.*
- *Check for loose ducts yearly. If necessary, secure loose flanges with sheet-metal screws and seal joints with duct tape.*
- *Adjust the pilot flame so it burns blue with a yellow tip.*

Tip

Forced-air ducts often have dampers that can be adjusted to ensure more even heat distribution. Position thermometers near the center of each room, then turn up the thermostat and allow the furnace to run constantly. Check the temperature in each room every thirty minutes or so. Open or close dampers as necessary until all rooms are roughly the same temperature.

Air Filtration Systems

If you have a forced-air system, your unit probably has a filter that strains out the particulates floating in the air. Although they don't trap noxious gases, like radon, such filters do remove household dust.

What makes up the dust in our houses? There are soil particles and lint, of course, but also some things that are even more unpleasant to contemplate: airborne cooking grease, tobacco smoke, pet hairs, pollen, mold spores, bacteria, viruses, skin flakes, carbon particles, dust mites, dust mite feces and insect scales. These particles range in size tremendously. While some particles (10 microns and larger) are visible, most cannot be seen with the naked eye. The common fiberglass filters most home-owners use are not very effective at trapping the smaller of these contaminants. Fortunately, there are other options:

Electrostatic media filters can be substituted for the standard fiberglass filters. Dust is attracted to the filter media, much as it is to the statically charged surface of a television screen. Most units withstand at least five years of the recommended monthly washings. A tight fit around the filter ensures maximum efficiency.

Paper cartridge filters usually consist of a loosely folded, paper-like media. They have an enormous surface area and an operating life of about one year. Moreover, the dirtier the filters get, the more effective they become—up to a point. The dust accumulation actually increases the surface area of the filter. Paper filters are especially effective at arresting particles that trigger common allergies: pollen and mold spores.

Two-stage ionization filters consist of a coarse metal mesh that ensnares and then ionizes particles so they cling to a network of metal plates. Popping noises, similar to

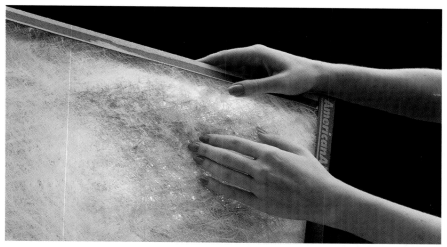

If you use your central-air system for both heating and air conditioning, it's a good idea to do a visual inspection once a month throughout the entire year. Use a bright light to check for clogged and dirty filter elements, and replace as necessary.

those made by a bug zapper, signal the need for cleaning.

Two-stage ionization filters are costly but very efficient—when kept clean. They eliminate a broad range of particulates and do the best job of keeping the furnace itself clean. They must be spliced into return-air ductwork by professionals.

Controlling Humidity

The amount of humidity in the air may not only affect your family's comfort and health, but it can also be harmful to wood objects, such as furniture and musical instruments. In winter, higher humidity can make a room seem warmer; in summer, lower humidity makes air seem cooler.

Forced-air heat systems dry out the air in your home, especially in dry climates and regions with cold winters. Forced-air furnaces can be equipped with automatic humidifiers to add moisture to the air. Some motorized models put a fine mist of water right into the airflow; others have a rotating water wheel that allows air moving from the furnace into the ducts to pick up moisture along the way. A humidistat measures moisture

levels and then turns off the humidifier when the preferred level is reached. For most people, humidity levels of 35 to 40 percent are most comfortable.

However, increasing indoor humidity is not always a good idea.

Molds and mildew can build up in the moist environment of the humidifier, and can be dispersed throughout the house by the ductwork. Clean furnace-mounted humidifiers as recommended by the manufacturer—at least once each month.

When outdoor temperatures dip below about 20°F, too much indoor humidity can become a serious problem, especially in newer, airtight houses. Moisture condensing on cold windows and wall surfaces can cause paint to peel, and if this moisture is trapped in wall and ceiling spaces, it can cause mold and wood rot. These problems are epidemic in thousands of newer houses, so watch carefully for these symptoms.

Portable room dehumidifiers, fresh-air vents, and bathroom and kitchen vent fans can all help reduce indoor humidity levels.

Hot-Water Systems

Hot-water heating systems are most common in older homes, but the technology is far from obsolete. New, high-efficiency boilers are available to replace older units when they fail.

Although "hydronic" or hot-water systems vary greatly in appearance, they all start with a gas, oil or electric boiler that heats water. As the water heats, it expands in volume. To prevent pressure from damaging the pipes, the system incorporates an expansion tank, much like the one that probably sits next to the radiator in your car.

Once the water has been heated, the next step is moving it to where it's needed. In older, *gravity hot-water systems*, simple physics moves the water: hot water rises, gives off its heat, then is pulled by gravity back down to the boiler to be reheated.

A newer and more effective way to move the water is by means of a *mechanical circulator*. The circulator

- *Make sure water levels in the boiler are at proper levels.*
- *Oil the circulator pump and motor twice a year.*
- *Clean and flush out your boiler at least once a year—or when you notice that the water in the glass gauge is cloudy.*
- *On hot-water systems, release any trapped air from any radiator that doesn't heat up. Radiators should also be "bled" whenever you are adding water to the system or starting the furnace up for the first time in the heating season.*
- *Test the safety relief valve yearly. If the valve drips when closed, replace it (shut off boiler and drain it first).*
- *Insulate pipes that run through unheated areas.*
- *Use standard paint to cover a radiator. Paint made specifically for metal objects can reduce the unit's heat-transfer properties by 25%.*
- *Vacuum radiators and convectors regularly to improve their efficiency.*

is an electric pump installed near the boiler. Controlled by a thermostat, it pushes the water through the pipe after the water reaches a specified temperature. Because the water doesn't need to lose heat to move back to the boiler, this forced-circulation system delivers a greater flow of hot water to room radiators or convectors.

If yours is a newer home, you are more likely to have convectors rather than radiators. Either in upright or baseboard style, a convector has a larger area of heated surface and is therefore more efficient.

Hot-water and steam heating systems can be configured to create zone heating in a home. Especially useful in large homes, zone control allows the homeowner to preset temperatures for different areas of the home based on the amount and type of use at various times during the day. Any number of zone lines can be created by tapping off the main supply pipe and installing a zone valve for each line. A thermostat opens or closes the zone valve, regulating the amount of hot water received in an area.

One of the most common zoned-heating plans splits heat in two zones: one for high-use areas and another zone for bedrooms and other areas that need less heat or are in use at different times.

Steam Heating

Steam heating uses most of the same principles and elements as a hot-water system. However, the boiler heats the water until it vaporizes. The vapor then rises and makes its way through the pipes and into the radiators or convectors. Upon hitting the cooler surfaces of these objects, the vapor condenses and runs back to the boiler in the form of water for reheating. If water gets trapped in the radiator and causes audible gurgling, drain the water from it.

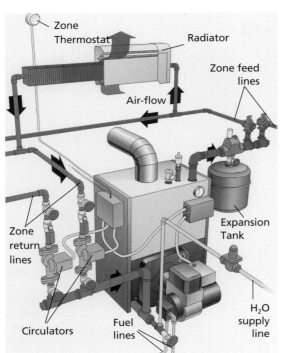

Zone Thermostat — Radiator — Zone feed lines — Air-flow — Expansion Tank — Zone return lines — Circulators — Fuel lines — H₂O supply line

Left: Modern boilers are highly efficient, and can be configured for two or more zones controlled by separate thermostats.

Radiant Hot-Water Heating

If you have a newer home, it might be heated by a new type of hot-water system—radiant heating. In a radiant hot-water system, water is pumped from a central boiler through a series of pipes imbedded in the floor of each room. Rather than heating air, this type of system radiates heat up through the floor to warm the objects in the room. The result is a more efficient and even distribution of heat, and enthusiasts argue, a more natural and comfortable environment. Because the heat originates at the floor and quickly warms our more temperature-sensitive lower extremities, house temperatures can be set lower: typically at 65°F.

If your home happens to have a radiant hot-water system, you're probably in harmony with a growing list of ardent supporters who sing its praises. For others, it's yet another option worth considering, particularly in new-construction situations.

Originally introduced in the 1940s, radiant heating systems were plagued by mechanical failures; iron and copper pipes and fittings tended to fail after extended use. Only recently has radiant hot-water technology improved to make this system practical and appealing for widespread use.

Today, radiant hot-water systems are most common in new construction of upscale homes. However, new methods of installation are available to make radiant heat a viable option for remodeling, especially if there is an existing boiler that can be used to supply the water.

The preferred method for new installation is to embed plastic or synthetic rubber/plastic tubing under the floor in a layer of mortar. A popular and less expensive alternative is called the *staple-up system,* in which the tubing is

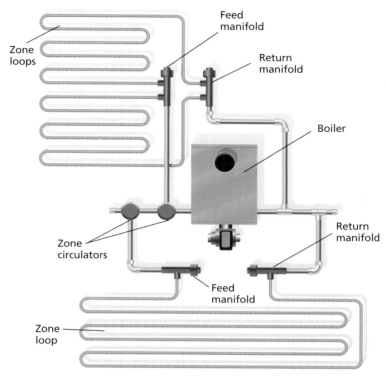

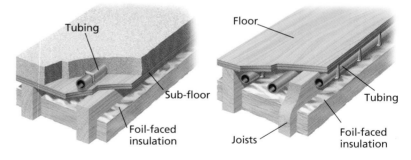

Radiant systems use circulators to move hot water, and manifolds to divide the system into zones that can be controlled independently. Installation variations include setting tubing in mortar, or placing it between flooring and a layer of foil-faced insulation.

stapled directly to the underside of the floor between the joists. The joist spaces are filled with foil-faced fiberglass insulation batts. Another variation is the *sandwich-over-frame* floor, which places the tubing between two flooring layers.

Advantages of radiant hot-water heat include:

• Air pressure isn't increased in isolated rooms. This means there is less heat loss through doors and windows.

• Moisture content of the air isn't affected.

• Dust circulation is reduced.

• Energy costs can be as much as 30 percent less than for conventional systems.

Heat Pumps

Another heating and cooling option for those living in areas with relatively moderate winter temperatures is a *heat pump*. Unlike combined forced-air heating and central air-conditioning systems, which simply share the same duct network and fan, a heat pump system uses a single unit to both heat and cool your home.

A heat pump operates something like a reversible kitchen refrigerator. The unit features a compressor and two refrigerant-filled pipe coils, one outside and one inside the house.

While in a winter heating cycle, refrigerant passes through outdoor coils as a gas, drawing heat from the air or ground. The refrigerant then passes into a compressor, which raises the temperature of the gas by pressurizing it. Next, the refrigerant moves into the indoor coil located inside a fan and duct system, where it releases its heat and condenses into a liquid. The liquid refrigerant now passes through an expansion valve, which allows the refrigerant to return to a gaseous state. The gaseous refrigerant is then sent back to the outdoor coil to begin the cycle again.

In summer, the refrigerant cycle is reversed, picking up heat from indoor air and releasing it outdoors. To improve the efficiency of the unit in summer, shield the outdoor condensing coil unit with a sun shade to improve heat dissipation. In winter, remove the shade so the coils absorb the sun's heat more readily.

In cooler climates, heat pump systems are not always sufficient. Here, a back-up heat source may be required by the local Building Code. A secondary heater kicks in when outside temperatures drop to a predetermined threshold.

The fans and compressor, of course, consume energy in this process. Depending on the outdoor temperature, an effective heat pump delivers 1 to 3 BTUs for every BTU consumed.

A heat pump should be inspected and serviced by a licensed contractor each year. You should also make sure the indoor and outdoor coils are regularly vacuumed clean and that the blower filter is changed when necessary. The fan motor should be lubricated and the belts adjusted annually.

Electric Baseboard Heat

Because electricity is considerably more expensive than other energy sources, electric baseboard heat is generally used in regions where the heating season is brief or mild, or as an auxiliary source in colder climates. For example, using baseboard heat in an attic or garage room expansion can be much

Fan motor

Compressor

Reversing valve

Pipe/fin coil

Published courtesy of Carrier Corporation

A heat pump works something like a reversible central air conditioner unit. In cold weather, it releases heat into the house; in warm weather, it releases heat outdoors.

SUPER-HIGH-EFFICIENCY FURNACES AND BOILERS

When you find yourself in need of a new furnace or boiler, there are a number of high-efficiency and super-high-efficiency designs you should consider.

With a standard furnace or boiler, the heat of the flue gases carries the exhaust fumes up the chimney by way of convection. Super-high-efficiency furnaces and boilers, however, circulate waste gases until nearly all of the heat is extracted. In most cases, super-high-efficiency furnaces and boilers need a vent fan to expel waste gases. There are several different types of high-efficiency heating units.

CONDENSING FURNACES AND BOILERS feature enlarged heat exchanger surfaces that lower the temperature of the exhaust gases to the dew point of the water vapor in the gas. This causes the vapor to condense into water—a reaction that provides 970 BTUs for every pound of water condensed.

RECUPERATIVE (PARTIALLY CONDENSING) FURNACES AND BOILERS work by adding a recuperative heat exchanger that captures the heat that is normally lost up the chimney flue. The exhaust gases are vented to the atmosphere by a fan. Some of the water vapor in the flue gases is condensed, providing additional heat. The captured water is disposed of by a condensate drain to ensure that corrosion doesn't develop in the furnace and flue.

POWER DRAFT FURNACES, instead of drawing air into the combustion chamber by natural draft, use a motor-driven fan at the burner level to push (forced draft) or pull (induced draft) air into the combustion chamber.

easier than spending the time and money to extend a forced-air or hot-water system.

Mounted at the floor level, usually beneath windows, baseboard heater elements use 240-volt electrical current to warm metal fins, which release their heat to the air that passes over them. Each heater is wired directly to the house electrical supply and is controlled by a thermostat. Periodically cleaning the fins will make these heaters more efficient.

Fireplaces

Despite its aesthetic appeal, a fireplace is not a very practical source of house heat. Even with the modern addition of glass doors, an outdoor source of combustion air and heat distribution fans, fireplaces are more for looks than performance. In most fireplaces, the warmth generated exits through the chimney—along with additional ambient house heat. In the minds of most energy experts, an open fireplace is an energy drain, not a source.

The good news is that some fireplace lover with a will found a way to increase heating efficiency by inventing the *fireplace insert*. A fireplace insert acts more like a wood stove, confining the fire and releasing warmed air through vents that circulate around the firebox. Better models have catalytic converters and secondary combustion chambers that extract maximum heat and reduce soot build-up in the flue. Although the view of the fire may be partially obstructed, the energy saved by a fireplace insert is well worth this inconvenience.

In any wood-burning fireplace, use well-dried, slow-burning hardwoods to reduce the buildup of creosote—an oily residue produced by burning wet or green wood—which can cause chimney fires. Check the flue regularly for signs of excess accumulation, and have your chimney cleaned professionally once each year if you use the fireplace regularly.

Although *gas fireplaces* are quite popular these days, not all generate significant heat. Their beauty is that they offer some of the ambiance of a log fire without the need to chop and haul wood or clean up ashes.

Gas units are housed in insulated metal cabinets and, therefore, can be installed nearly anywhere. Some models are designed as fireplace inserts, other as freestanding stoves with a vent pipe that runs through the roof or an exterior wall. Inside the firebox are several ceramic logs and a burner assembly that delivers a reasonably realistic, yellow flame instead of the short, nearly invisible blue flame found in other gas appliances.

Wood Stoves

During the energy crunch in the 1970s and 1980s, wood stoves enjoyed a surge in popularity. It's possible your home has a wood stove. Although their popularity has waned, many wood stoves remain in service. A good percentage of these stoves were installed by weekend do-it-yourselfers and have never been inspected. Some have improper clearances or improper chimneys and connectors. If you have a wood stove, have it inspected soon, and serviced annually if you use it regularly.

WOOD STOVE CLEARANCES

To prevent fire hazards, it's important that proper clearances be maintained between wood stoves and nearby combustibles. Wood in walls and furniture undergoes a physical change when continually exposed to elevated temperatures, and this reduces its ignition temperature. Under normal circumstances, wood begins to burn between 400°F and 600°F. However, when it is continually exposed to temperatures between 150°F and 250°F, its ignition temperature can be lowered to 200°F.

It can take years for wood's ignition temperature to be lowered, so homeowners can acquire a false sense of security. But when the wood's temperature coincides with the lowered ignition temperature, it will ignite and burn spontaneously. With this in mind, there are basically two sets of standards for clearances around wood stoves: clearances for stoves that have been listed to UL Standard No. 1482, and clearances for stoves that have not been listed to this standard. The label also will tell you what clearances to use around the appliance (generally these are in the 12- to 36-inch range). For stoves that have not been tested and listed to the UL standard, minimum clearances often are defined by local codes; so check with your local building authority before proceeding.

36"

12" min. with protection

Masonry or Sheetmetal

Air Conditioning

In the same way that your heating unit can take the chill off a cold winter day, a central air-conditioning system can make your home a cool oasis in the midst of sweltering summer heat. In very warm climates, air conditioning can be nearly as essential to basic survival as a furnace is to a homeowner in the far North.

Most central air-conditioning systems run on 240-volt electrical current, though natural-gas powered designs are available. A single-duct, forced central-air system is the most common. In this design, the same ductwork used for heating also distributes cool air throughout the house.

In essence, your central air conditioner is a two-part refrigerator, with a cooling unit (evaporator) installed inside your furnace and the heat transfer unit (condenser) mounted outdoors.

When the thermostat turns the system on, refrigerant flowing through a network of copper pipes picks up heat from air blowing over the evaporator coil located inside the furnace. The gaseous refrigerant then flows to the outdoor unit, where a compressor forces it into a liquid state and a condenser coil releases the heat in the refrigerant to the outside air.

Maintaining a central air conditioner is relatively simple:

• Remove the covers from the condenser unit and vacuum the coils clean at the start of each cooling season. Also clean leaves and debris out of the housing.

• For best efficiency, shade the condenser unit from the sun.

• Clean the evaporator coil inside the furnace on a regular basis.

Ductless Systems

Homes with hot-water or steam heating systems and no furnace ductwork can be centrally air conditioned using a ductless system. Instead of ducts, small tubes run between the outdoor condenser and multiple indoor evaporator units, forming a closed-loop cooling system. The cooling units, mounted on the wall, resemble window-mounted air conditioners but are much quieter because the loud compressor component is outside.

A ductless system is a good option for retrofitting an older home with central air conditioning.

The components of a ductless air-conditioning system should be cleaned and serviced in the same fashion as ducted air-conditioning systems (opposite page).

Air-Conditioning Ratings

Your central air-conditioning unit has a variety of ratings that can be used to evaluate its efficiency and capacity.

Your air conditioner's Energy Efficiency Rating (EER) is a measure of how much electricity an air conditioner consumes per unit of heat removed from the room. On newer units, you'll find this rating on a yellow Energy Guide label. It is expressed in BTUs per watt. Ratings of 12 and 13 are considered highly efficient EERs.

Air conditioners also are rated by the number of BTUs of heat they remove from the house. This BTUs-per-hour rating can be found on the Energy Guide, too, along with a comparison between your particular model with others of the same capacity.

Determining if your central air-conditioning unit has an appropriate capacity for your home is a more complicated process.

Before your air-conditioning system was installed, a number of factors were taken into consideration. Total floor area, ceiling height, window area, insulation values of walls and ceilings, amount of

Published courtesy of Lennox International, Inc.

An outdoor condenser unit on a central air conditioner releases the heat absorbed by the indoor evaporator unit.

Condenser fan

Outdoor fin/coil

Compressor

shade, family size and lifestyle are all considered by a good HVAC contractor planning installation. If you want to do this for yourself, consult a copy of "Manual J," published by the Air Conditioning Contractors of America; this is the reference contractors use to plan HVAC installations.

In determining whether to keep your old unit or buy a new one, base your analysis on a reasonable estimate of operating costs for the cooling season. Higher-efficiency models often cost more initially but can save you money in the long run.

Central-Air Maintenance

Of the major appliances, central air conditioners probably suffer the most from poor maintenance. The most common problem is dust build-up. Within a single cooling season, compressor fin tubes can become completely clogged with dust, leading to gradual deterioration of performance and, eventually, the unit itself.

With this in mind, it is best to clean your compressor once each spring, then again midsummer. Before conducting any maintenance procedures, shut off the power, using either the compressor's main disconnect switch or the circuit breaker at your house's main service panel.

While servicing the condenser unit using the above procedures, it's also a good idea to tighten loose fan blades and make sure the fan rotates smoothly and steadily. Once a year, lubricate the fan motor, using 20-weight oil. Add about 10 drops per oil port. These ports can usually be identified by their small rubber or metal caps.

Before starting your unit each spring or after any long shutdown period, first restore power to the air conditioner for 24 hours. This allows heat to build up, which helps the oil separate from the refrigerant in the compressor.

Tips

• First and foremost, don't run your air conditioner unless you really need it. If the temperature outdoors is 80°F or less, simply opening windows to provide cross-ventilation will be sufficient.

• Experiment with slightly raising the temperature setting. Studies show that raising settings even two or three degrees can provide between 10 and 25 percent savings in operating costs.

• Keep windows closed when you're not running your unit during the day.

• Keep shades or blinds closed, particularly south- and west-facing windows in the summer months.

• Keep the air filter clean and, whenever possible, run the air conditioner in the recirculating mode rather than the ventilating mode.

Carefully lift the top panel and remove by hand any debris from inside the condenser coil and below the fan.

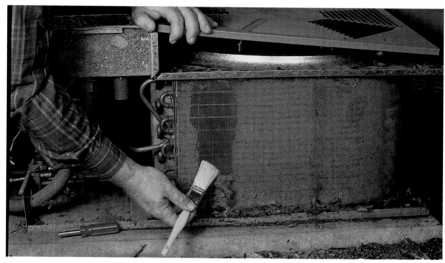

Remove the condenser side panels and use a hose and/or a soft brush to remove the dust on the fins and tubes.

Solar Energy

When you consider that an entire structure becomes a solar collector in a passive heating system, it's probably worth considering whether your home has some features or potential for tapping into this, the world's most abundant, reliable and cleanest fuel source.

We continue to harness but a small fraction of the 170 trillion kilowatts of electromagnetic radiation that strike the Earth annually (about 35,000 times more energy than that produced by humans each year). Yet, if you're looking for an environmentally conscious and, in many cases, economical, source of energy, solar power remains a viable and worthwhile option when applied correctly and under the proper circumstances.

The sun's energy must be collected over relatively large areas. How effectively you are able to do this depends on a number of factors:

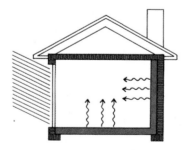

Passive direct-gain heating through a south-facing window.

• Your location's altitude, latitude and longitude.
• The time of the year.
• Weather patterns in your area.
• The proximity of light-blocking elements like trees or buildings during peak collection hours.

While some locations are better suited to solar energy than others, nearly every home could benefit from at least a limited solar application—and certainly by many of the energy-conservation practices that are a large part of any modern solar energy system. We will primarily focus on large structural solarization techniques in this book, even though many other applications bear investigation if you're looking for cost-effective, energy-saving alternatives.

An effective solar heating system requires about 200 square feet of collector area for every 1,000 square feet of space to be heated. When considering solar power, you will want to carefully evaluate your proposed or present structure and location. This should include conducting such things as Degree Day and Home Heating Index calculations to determine how much energy your home requires and if it is indeed ready for solarization. Conduct an *energy audit* to see how effectively and at what rate your home processes environmental changes, and follow up with any needed weatherproofing, insulating or air-tightening remedies (see related chapters). You

may opt for a more complex—and therefore, generally more expensive—*active* solar energy system that uses mechanical devices to collect, store and distribute the sun's energy. But more popular in recent years are *passive* systems in which an entire structure functions as a self-contained, natural heating, ventilation and air-conditioning system. These systems quickly respond and adapt to the ever-changing environment, taking maximum advantage of the sun's motion and position in the sky. The key is to strike a balance between adequate solar energy collection and the methods for controlling this "living and breathing" environment. In a passive design, the environment must be especially free of drafts or cold surfaces, which makes an energy audit and resulting improvements so critical.

As much as one-third of incoming radiant heat is stored in thermal mass materials like large floor slabs, masonry, water- or chemical-filled containers or other elements of the home, and then slowly released during non-collection periods. Control devices such as movable insulation in the collection area, thermostats, adjustable vents, awnings, shade-producing landscaping and overhangs complete the system by regulating air flows. The result is an indoor environment that remains comfortable year-round.

PASSIVE SOLARIZATION HOME AND LANDSCAPING TIPS

• Design the home so the long axis of the structure faces north and south.
• Limit windows to 15 percent of the floor space.
• Put the bulk of your window space on the south side of your house and the smallest amount on the north side. Consider a porch or car port as a buffer.
• Make use of overhangs that block the hot summer sun but don't obstruct needed winter sunshine.
• Design your home so temperatures in main activity rooms

remain consistent.
• Consider the use of a radiant barrier in the attic, which can significantly cut heat transfer through the ceiling.
• Use trees and dense landscaping materials on east and west sides to reduce the effects of the sun and wind.
• To increase shade, plant trees seven to 20 feet from the home (depending on height) or in colder climates, at a distance three times the tree's expected height at maturity.
• Use plantings near the foundation to keep it cool.

Ventilation

Your house needs to breathe. It needs to get rid of internal moisture, odors, smoke and other contaminants, and it needs to bring in fresh air to keep you and your family healthy and to provide combustion air for furnaces, water heaters and other fuel-burning appliances.

Ironically, air quality in old houses is often much better than that in new, modern homes. In old houses, fresh air enters through cracks in walls, through seams around windows, doors and chimneys. You may curse the drafts you feel in an old house, but in fact these drafts are providing you with ample amounts of fresh, healthy air.

New houses, however, are sometimes insulated and sealed so tightly that there is very little exchange of fresh air. In a tightly sealed home that uses fuel-burning appliances, carbon monoxide poisoning is a very real danger. Carefully evaluate your home's ventilation, and call in an HVAC expert if you feel your family or home is at risk.

All homes should have at least one functioning carbon monoxide detector.

Signs of possible air-quality problems include:

• Frequent condensation on windows. This indicates a buildup of air moisture.

• Persistant odors of foods or cigarette smoke. If these odors are still detectable after a few hours, it means there is insufficient air exchange in your home.

• Mold and mildew in carpets or on walls. These pollutants are the result of excessive air moisture, and can cause allergies and asthma.

Exhaust Ventilation

Local codes usually require electric exhaust vents in bathrooms and kitchens, but a surprising number of those in existence are

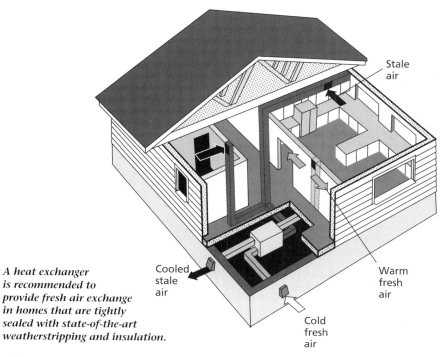

A heat exchanger is recommended to provide fresh air exchange in homes that are tightly sealed with state-of-the-art weatherstripping and insulation.

Stale air

Cooled stale air

Warm fresh air

Cold fresh air

either not used or do not function correctly. Among the most common mechanical exhaust-only fans are those installed in kitchens and bathrooms. Vent fans should exhaust directly to the outdoors. A vent fan that exhausts moist air into the attic poses a very serious problem and should be replaced immediately. Self-circulating kitchen fans are virtually useless; they should be replaced with fans that vent to the outdoors.

Make sure you use your kitchen and bathroom vent fans. You should make sure, however, that the units are not so powerful that they create a situation called *backdrafting*, in which negative pressure created by the pull of the vent fans can draw combustion gases down through furnace and appliance chimneys into your home. This problem sometimes occurs in new houses that are tightly sealed; consult your local building inspector for guidelines.

Appliance Ventilation

Make sure all fuel-burning heating appliances, including furnaces and water heaters, have an adequate supply of air for combustion. In older homes, these appliances can safely draw combustion air from the indoor air around the appliance. So long as the immediate spaces around these appliances are open and the house has a ready supply of fresh air, these appliances rarely pose a problem.

But in a tightly sealed home, older heating appliances can seriously degrade the quality of the inside air you breathe. In this situation, the furnace, water heater, fireplace and any other fuel-burning appliances should have sealed combustion chambers that draw air directly from the outdoors.

Heat Exchangers

So what do you do if you have a home with state-of-the-art insulation and weathersealing that has created an air-quality problem? Replacing old appliances with newer ones that draw outdoor air will help, but it may not be enough to correct a bad-air situation.

The best solution may be a system known as an air-to-air heat exchanger (*illustration, above*). A heat exchanger uses a blower fan and ductwork to exhaust stale interior air to the outside while simultaneously drawing in fresh outside air. Inside the exchanger unit—which contains two sets of parallel, baffled ducts—the incoming fresh air absorbs the heat of the outgoing moist air (*inset, above*). Heat exchangers are also used to eliminate radon problems in basements.

Tin
ceiling
tile

Acoustical
ceiling
tile

Resilient
vinyl
tile

Wood
parque
floorin

Ceramic
floor
tile

Carpeting

INTERIOR SURFACES

Most of the mechanical and structural systems in your house serve their functions more or less invisibly.

Not so with the last system installed—the interior wall, ceiling and floor surfaces. Because the interior surfaces are visible at all times, they are expected to serve important aesthetic functions as well as practical ones. Your interior is a marriage of form and function. You want it to be visually appealing and yet stand up to all the expected wear and tear of daily living.

A high-quality interior should be durable, easy to clean, fire-resistant and repairable. Interior surfaces also insulate your house from temperature extremes and noise.

In this chapter we'll investigate walls, floors and ceilings. We'll point out what lurks beneath their surfaces. And, as usual, we'll show you what to pay attention to in your house.

Walls

Give your walls a gentle rap with your knuckles. You're almost certainly tapping on either plaster or wallboard.

Wallboard

Wallboard, or gypsum drywall, has nearly made plaster extinct in most new construction. Wallboard earned its name by the fact that it is manufactured in sheets generally four feet wide and up to 14 feet long. It has a core of gypsum and a backing of paper. Water-resistant wallboard has a gypsum-asphalt core and paper backings designed to repel moisture. Wallboard is fastened by screws or nails and its edges are taped and smoothed with joint compound. Standard wallboard has a tapered edge to eliminate bulging under the tape.

Wallboard dominates new construction because it takes less skill and is much faster (and therefore cheaper) to apply than plaster.

Plaster aficionados look down on wallboard as a cheap substitute that is easily dented. But wallboard does reduce construction costs, an important point if you are looking for a new home or planning to remodel. And wallboard can be applied more easily by do-it-yourselfers.

Plaster

Common in older houses, plaster is a mixture of calcined gypsum, water and aggregate such as sand. It is prized for its hardness, quietness and its plasticity—it can be textured in many different ways. Although most new homes have walls of wallboard, more luxurious new homes may have plaster walls. Properly cared for, plaster lasts for decades and shrugs off slight impacts. Plenty of century-old-houses have plaster walls in flawless condition. That being said, plaster is susceptible to cracking and chipping. It can also separate from the lath over time.

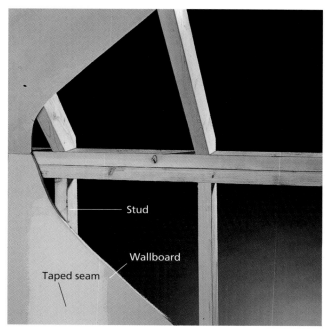

A wallboard system, also known as drywall, consists of gypsum panels attached directly to framing members. Wallboard thickness varies from ¼ to ¾ of an inch.

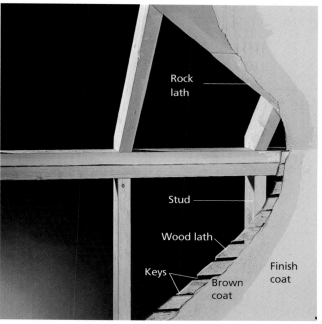

Plaster is applied in layers onto a base of lath. The lath can be rock, wood or metal. Plaster gets its grip from being squeezed into the spaces (called keys) between the lath strips or metal.

Plaster can be applied directly to masonry walls, but it is usually applied to thin wood strips (wood lath) or a wire mesh (metal lath) that allow the plaster to "grip" the wall. Like its outdoor cousin, stucco, wet plaster is troweled onto a wall in layers. The first coat, called the *scratch coat*, adheres to the lath. The second coat, or *brown coat*, provides a level base. The third coat, called the *finish coat*, is a thin layer that can be textured or smoothed to be painted or papered.

Water, of course, is an enemy to both plaster and wallboard. Even in small amounts, water can stain either surface. In large amounts, water will dissolve the gypsum in wallboard, producing weak spots or holes, and it will cause plaster to lose its grip with the lath and fall.

Wood Paneling

Unlike plaster or wallboard, wood paneling has great variety. Paneling can be thick, elegant hardwood. Or, it can be thin sheets of plywood with a simulated wood veneer.

Wood paneling is used because it offers textures and patterns not available from paint or wallpaper. It also fends off abuse better than most other wallcoverings.

Wood paneling is applied directly to studs glued to finished walls or attached to furring strips nailed to an existing wall.

Most real wood paneling is softwood, such as cedar, pine or redwood, but pricier hardwoods are also common. Veneer paneling can have any number of manufactured wood bases.

Tiled Walls

You'll find ceramic tile walls in bathrooms and kitchens. Ceramic tile creates a very durable and water-resistant surface, so long as the cement grout filling cracks between tiles is intact. Moisture seeping behind tiles is the single greatest threat to a ceramic tile wall.

Missing or old grout needs to be repaired before moisture can penetrate behind it. To make this repair, scrape out old grout with an awl or utility knife. Clean and rinse the

REPAIRING WALLBOARD AND PLASTER

Wallboard

Wallboard is easier to repair than plaster. Unlike plaster patch, wallboard compounds stick to painted surfaces, which means you can patch directly over paint.

• TO PATCH A HOLE: Create an outline around the damaged area with a straightedge. Using a wallboard saw, remove the damaged area by cutting along the lines. Cut a piece of 'backer,' wallboard that is longer and narrower than the hole. Apply contact cement or hot glue to the backer and insert it into the hole, attaching it to the back side of the undamaged wallboard. Now cut a patch of wallboard to fit the hole. Apply hot glue to the back of the patch and press it against the backer until glue sets. Apply fiberglass wallboard tape directly to seams. Cover the tape with premixed wallboard compound, let dry, apply a second layer, then sand. Repaint.

• TO RESET POPPED NAILS: Press the wallboard tightly against the stud or joist. Drive a new screw about 2 inches from the popped fastener. The screw head should be indented slightly. Then, hammer in the popped nail, leaving a slight indentation. Fill dents with taping compound. Sand, then paint.

Plaster

Cracks in plaster walls and ceilings are usually caused by movement in the house's framing. Holes in plaster can be caused by impacts or water.

• TO PATCH A HOLE: Scrape away all loose or scaling plaster to expose firm base plaster or lath. Make certain the damaged area does not extend beyond the scraped area. Brush latex bonding liquid into the patch area. Fully coat the edges of the old plaster. (Do not wet the patch area after coating it.) Mix patching plaster stiff enough to hold its shape. Firmly trowel the patching plaster into the hole with a wallboard knife. Smooth the plaster, then let it dry. For holes deeper than ¼ inch, apply a second coat. Let the plaster set, then sand lightly and repaint.

• TO REPAIR CRACKS: Self-adhesive fiberglass tape helps prevent recracking. Apply the tape directly to wall and press it smooth. Use a taping knife to cover tape with one or two thin layers of premixed wallboard compound. Sand the patch area until smooth. Repaint.

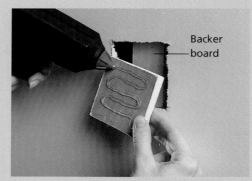

Backer board

joints with a sponge. Use a foam grout float or sponge to spread a mildew-resistant, premixed grout over the entire tile surface. Let it set slightly, then wipe away excess with a damp cloth. Let dry completely. Wipe away residue with a clean cloth. Wait a day before getting the wall wet.

Similarly, cracked ceramic tiles should also be replaced before moisture migrates into the substrate. It helps to keep a few spare tiles around the house for this purpose: ceramic tile is brittle, and sooner or later you'll probably need to replace a cracked tile or two.

Ceilings

Most ceilings are made of the same stuff as walls—plaster or wallboard. Sometimes the only difference is that ceilings may have a final layer of texture paint or sprayed-on texture, some of which is made of polystyrene bits suspended in a bonding agent. Other ceiling types include suspended panels, acoustic ceiling tiles and, in some restored homes, tin ceilings.

Suspended ceilings and acoustic tiles are easier to install than a new plaster or wallboard ceiling. And if a minor leak develops above the ceiling, replacing a single suspended panel or tile is a lot easier than repairing water damage to a plaster or wallboard ceiling, where the entire surface may sag away from the lath or framing.

Damaged sections of plaster can be replastered, or you can try to repair the area with plaster washers. Plaster washers are perforated disks attached with wallboard screws, which can be used to pull sagging plaster back in place. Encircle the sagging area with washers spaced 6 to 10 inches apart. Once the outside perimeter is secure, move inside and repeat the process in concentric circles until the sag is fully supported. Spackle over the washers.

Wall Hangers

The type of hanger you use depends on how much weight you will be hanging and whether you have plaster or wallboard.

Plaster is very brittle and will crumble if you attempt to drive a nail or screw into it. You must drill pilot holes and install plastic anchors before driving nails or screws.

The most secure hanger is attached directly to a stud beneath the wallboard or plaster. Sometimes that is not possible.

The top row shows wall hangers for lightweight objects that will be attached between studs. Lightweight hangers should only be used for items such as small pictures or very light mirrors.

The middle row shows hangers for mediumweight objects, such as curtain rods.

The bottom row shows hangers for heavier items, such as hanging planters.

Make certain to follow the weight instructions supplied by the manufacturers. Never overstress either a hanger or a wall surface. Never attach a heavy item like a bookshelf without first finding studs (see page 25).

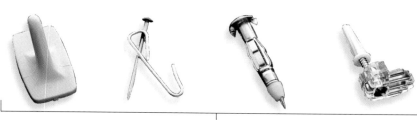

Hangers for lightweight objects.

Hangers for medium-weight objects.

Hangers for heavy-weight objects.

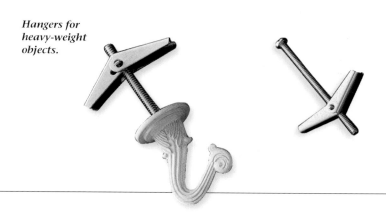

Paint & Wallcovering

Paint

A fresh paint job can do an amazing job of transforming a room, but you'll need to use the right paint to get the best results.

Interior paint can be divided into two categories: latex and oil-base (or alkyd). Latex paint is much easier to apply and clean up, and it produces fewer foul odors. Latex paint seems to last just as long as oil paint in most applications, but oil-base primers are still preferred where staining is a problem, and oil-based enamels are often preferred on flooring.

Both latex and oil-base paint come in three general finishes: flat, semi-gloss and high-gloss. A simple rule of thumb states that flat paint is used on walls while semi-gloss and high-gloss paints are used on trim or where walls get wet or or endure lots of handprints. A gloss paint applied to walls will reveal more imperfections in the surface, but higher gloss paint will not get dirty as easily.

If you're planning to repaint, remember these hints:

• Paint will not stick well to a surface that is too glossy. If the surface has a high sheen, sand the surface or use a chemical deglosser.

• If stains bleed through walls or trim, seal the area with white pigmented shellac. *Do not use clear shellac.*

• Use a solution of trisodium phosphate to remove dirt and cut grease before repainting.

• Painting over wallpaper is not recommended. Wallpaper can show through paint, and the solvent in paint can loosen wallpaper or cause dyes to bleed through the paint. Wallpaper should be removed before painting, and plaster should be sealed with an alkyd primer.

Wallcovering

Wallcovering produces texture and patterns that painters cannot produce—unless they are very experienced artisans working with thick paint. Wallcoverings are available in a vast number of types. The right wallcovering can give your rooms a rich and unique appearance. The downside is that wallcovering can be very time-consuming to apply—and to remove.

Removing wallcovering is not as tricky as hanging it, but can be even more tedious. Some wallcoverings will melt off with a steamer or spray-on chemical remover, while others will tenaciously grip the wall. If you are stripping wallcovering, test a small, inconspicuous area in order to budget your time.

To repair wallcoverings:

• Clean dirty wallcoverings with a gum eraser or wallpaper dough, which can be found at decorating centers.

• Fix loose seams by squirting a line of adhesive under the paper and pressing with a small roller.

• Flatten bubbles by slitting the paper, then repairing it like a loose seam.

• Patch by taping replacement paper, aligned correctly, to the damaged section. Cut out the damaged section and the patch together. Remove the damaged section and apply the patch.

LEAD PAINT

Lead was used extensively in house paints and stains until it was banned in 1978 due to a growing awareness of its role in lead poisoning.

Lead is very dangerous to youngsters. Lead levels can have a direct impact on children's brains and physical development, their learning abilities and attention spans. Medical researchers have found correlations between elevated lead levels and mental and physical retardation.

To make matters worse, children are very susceptible to the effects of lead in paint. Some children will eat paint chips, but all children can ingest lead dust through their daily activities. For example, a child, while peering out a window, can grab a dust-covered windowsill and later suck a thumb. If the dust is from lead paint, the child will ingest it.

A 1997 study published in the Journal of the American Medical Association noted: "The most common source for lead exposure for children is lead-based paint that has deteriorated into paint chips and lead dust. In the United States, approximately 83% of privately owned housing units… built before 1980 contain some lead-based paint."

If you have young children, ask their doctor about having a blood lead test performed. Lead tests are now commonly prescribed by pediatricians.

Lead is also toxic to adults, but to a much smaller degree.

As a homeowner, you need to reduce or eliminate lead exposure. Lead paint should be removed or adequately contained by repainting. Flaking lead paint must be removed. Home testing kits, while not 100% accurate, will give you a good idea if you have lead paint. A more reliable test can be done by toxicology centers or public-health laboratories.

Another guard against lead ingestion is to regularly wipe down windowsills, baseboards, floors and anywhere children play, because lead-filled dust can accumulate in these areas.

Exterior soil is another source of lead. Dirt directly around the house can be contaminated by lead from runoff caused by weathering and past scraping. Older urban areas with heavy auto traffic nearby also often have high lead levels in the soil (leaded gasoline was also outlawed in the 1970s). One tip: planting shrubbery around the perimeter of your house will make the soil there an unattractive play area.

If you scrape old siding, keep children and pregnant women away. Wash your hands before eating and change into clean clothes before playing with children. Of course, remove all the paint chips. Contact your local waste management department for information on disposing of lead paint.

INTERIOR DESIGN BASICS

Among their other tricks, interior designers know how to alter our perceptions of space. They realize that different colors, tones and patterns can dramatically alter how large or small a room appears, as well as the mood it conveys.

The photos below give a few simple examples. The room with white walls appears larger and more open. The white walls also reflect more light, which gives the space a brighter feel. Compare it to the room with dark brown walls. The dark walls create the illusion of a smaller, more intimate room. The walls seem closer and the ceiling appears to be lower. And because the darker color absorbs light, the room has a heavier, quieter atmosphere.

The types of wallpaper patterns will produce similar illusions. The bottom photos depict the same room. The wallpaper with the small print pattern will cause the walls to recede visually, making the room appear larger. When the wallpaper has a large, bold print, the room seems smaller and more intimate.

Other decorating illusions:

• Vertical stripes increase the height of the walls; horizontal stripes make a wall seem wider.

• Warm tones appear closer; cool tones recede.

• A dark ceiling appears lower, a light ceiling looks higher.

These techniques can help the designer make small, claustrophobic rooms appear larger or make larger spaces less intimidating.

Light tone

Dark tone

Fine pattern

Bold pattern

Flooring

Your floor is composed of layers.

Joists support the weight of your floor. A full treatment on joists is found in the chapter on Framing (pages 18 to 29).

Subflooring, laid over joists, provides a flat surface. In houses built before the 1970s, subflooring tends to be one-inch wood planks nailed diagonally across the joists. If you have a newer house, your subflooring is probably ¾-inch tongue-and-groove plywood.

Underlayment is often put on top of the subflooring. An underlayment, normally ½-inch plywood, needs to be smooth and flat. Adhesive or mortar is applied on the underlayment. When reflooring, the underlayment is often replaced, while subflooring, unless it is damaged, usually stays in place.

Floor coverings cover a huge range of options, and include a wide variety of carpeting, wood, tile and resilient flooring.

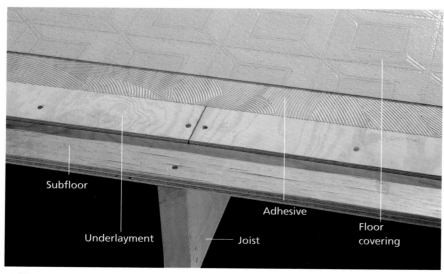

A floor is typically composed of several layers. At the bottom are the joists, which support the weight of the floor. Then comes the subfloor, made of plywood or wood planks. Many builders also place a layer of ½-inch plywood on top of the subfloor, which serves as a base for the adhesive holding the floor covering.

Buckling indicates that boards have come loose from the subfloor. Buckles can be flattened by drilling pilot holes and driving 8d finish nails into the boards.

Squeaky Floors

Squeaky floors are one of the leading complaints of homeowners. Hardwood flooring is notoriously squeaky.

Floors squeak when someone walks over floor strips, which causes them to rub together or rub on a nail. Another source of noise is when the subfloor moves against the joists. Diagnosing the cause of a squeak is fairly easy. If the squeak is in one or two hardwood strips, it's likely that they are rubbing together. If the floor squeaks when you walk over an area that is one to two feet wide, the cause is probably subfloor movement.

Correcting a squeak caused by movement in the subfloor will require that you reattach the subfloor to the joists. This is easy to do if the squeaky floor is on the ground level and you have an unfinished basement. Otherwise, you'll have to expose the floor joist, which will result in a big mess and damage to your ceiling. Whatever your choice, simply extend screws through the joists into the subfloor. Use the correct screw length, or you'll poke the screw head through your floor.

An alternative method is to fasten the subfloor from above. This can be done with a hardwood floor, or when replacing other surfaces such as carpet. Drive finishing nails through the floor into the joists. Locating the joists can be tough, but the newest electronic stud finders can help. Once you locate a joist, bore a pilot hole at an angle through the floor, subfloor and joist. Drive and set a finish nail, and putty over it.

When the squeak is caused by movement in the strips of a hardwood floor, pour talcum powder, liquid wax or powdered graphite between adjacent flooring strips where the noise occurs.

Floor Coverings

Your house probably has several different types of flooring. Ideally, each floorcovering should be both durable and aesthetically pleasing. Flooring options can be put in four categories: resilient flooring, hardwood, carpet and tile. Let's take a quick look at their highlights:

Resilient flooring is a flexible flooring made primarily of vinyl. It ranges in thickness from 1/16 inch to 1/8 inch. It is usually glued to an underlayment. In some cases, the entire project area is covered with an adhesive (called *full-spread*); in other installations, only the edges are glued (called *perimeter bond*). This flooring is one of the least expensive options, and it is preferred where water is prevalent, such as in kitchens or bathrooms.

NOTE: If you have older vinyl floor tiles made of asphalt, have a professional replace them. Asphalt tiles often had cancer-causing asbestos fibers in the backing. The asbestos poses no risk while the tile is in place, but it can become airborne during removal.

Hardwood flooring is durable enough to hold up well in high-traffic areas, and it looks warm and elegant. Hardwood flooring is available in solid or laminated planks, and in laminated parquet squares. Most hardwood floors have tongue-and-groove joints. Installing hardwood floors can be expensive, and the availability of hardwood is decreasing, driving prices up. The benefit is that solid flooring can be resurfaced several times—it may well last the life of your house. Laminated flooring must be replaced when the surface wears out.

Carpet is usually made of synthetic fibers, but some is woven from natural fibers like wool. The two basic types of carpeting are loop pile, which uses uncut loops of yarn to create a textured look and feel, and cut pile, which has trimmed fibers that give a more uniform appearance. Some carpeting comes with a cushioned backing already attached and designed for gluing down.

Standard carpeting is installed with tackless strips and padding. If you ever plan to install carpet over hardwood floors, don't glue the carpeting or it can ruin the hardwood for future use. New carpeting can have a chemical smell. If you are sensitive to chemicals, or you have a respiratory ailment such as asthma, talk to a reputable flooring dealer about options.

Ceramic tile and stone are the most durable and water-resistant of floor coverings. Ceramic tile is commonly installed in bathrooms, kitchens and entryways. Traditional ceramic tiles are made from oven-baked clay. Thickness of the tiles ranges from 3/16 to 3/4 inch. Tile tends to be among the most expensive floor coverings, and installation is time-consuming. The underlayment must be perfectly flat and level, and the layout must be planned and executed very carefully. Natural stone flooring requires the same care and attention as tile. Natural stone tiles include marble, slate and granite.

EVALUATING OLD FLOORING

Installing new flooring can be simple or difficult, depending upon your choice of new floor coverings and the type and condition of your existing floor.

OLD HARDWOOD FLOORING
• If the flooring is secure and the boards are tight, you can lay carpeting directly over the flooring.

• To install resilient flooring or ceramic tile over hardwood flooring, you can attach new underlayment over the existing hardwood before installing the new flooring.

• If the existing hardwood floor is a 'floating' hardwood surface with a foam-based underlayment, it must be removed completely before any type of new flooring is laid.

OLD RESILIENT FLOORING
• Your existing resilient floor can serve as the foundation for most new floorings, including carpet, resilient flooring, even hardwood, but only if the existing surface is smooth and sound. The surface must be free of loose seams, tears, chips, air bubbles and other areas where the adhesive bond has failed. If these loose spots constitute less than 30% of the total area, then you can remove the flooring in these spots only and fill the voids with floor-leveling compound.

• If your existing floor is suspect, install a new underlayment after repairing obviously loose areas.

• If you plan to install ceramic tile or the existing surface is in very poor shape, the old resilient flooring should be removed. If the old flooring was glued down with full-bond adhesive, it is usually easiest to remove both the flooring and the underlayment at the same time. Then, of course, you'll have to install a new underlayment.

OLD CARPET
Without exception, carpet must be removed before you install new flooring. For traditional carpet, cut the carpet into pieces and remove the padding and tackless strips. Remove glued-down cushion-backed carpet with a floor scraper.

CERAMIC TILE & STONE
If surface is relatively solid, new flooring can usually be laid over old tile. Loose tiles should be removed, and the voids filled with a leveling compound. If laying resilient flooring, apply an embossing leveling compound over the ceramic tile before installing the new flooring. If more than 10 percent of the old tiles are loose, it is best to remove all the tiles and underlayment before installing new flooring.

TROUBLESHOOTING

No matter how well built your home is or how carefully you maintain it, eventually things break or just plain wear out. When that happens, this chapter will guide you to possible causes and suggest solutions for common household problems.

The chart is organized to coordinate with previous chapters, and problems are listed according to the element of your house that is affected by the problem. Since many problems affect more than one element of your house, some issues are discussed in several places. For example, inadequate attic ventilation can create problems ranging from mold on interior walls (Interior Surfaces) to buckling shingles (Roofing and Ventilation).

The old medical adage, "When you hear hoofbeats, think horses" applies to home repairs, too. In other words: start with the obvious. You may be surprised at how often the simplest remedy solves the problem. In some cases, though, the problem is more difficult and the solution more complex than we can adequately address here. If you need further information, refer to a how-to book you can trust. We recommend the Popular Mechanics books, *Home Answer Book*, and *Home How-To.* You'll also find helpful information in the Home Improvement section of every issue of *Popular Mechanics.*

Problem	Possible Cause	Solution
Foundations (pages 8 to 17)		
Concrete blocks severely damaged or defaced. (pages 10, 15)	Moisture trapped in wall or blocks.	Eliminate source of moisture. Chip out face of block and replace with paver of same dimensions.
Concrete patch has separated. (pages 10, 15)	Source of original problem not resolved.	Find and eliminate cause of stress on structure; repeat repair.
Cracks in foundation. (pages 10-13, 15)	**Hairline cracks:** occur naturally in poured foundations.	Monitor for further movement.
	Open cracks: excessive water pressure.	• Improve grading to direct water away from house; repair cracks. • Add external or internal drain system; repair cracks.
Insects or other pests entering home through foundation (pages 10-15)	Exterior gaps providing access.	Fill cracks in foundation with concrete patching caulk; seal gaps around outside faucets, telephone and TV lines, electrical conduits and vents with expandable foam or caulk.
Moisture on basement walls. (pages 12-13)	Insufficient basement ventilation.	Add fans or windows.
	Water seeping through walls.	Seal walls and floors; add drain system in extreme cases.
	Unvented clothes dryer and/or sweating pipes contributing too much humidity.	• Vent dryer and/or insulate pipes. • Install dehumidifier.

Problem	Possible Cause	Solution
Mortar joints deteriorating. (page 15)	Mortar exposed to stress and moisture.	Eliminate stress; tuck-point joints.
Water in basement. (pages 12-13)	Poor grading around foundation.	Raise grade around foundation. Ground should fall one-half inch to the foot, for at least six feet.
	Water seeping in from basement window wells, stairwell openings or other basement entries.	Build up curb around window well perimeters; caulk around metal cellar doors.
	No gutters; broken or clogged gutters.	Install gutters; clean and repair gutters and downspouts.
	Downspouts release water too close to foundation walls.	Direct water away from house with extended outlet pipe, concrete splash block or dry well system.
	Cracks in basement walls.	Repair cracks and waterproof walls.
	Cracks in joints between basement walls and floor.	Widen joint, fill with epoxy cement and seal with patching cement.
	Clogged or broken drain tile.	• Clean out or repair drain tile. • Install new internal drain system.
	House located at foot of hill.	Install French drain to direct water around house.
	House built on ground with high water table or over underground spring.	Install new internal drain system.

Framing (pages 18 to 29)

Problem	Possible Cause	Solution
Cracks (diagonal) in corners of drywall or plaster. (pages 20-22)	Uneven settling of basement support columns.	Shim columns in basement or crawl space to re-level house frame.
Floor bounces. (pages 20-21)	Joists span too great a distance.	Add another support beam in the middle of the joist span.
Floor bounces severely. (pages 20-21)	Insufficient structural support.	Consult structural engineer.

Problem	Possible Cause	Solution
Framing Cont.		
Floor buckling. (pages 20-21)	Subfloor plywood does not have room to expand and contract with changes in humidity.	• Create expansion gaps in subfloor, if possible. • Replace subfloor with underlayment plywood.
Floor creaks or squeaks when someone walks on it. (pages 20-21)	Floor bridging members rubbing against one another under load.	Renail bridging.
	Gaps between subfloor and floor joists.	Place shims between joists and subfloor.
	Plumbing pipes rubbing against pipe hangers.	Adjust or cushion pipe hangers.
	Hardwood floor boards too tight.	Lubricate with liquid wax, talcum powder or powdered graphite.
	Hardwood floor boards too loose.	• Drive finish nails through boards at an angle; fill holes with wood putty. • Drive wood screws up through subfloor and into loose boards.
Nails popping out of wallboard walls. (pages 22-23)	Framing members shrinking as they dry.	Remove nails; replace with wallboard screws; spackle, sand and paint.
Stair tread creaks. (page 26)	Uneven plane across stringers.	Shim under tread to create level plane.
	Tread rubbing against riser above or below.	• Glue small blocks of wood to corners between riser and tread. • Drill holes through bottom of tread into riser above; drive screws into these holes, securing tread to riser above.
Walls separating from ceiling in center of house. (pages 22-23)	Truss uplift pulling ceiling away from walls.	Be patient and observe. Usually occurs during home's first heating season and remedies itself in the spring. If problem continues in subsequent years, the trusses were probably constructed from young, unseasoned wood. Cracks can be hidden. Hide crack by nailing or gluing crown or cove molding to ceiling.

Problem	Possible Cause	Solution

Roofing (pages 30 to 39)

Problem	Possible Cause	Solution
Downspouts clog repeatedly. (page 37)	Leaves and other debris accumulating in gutters.	Install downspout strainers and gutter guards.
Ground worn away near end of gutter's outlet. (page 37)	Runoff eroding soil.	Position splash block under outlet pipe.
Gutters filled with tiny gravel. (page 37)	Shingles deteriorating.	Clean gutters; if asphalt is showing on shingles, replace them.
Gutters leaking. (page 37)	Joints separated.	Take joint apart, caulk and reassemble.
	Holes in gutter.	Patch holes or replace section.
Gutters sagging. (page 37)	Fascia damaged or support hangers are loose.	Remove gutters and replace damaged sections of fascia; raise and rehang gutters; replace damaged hangers.
	Gutter clogged.	Remove clog and clean gutters; reseal and patch where necessary.
Ice forms on roof sheathing inside attic. (pages 32, 38)	Inadequate or missing vapor barrier between heated space and insulation.	Replace or add vapor barrier; replace damp insulation.
	Inadequate attic ventilation.	Add attic and soffit vents.
Ice dams on roof. (page 38)	Inadequate roof ventilation.	• Clear obstructions and replace damaged vents; replace damaged sheathing or shingles.
		• Install additional vents, if necessary; replace damaged sheathing and/or shingles.
Shingles buckling and/or cupping. (pages 32, 34-35, 38-39)	Flashing loose or damaged.	Replace damaged flashing; reseal loosened areas.
	Worn or damaged shingles causing leaks and trapping moisture.	**Isolated damage:** repair leaks and replace damaged shingles.
		Widespread damage: reshingle roof.

Problem	Possible Cause	Solution
Roofing Cont.		
Soffits deteriorating. (page 38)	Moisture buildup.	Install soffit vents.
	Pest damage.	• Consult pest control expert.
		• Replace damaged sections of soffit.
		• Install new soffit system.

Doors & Windows (pages 48 to 57)

Problem	Possible Cause	Solution
Bi-fold doors stick. (page 50)	Track dirty and/or lacks lubrication.	Clean track; lubricate track and rollers or pins.
Bi-fold doors hang unevenly. (page 50)	Doors aligned poorly.	Adjust pivot blocks in track at top of doors.
Door doesn't latch when closed. (page 53)	Lockset malfunctioning.	Open lockset; clean and lubricate moving parts.
	Latchbolt binding within faceplate.	Align latchbolt and strike plate; if door is hanging at an angle, shim hinges as necessary.
	Hinges sagging.	Tighten hinge screws.
	Door swelling during humid conditions.	Sand and plane door; seal edges with clear sealer.
Doors or windows have drafts around them. (pages 45, 52)	Missing or faulty weather-stripping.	Add or replace weatherstripping.
	Inadequate insulation around frames.	Remove casing moldings and stuff open spaces with fiberglass insulation; replace moldings.
Sliding glass door sticks or slides poorly. (page 52)	Track dirty and/or lacks lubrication.	Clean track with toothbrush and damp cloth or hand vacuum; lubricate rollers.
	Roller mechanism bent or worn.	Replace rollers.
	Uneven gap along bottom edge of sliding glass door.	Rotate mounting screw to raise or lower door edge.
Windows have condensation or frost buildup on inside. (pages 54-57)	Missing or failed weather-stripping.	Add or upgrade weatherstripping.
	Inadequate ventilation.	Create outlet for moisture by drilling one or two small holes in lower rail of storm windows.

Problem	Possible Cause	Solution
Window sticks when opening or closing. (page 55)	Tracks dirty.	Clean with toothbrush and hand vacuum.
	Paint in tracks.	Clean tracks with small amount of paint remover; let dry thoroughly; lubricate.
Window will not stay open. (page 55)	Sash cord missing or broken.	Replace sash cord.
	Misaligned.	Adjust screw on track insert until window is properly balanced.

Siding & Trim (pages 58 to 65)

Problem	Possible Cause	Solution
Bricks have white, powdery coating (efflorescence). (page 64)	Evaporated moisture leaving minerals on surface of bricks.	Eliminate sources of moisture; clean with stiff brush and household cleaner.
Gaps between windows and siding. (page 61)	Caulk failed or missing.	Clean gap and seal with appropriate exterior caulk.
Paint blistering and/or peeling. (pages 62-63)	Trapped moisture leaking from roof, gutters, soffits or interior pipes.	Identify and repair leaks; scrape and touch up affected areas.
	Poor surface preparation.	Scrape and touch up affected areas.
	Failed or inadequate vapor barrier.	Correct moisture problems; remove paint down to bare wood; prime and paint.
Paint cracking and/or chipping. (pages 62-63)	Too many layers of paint.	Remove paint down to bare wood; prime and paint.
Siding joints are separating. (page 60)	Gaps between ⅛" and ¼" occur naturally.	Fill with caulk.
	Gaps more than ⅜" indicate shifting or moisture problems.	Consult siding contractor or structural engineer.
Siding or trim spotted with rust. (pages 60-65)	Popped nails rusting out.	Remove nails; sand out rust; replace with galvanized ring-shank siding nails; prime and repaint.

Problem	Possible Cause	Solution

Siding & Trim Cont.

Problem	Possible Cause	Solution
Siding (vinyl) buckling. (page 65)	Inadequate expansion gaps between joints or where siding fits into trim or channels.	Move channel slightly. If not possible, remove siding, trim slightly and reinstall. If professionally installed, contact original contractor for repair.
Siding (wood) cracking. (pages 60-61)	Natural aging process.	Apply glue to both sides of crack and brace together until dry; drive galvanized deck screws on each side of crack; fill holes; sand and paint.
	Nails improperly positioned in wide horizontal siding.	• If siding was Do-It-Yourself project, reposition nails so they do not penetrate underlying row of siding; repair cracks as described above. • If siding was professionally installed, consult original contractor.
Stucco has hairline cracks. (page 64)	Naturally occur as house settles or goes through wide fluctuations in temperature.	Fill cracks with concrete caulk; feather until flush.
Wood trim damaged or rotted. (page 61)	Moisture damage or inadequate surface protection (such as failed paint).	Eliminate source of moisture; remove damaged areas; patch with wood filler; sand and paint.

Plumbing (pages 66 to 85)

DRAINS

Problem	Possible Cause	Solution
Fixtures drain slowly throughout home. May notice foul odor at fixtures. (pages 80-85)	Partial clog in connection to sewer system or roots in line.	Contact licensed plumber.
	Septic tank filled to capacity.	Contact septic system service company.
Sink or tub doesn't drain or drains slowly. (pages 80-85)	Drain assembly clogged.	Remove and clean drain assembly.
	Drain assembly faulty.	Remove and adjust drain assembly.
	Drain line clogged.	Clear with plunger or hand auger.
	Drum trap blocked.	Remove drum trap cover and clear line with hand auger.
Sink or tub will not hold water. (page 80)	Drain assembly faulty.	Remove and adjust drain assembly.

Problem	Possible Cause	Solution
Two or more fixtures attached to same branch drain seem to be clogged. (page 84)	Branch drain blocked.	Clear with drain auger.
Water backed up onto basement floor. (pages 82-85)	Floor drain line or drain trap clogged.	Clear with hand auger.
	Sewer service line clogged.	Call licensed plumber.

FIXTURES

Problem	Possible Cause	Solution
Faucet drips from spout or around handle. (pages 76-77)	Seals or washers worn or dirty.	Replace seals and washers. If leak continues, replace faucet.
Faucet's water pressure seems low or water flow is partially blocked. (pages 76-77)	Buildup or sediment blocking aerator.	Take faucet apart and clean aerator thoroughly.
	Galvanized pipes corroded.	Replace with copper piping.
Hose bib or valve drips from spout or leaks around handle. (pages 72-73)	Washers or seals worn out.	Replace washers or seals.
Sink sprayer leaks from handle or has low water pressure. (pages 76-77)	Buildup or sediment blocking sprayer head.	Take sprayer apart and clean thoroughly.
Toilet does not flush completely. (pages 78-79)	Lift chain too loose.	Adjust chain.
Toilet overflows or flushes sluggishly. (pages 78-79)	Toilet trap clogged or partially blocked.	Clear trap with plunger or closet auger.
	Waste-and-vent stack clogged.	Clear stack by running hand auger down through roof stack vent.
Toilet handle loose. (pages 78-79)	Handle mounting nut loose.	Tighten mounting nut.
Toilet handle sticks or is hard to push. (pages 78-79)	Handle mounting nut dirty or corroded.	Replace mounting nut.

Problem	Possible Cause	Solution
Plumbing Cont.		
Toilet leaks water onto floor. (pages 78-79)	Tank bolts and/or water connections loose.	Tighten bolts.
	Condensation forming on tank.	Insulate interior of tank with foam panels.
	Wax seal defective.	Remove and replace wax seal.
	Tank or bowl cracked.	Replace toilet.
Toilet runs continuously. (pages 78-79)	Lift chain or lift wire too tight.	Adjust lift chain.
	Float ball improperly adjusted or leaking.	Reposition or replace float ball.
	Water level improperly set.	Adjust float ball or float cup.
	Flush valve improperly adjusted or tank ball cracked.	Clean flush valve and reposition tank ball; replace, if necessary.
	Ballcock faulty.	Repair or replace ballcock.
Water leaks onto floor underneath faucet. (pages 76-77)	Sprayer hose cracked.	Replace sprayer hose.

HOT WATER HEATER

Problem	Possible Cause	Solution
Burner will not light or burns poorly. (pages 74-75)	Thermocouple worn out.	Replace thermocouple.
Delay before hot water arrives at fixtures, especially upstairs. (pages 74-75)	Inefficient hot water distribution system.	Install return loop on distribution line.
Leak at base of tank. (pages 74-75)	Tank corroded or damaged.	Replace immediately.
No hot water or not enough hot water. (pages 74-75)	Excessive sediment in tank.	Flush water heater to remove sediment.
	Excessive heat loss through pipes.	Insulate hot water pipes.
	Gas heater: Gas off or pilot light out.	Check gas supply and relight pilot light.
	Electric heater: Power off or thermostat set improperly.	Check power; adjust thermostat.
	Thermostat defective.	Replace thermostat.
	Heating element burned out.	Replace heating element.

Problem	Possible Cause	Solution
Pressure-relief valve leaking. (pages 74-75)	Temperature setting too high.	Lower thermostat setting.
	Valve defective.	Install new valve.

PIPING

Problem	Possible Cause	Solution
Pipes corroding near junction of dissimilar metals. (pages 70-71)	Galvanic action causing corrosion.	Replace damaged piping; use proper transition fittings or dielectric unions to join pipes of dissimilar metals; support pipes with brackets and straps made of matching materials.
Pipes knock or bang loudly. (pages 70-71)	Pipes too close to framing members.	Install foam rubber cushions between pipes and boards.
	Pipe hangers too loose.	Tighten hangers.
	Sudden changes in water pressure causing pipes to knock against framing members.	Install air chamber or water hammer arrestor.
Pipes leading to outside faucet rattle at low pressure. (pages 70-71)	Loose washer on water line, probably on shut-off valve.	Remove valve stem and tighten washer.

WATER PRESSURE

Problem	Possible Cause	Solution
Pressure from faucets and/or spigots too high. (pages 68-69)	Excessive municipal pressure.	Install pressure-reducing valve to house side of water meter and main shut-off valve.
Pressure from faucets and/or spigots too low. (pages 68-69)	Main valves dirty.	Clean valves and aerators.
	Pipes undersized.	Replace undersized pipe.
	Insufficient municipal water pressure.	Install pressure-boosting pump.

Problem	Possible Cause	Solution

Electrical System (pages 86 to 115)

Problem	Possible Cause	Solution
Doorbell doesn't work. (page 112)	Loose or worn wire connections.	Secure connections or replace switch.
	Transformer faulty or burned out.	Test; secure wire connections; replace transformer, if necessary.
	Chimes dirty, worn or broken.	Remove cover and clean chime plungers; if bell still does not work, replace chime unit.
Fluorescent light fixture has black substance around ballast. (pages 108-109)	Ballast worn out.	Replace ballast or entire fixture, depending on respective costs.
Fluorescent light fixture doesn't light. Or, flickers, and hums. (pages 108-109)	Wall switch defective.	Repair or replace switch.
	Light tube poorly seated.	Rotate tube to make sure it is seated properly in sockets.
	Light tube burned out.	Replace tube and starter (where present).
	Socket cracked or chipped.	Replace fixture.
Fuse blows or circuit breaker trips repeatedly. (pages 94-99)	Circuit overloaded.	Move several plug-in appliances to another circuit; if no other circuit is available, add circuits.
	Electrical short in circuit.	• Replace faulty appliances, switches or receptacles. • Check for loose wire connections. • Clean dirty or corroded wires and replace taped connections with wire connectors.
Fuse blows when high-demand appliance (such as electric shop tool or window air conditioner) is turned on. (pages 94-99)	Circuit overloaded by surge in power demand.	Install time-delay fuse.
Fuse box or service panel has rust stains on the inside. (page 95)	Water seeping into service head, then leaking into service panel.	Call licensed electrician to examine service head and service panel.

Problem	Possible Cause	Solution
Lamp or plug-in appliance doesn't work. (pages 96-99)	Cord worn or plug damaged.	Cut away damaged portion of cord and replace plug.
	Loose or dirty wire connections to receptacle.	Clean wire ends and secure connections.
	Receptacle faulty.	Replace receptacle.
	Lamp or appliance defective.	Test on different circuit; repair or replace lamp or appliance, if necessary.
Light fixture or permanently installed appliance doesn't work. (pages 94-95, 108-109)	Light bulb loose or burned out.	Tighten or replace bulb.
	Fuse blown or circuit breaker tripped.	Replace fuse or reset circuit breaker.
	Switch faulty.	Make sure all wires are securely connected and properly grounded; replace switch, if necessary.
	Socket, light fixture or appliance defective.	Repair or replace socket, fixture or appliance.
Light fixture flickers. (pages 108-109)	Light bulb loose in socket.	Tighten bulb.
	Faulty wire connections on socket.	Clean wire ends and tighten connections; replace taped connections with wire connectors.
	Socket, fixture or switch defective.	Repair or replace socket, fixture or switch.
Lights flicker when major appliance cycles on. (page 95)	Circuit overloaded.	Add circuits.
Phone lines have excessive static. (page 114)	Line resistance and/or voltage loss.	Reduce phone lines to less than 250 ft.
	Lines service too many phones.	Reduce to fewer than four phones per line.
Receptacle does not hold plugs firmly. (pages 106-107)	Receptacle aged or damaged.	Replace receptacle.
Receptacle is warm; buzzes or sparks when plugs are inserted or removed. (pages 106-107)	Excess dirt or dust in electrical box overheating.	Pull receptacle out and vacuum electrical box.
	Switch has loose, corroded or damaged wires.	Clean wires and secure connections; replace damaged wires.
	Receptacle defective.	Replace receptacle.

Problem	Possible Cause	Solution
Electrical Cont.		
Switch buzzes or is warm to the touch. (pages 104-105)	Loose wire connections to switch.	Clean wires and secure connections; test switch and replace, if necessary.
Switch lever does not stay in position. (pages 104-105)	Switch worn out.	Replace switch.

HVAC System (pages 116 to 129)

FORCED AIR FURNACE (GENERAL)

Problem	Possible Cause	Solution
Blower making noises, especially when burner is off. (pages 118-121)	Pulleys loose.	Tighten setscrews.
	Blower mounts defective.	Replace mounts.
	Belt damaged or defective.	Replace belt.
	Belt too tight.	Adjust belt tension.
	Bearings lack lubrication.	Oil blower bearings.
Excessive dust in house. Or, soot visible in air or on furniture. (pages 118-121)	Filter dirty.	Clean or replace filter.
	Ducts dirty.	Have ducts professionally cleaned.
	Furnace dirty.	Vacuum inside furnace cabinet, removing dust and debris; vacuum or brush dust from fan blades.
	Heat exchanger defective.	Call HVAC contractor for repairs.
No heat. (pages 118-121)	Thermostat set improperly.	Adjust thermostat setting.
	Thermostat defective.	Replace thermostat.
	No power to blower motor.	Reset circuit breaker or replace blown fuse.
	Blower belt broken.	Replace blower belt.
	Blower motor defective.	Repair or replace blower motor.

Problem	Possible Cause	Solution
Not enough heat. (pages 118-121)	Filters dirty.	Clean or replace filters.
	Duct dampers or registers partially or completely closed.	Open dampers and registers.
	Registers dirty.	Remove covers and vacuum ducts as much as possible. Clean and replace register covers.
	Ducts leaking warm air.	Insulate ducts or wrap joints with duct tape.
	Blower belt loose.	Tighten belt.
	Blower improperly adjusted.	Adjust blower speed.

ELECTRIC FORCED AIR FURNACE

Problem	Possible Cause	Solution
No heat. (pages 118-121)	No power.	Reset circuit breakers or replace blown fuse.
	Heating elements defective.	Call HVAC contractor.

GAS FORCED AIR HEATING SYSTEMS

Problem	Possible Cause	Solution
Detectable gas odor. (pages 118-121)	Pilot light out.	Relight pilot.
	Gas leak.	Turn furnace off and close main gas valve; call gas company immediately.
No heat. (pages 118-121)	Pilot light out.	Relight pilot.
	Gas supply interrupted.	Call gas company for service.
Pilot light won't stay lit. (pages 118-121)	Dirty pilot port.	Clean pilot port.
	Defective thermocouple.	Call gas company for service.
	Pilot flame needs to be adjusted.	Call gas company for service.

Problem	Possible Cause	Solution
HOT WATER HEATING SYSTEM		
No heat. (pages 122-123)	Power off.	Reset circuit breaker or replace blown fuse.
	No fuel.	Call utility company or fuel supplier.
	Thermostat defective.	Replace thermostat.
	Circulator pump defective.	Repair or replace circulator pump.
	Pump motor or coupling defective.	Replace motor or coupling.
	Zone valves defective.	Turn valves to manual and call HVAC contractor.
Pump leaking. (pages 122-123)	Seal or impeller defective.	Drain system and replace seal or impeller.
Pump making clattering noises. (pages 122-123)	Circulator coupling defective.	Replace coupling.
Radiators gurgling or clanking. (pages 122-123)	Excess air in lines or in hot water boiler.	Open petcocks at each radiator or open air-eliminator valve on boiler.
Safety relief valve leaking. (pages 122-123)	Water in expansion tank.	Drain tank.
	Valve defective.	Replace valve.
Steam radiator not delivering heat. (pages 122-123)	Air blocking steam flow.	Open air vent to bleed air from line.
	Trapped water blocking steam.	• Open inlet valve completely.
		• Position radiator properly—older radiators should be pitched slightly toward the valve; newer radiators should be level.
HUMIDIFIER		
Humidifier doesn't work at all. (page 121)	No power.	Reset circuit breaker or replace blown fuse.
	Humidistat defective.	Replace humidistat.
	Motor defective.	Repair or replace motor.

Problem	Possible Cause	Solution
Insufficient humidity. (page 121)	Water supply cut off.	Check supply hose and pump; clean water pan.
	Float valve clogged.	Clean valve.
	Screens, pads or plates clogged.	Clean unit thoroughly.
Unit runs constantly. (page 121)	Insufficient capacity for square footage requirements.	Replace with larger unit.
	Humidistat defective.	Replace humidistat.
	Humidity levels set too high.	Adjust controls to lower setting.

VENTILATION

Problem	Possible Cause	Solution
Air stale. Cooking or smoking odors linger for days. (page 129)	House sealed too tightly.	Add air exchanger to HVAC system.
Deteriorated metal stack pipe on gas furnace. (page 129)	Excess condensation.	Replace damaged sections.
Electronic air filter making zapping noises and leaving burning smell in air. (page 129)	Filters dirty.	Clean thoroughly.
Smoky smell in rooms even when fireplace not in use. (page 129)	Backdrafting—too many vents pulling air out of house, so air drawn into house through chimney or furnace vent.	• Improve air flow throughout house. • Add air exchanger to HVAC system.

CENTRAL AIR CONDITIONING

Problem	Possible Cause	Solution
Air conditioner cycles on and off repeatedly. (pages 126-127)	Fan blocked or evaporator unit dirty.	Clean evaporator unit.
	Direct sun overheating evaporator unit.	Add bushes, trees or wall to provide shade for unit.
	Insulation on feed line damaged or missing.	Replace insulation.

Problem	Possible Cause	Solution
Central Air Conditioning Cont.		
Air conditioner does not run. (pages 126-127)	No power to unit.	Reset circuit breaker or replace blown fuse.
	Thermostat defective.	Test thermostat and replace, if necessary.
	Short in wiring.	Check wires and tighten all electrical connections.
	Capacitor defective.	Test capacitor and replace, if necessary.
	Refrigerant level too low.	Call HVAC contractor.
	Compressor defective.	Call HVAC contractor.
Air conditioner runs but does not cool. (pages 126-127)	Filter and/or condenser dirty.	Clean filter and condenser.
	Blower fan loose.	Check fan and adjust.
	Refrigerant low or leaking.	Call HVAC contractor.
Fan runs, but compressor does not. (pages 126-127)	Thermostat defective.	Test thermostat and replace, if necessary.
	Condenser coils dirty.	Clean interior and exterior of condenser cabinet.
	Compressor defective.	Call HVAC contractor.
Water leaking onto floor around indoor portion of unit. (pages 126-127)	Drain hose from condenser pan clogged.	Clean hose and make sure it drains freely.

Interior Surfaces

Ceiling stain bleeds through after repainting. (page 133)	Paint coverage inadequate.	Prime with pigmented shellac; wait at least two weeks; repaint.
	Recurring leak in area.	Eliminate leak; repaint as described above.
Mildew on interior walls. (pages 44-45, 131-132)	Attic ventilation inadequate.	Add a combination of soffit and gable vents or soffit and ridge vents.
	Excessive humidity in house, especially at temperatures below 20°F.	• Use vent fans when using bathroom and kitchen. • Add fresh-air intake ducts.

Problem	Possible Cause	Solution
Nails popping out of wallboard surfaces. (pages 134-135)	Framing members shrinking as they dry.	Remove nails; replace with wallboard screws; spackle, sand and paint.
Paint on windows and sills cracks and peels repeatedly. (pages 44-45, 131-132)	Moisture or excess sun damaging paint surface.	• Caulk windows. • Add window shades. • Install storm windows. • Sand, clean and thoroughly prepare surface before repainting.
Rust spots on walls. (pages 44-45, 131-132)	Trapped moisture rusting nails.	• Maintain one-inch gap between ceiling insulation and roof sheathing. • Improve attic ventilation. • Remove ceiling surface and rebuild with vapor barrier and properly placed insulation.
Significant drafts around electrical outlets. (pages 44-45, 131-132)	Inadequate wall insulation.	Add insulation, probably by blowing it in through holes drilled in the exterior walls.

ADDITIONAL RESOURCES

Helpful Books on Home Improvement

Popular Mechanics Home How-To

Hearst Books/
William Morrow
1-800-843-9389

Advanced Home Wiring

Basic Wiring & Electrical Repairs

Bathroom Remodeling

Building Porches & Patios

Built-In Projects for the Home

Carpentry: Remodeling

Carpentry: Tools • Shelves • Walls • Doors

Decorating with Paint & Wallcovering

Everyday Home Repairs

Exterior Home Repairs

Home Masonry Repairs & Projects

Home Plumbing Projects & Repairs

Kitchen Remodeling

Landscape Design & Construction

Cowles Creative Publishing, Inc.
1-800-328-3895

Helpful Internet/Web Sites

Code Check
www.CodeCheck.com

Council of American Building Officials
www.cabo.org

Department of Energy
www.doe.gov

The Energy Outlet
www.energyoutlet.com

EPA Indoor Air Quality
www.epa.gov/iedweb00/pubs/insidest.html

Habitat for Humanity
www.habitat.org

Home Improvement Net Tips
www.nettips.com

Home Improvement Highway
www.csz.com/hih/

Home Improvement Links
http://www.surfinglinks.com/homeimp.htm

House Net
www.housenet.com
or 410-745-2037

Plumbing Online
www.plumbingonline.com

Popular Mechanics Magazine
www.popularmechanics.com

U.S. Department of Housing & Urban Development (HUD)
www.hud.gov/

NOTE: *World Wide Web (WWW)/Internet sites appear and disappear rapidly. On-line searches conducted using the key word "home improvement" will provide the most up-to-date listing of web sites.*

Code Books and Technical Manuals

BOCA National Building Code
(Northeast and Eastern regional)
Building Officials & Code Administrators
708-799-2300

Standard Building Code
(Southeastern Region)
Southern Building Code Congress
205-291-1853

Uniform Building Code
(Western Region)
International Conference of Building Officials
310-699-0541

National Electrical Code Handbook
McGraw-Hill
1-800-722-4726
www.books.mcgrawhill.com

Practical Electrical Wiring
Richter & Schwan
McGraw-Hill
1-800-722-4726
www.bookstore.mcgraw-hill.com

Uniform Plumbing Code
International Association of Plumbing
 & Mechanical Officials
5032 Alhambra Avenue
Los Angeles, CA 90032-3490

National Plumbing Codes Handbook
Woodson
McGraw Hill
1-800-722-4726
www.bookstore.mcgraw-hill.com

Professional Associations

American Institute of Architects
(AIA)
202-626-7300
fax 202-626-7518

American Subcontractors Association
703-684-3450
fax 703-836-3450

Association of Energy Engineers
707-447-5083

**Independent Electrical
Contractors Association**
800-456-4324
fax 703-549-7448

National Association of Home Builders
202-822-0200

National Kitchen & Bath Association
908-852-0033
fax 908-852-1695

National Safety Council
630-285-1121
fax 630-285-1315
www.nsc.org/

American Institute of Building & Design
203-227-3640
fax 203-366-2423

Underwriters' Laboratories
847-272-8800
www.ul.com

NOTE: *National offices of professional organizations may be able to help you locate the local chapter nearest you. Your local chapter can provide you with a directory of qualified professionals in your area.*

INDEX